D1644034

city baby l.a.

The Ultimate Guide
for L.A. Parents from
Pregnancy to Preschool
Second Edition

By Linda Friedman Meadow
and
Lisa Rocchio

Universe Publishing

This edition first published in 2005
by UNIVERSE PUBLISHING
A Division of Rizzoli International Publications, Inc.
300 Park Avenue South
New York, NY 10010
www.rizzoliusa.com

Copyright © 2005, 2003 by Linda Friedman Meadow and Lisa Rocchio
Previously published by City and Company
Based on City Baby, copyright © 2003, 2001, 1997 by Kelly Ashton and Pamela Weinberg
Portions of City Baby L.A. have been excerpted from City Baby, and are used with the
express permission of the publisher and authors thereof.
Design by Paul Kepple and Jude Buffum @ Headcase Design
www.headcasedesign.com
Cover illustration by Sujean Rim

All rights reserved. No part of this publication may be reproduced,
stored in a retrieval system, or transmitted in any form or by any
means, electronic, mechanical, photocopying, recording,
or otherwise, without prior consent of the publishers.

2005 2006 2007 2008 / 10 9 8 7 6 5 4 3 2 1
Second Edition
Printed in the United States of America

ISBN: 0-7893-1347-2
ISBN-13: 978-0-7893-1347-8

Library of Congress Catalog Control Number: 2005907422

Publisher's Note:
Neither Universe nor the author has any interest, financial or personal, in the locations listed in this book. No fees were paid or services
rendered in exchange for inclusion in these pages. While every effort was made to ensure that information regarding phone numbers,
rates, and services was accurate and up-to-date at the time of publication, it is always best to call ahead and confirm.

contents

part one

Preparing for Your L.A. Baby: Everything You Need to Know!

Acknowledgments

We would like to thank the following people for their encouragement and support in the writing of the second edition of this book:

Our husbands, John Rocchio and Cary Meadow, for being so patient while we did all of our research, and for allowing us to monopolize the computer every night! Our children, for being our willing guinea pigs. As always, Kelly Ashton Sant Albano and Pamela Weinberg, authors of the original New York edition of *City Baby*. And Kingsley Baker, Lisa's father, for being better than any delivery person we could have hired!

Special thanks to all of our moms "in the know," who advised us and filled us in on all their favorite places from Sherman Oaks to Pasadena, and everywhere in between! Thanks especially to Ling in Los Feliz, Kristy in Manhattan Beach, and Kimberly and Kristin in Pasadena. Also thanks to our favorite retailers for their endless support from day one. And most of all, thanks to our readers for telling us what they liked (and didn't like!) in the previous edition.

Finally, thanks to Kathleen Jayes and Caitlin Leffel, whose patience and persistence made this book possible.

Preface to the Second Edition

It's hard to believe that three years have gone by since our first edition was published. My, how things have changed! From maternity fashions to strollers, everything keeps improving! Since our first edition came out, we have received countless thank-yous from our readers—who have called, emailed, and stopped us on the street—and we have been overwhelmed by the number of books sold in such a short time. So we decided it was time for an update. It has been so rewarding for us to find out that we weren't the only people to see the need for an up-to-date resource guide for L.A. parents. With all the "knock-offs" that have come out since *City Baby L.A.* was first published, we want to thank our readers and retailers for their loyalty. In a trendsetting city such as Los Angeles, things change quickly. And our readers have not been shy about letting us know what they liked and disliked about the previous edition. Believe us, we listened! You wanted more emphasis on different geographic areas in L.A., so in this edition we've expanded the resources in areas from Los Feliz to Pasadena. Plus, many of our loyal readers who had infants when the first edition came out are now interested in activities for school-age children, so we've expanded the indoor activities chapter to include transition classes and after-school programs for older kids. So keep the feedback coming (email us at realmomsink@yahoo.com)—we love to hear from you—and keep on reading!

Linda Meadow
Lisa Rocchio
2005

introduction

By the time you become an L.A. mom, you've probably earned a degree or two, negotiated a few promotions and raises for yourself, planned your wedding, mastered the Internet, bought a home . . . So why should having a baby in L.A. suddenly seem so daunting?

Well, perhaps it is, because no matter how well you think you know L.A., pregnancy and parenthood aren't neighborhoods you have visited yet. If you're like us, the moment you found out you were pregnant, you wanted to know everything: where to go, what to buy, and who to see.

We were once in your shoes. We met in a Mommy and Me class when our children Sarah (Linda's daughter) and Jack (Lisa's son), were just four months old. We bonded over how overwhelmed we felt by the prospect of raising a child in L.A. One of us moved to L.A. from Chicago and one is originally from New Orleans, so neither of us had our families, old friends, or our trusted family doctors nearby, and it was intimidating. However, this hasn't stopped us from having more children:

Linda's daughter, Eve, and Lisa's son, Will, were born before their older siblings were two years old. And Lisa just gave birth to a baby girl named Sarah, and Linda is pregnant with her third child. With this many children between the two of us, we have learned a lot. Among other things, we have come to see how much time, energy, and expertise it can take to prepare for and raise a child in the City of Angels. If only we had had one book that told us everything we wanted to know! And that is why *City Baby L.A.* was born; it is the result of our extensive research, and, most importantly, our experience.

Join us in the land of *City Baby L.A.*, the "offspring" of the New York edition of *City Baby*, a successful resource guide for New York City parents, now in its third edition. Because of L.A.'s geography, it is virtually impossible to discover everything the city has to offer your new family just by strolling around your neighborhood. That's why this new edition covers more ground, from the Palisades to Pasadena, including Silver Lake, Sherman Oaks, Manhattan Beach, and everywhere in between. And oh, what is in between! It probably won't surprise you to find out that L.A. is home to some of the hippest maternity stores, the best prenatal yoga, the most beautiful parks, and the highest-quality medical care in the country. Trust us: Being a mom in L.A. is fun!

Let *City Baby L.A.* help to make these first years of parenthood easier. Use it as a resource at home while you prepare for your new life, and throw it in your bag as you venture out shopping. We will tell you about the important products you will need, where you can find them, and how much you should—and shouldn't—pay for them. We will take you through the ins and outs of parenting, including finding the right nanny, day-care center, or baby-sitter, and walk you through the important choices regarding health care professionals. Want to save some money? We will tell you how and what you can borrow, trade, make do without, or re-use. Remember, it's expensive to live in this great city, and if you can save a bit here and there, all the better. After all, fashionable clothes and state-of-the-art cribs are not what make a happy, well-adjusted baby. You,

the loving parent, are the most important component in your child's life. The intention of this book is to help you make the most of these special first years as a parent.

This book is not a complete listing of every store and resource in L.A., but those that are tried and true; we've only included entries that either we or our friends recommend. Throughout the book, we've starred (*) our favorite selections to indicate what we view as the best in each category. Whenever possible, we provide an address, phone number, website, and ballpark price for every item or service, but please call ahead to confirm. While we did our best to give you the most up-to-date information, keep in mind that prices and services change constantly.

Now, it's time to enjoy yourself! We'll shop, do lunch, register for classes, decorate a nursery, and plan a birthday party. With *City Baby L.A.* by your side, you'll be able to sit back and relax before you embark on the zaniest, most amazing and fantastic adventure of your life—being a parent!

Chapter One

from obstetric
care to childbirth

You just found out you're pregnant!
Congratulations! Before you tell everyone you know, you need to make some decisions about your pregnancy and childbirth. We know it can seem overwhelming, especially living in a city like Los Angeles, where there are so many options for pre-natal care and childbirth. But have no fear. We're here to help! In this chapter, we will provide you with all you need to know about giving birth in Los Angeles, including information about doctors, midwives, hospitals, birthing centers, childbirth preparation classes, lactation consultants, labor coaches, and more. You can make an informed decision about how you want to care for yourself and your baby before, during, and after your pregnancy without even breaking a sweat.

First of all, you need to decide who will take care of you and your baby during your pregnancy and help with the delivery. You can either see a doctor or a midwife; these professionals will meet with you during your pregnancy to monitor your progress and be there on the big day.

Where your baby will be born—hospital, birthing center, or your home—is another choice to make. We've all heard the stories about a woman who is forced to deliver while stuck in rush-hour traf-fic on the 405, but don't worry, that is only a remote possibility. Chances are you will make it to the right place in time—especially if it is at home!

While finding excellent care won't be a prob-lem, the best advice we can give is to make sure you find a doctor or midwife that you feel comfort-able with and have confidence in. We also know how important it is to find a good hospital with an excellent neonatal intensive care unit (NICU). We both had one fairly complicated birth followed by an easier birth, so we know firsthand how essential this is.

the birth attendant

Whether you choose to use an obstetrician or a midwife, you should find one as soon as you know you're pregnant.

Obstetrician

You probably already have an obstetrician/gynecol-ogist (ob/gyn) that you see for annual checkups, and you may be perfectly happy with this person and want to continue seeing her or him throughout your pregnancy. But there are many reasons why you may want to switch. Maybe seeing this doctor once or twice a year was more than enough for you; perhaps you don't like the doctor in question enough to want to make it a monthly and, once you're nine months pregnant, weekly visit. Perhaps your current doctor isn't an expert in high-risk pregnancy, or the practice is so large that you never see the same doctor twice. If you want to find someone else, now is the time. Most low-risk patients will see their doctor once a month for the first three trimesters, every two weeks during the eighth month, and every week during the final month(s). Factors such as age, previous preg-nancy history, obesity, diabetes, and other serious health problems determine high-risk pregnancies. If you do have a high-risk pregnancy—and both of us had one—you will be visiting the doctor more often. In any case, your ob/gyn will be privy to some of the most private moments of your life, so you better make sure you are at ease with him or her. We have heard stories of people who were unhappy with their doctor before, during, or after their first birth, but were too afraid to look for a new doctor. This can lead to anxious feelings about your appointments and even childbirth in general. Don't let this happen to you. Take the extra time to meet a few doctors and ask the tough questions so that you can be sure to choose the right doctor for you and your baby.

You'll want to look for a doctor with a good bedside manner, especially if you are a first-timer. Make sure the doctor has time to get on the telephone and answer your questions. You should also be sure that you feel comfortable calling your ob/gyn in the middle of the night (perhaps more than once). This is the nature of an ob/gyn's job, so be sure he or she won't make you feel uncomfortable when you make those late-night calls.

Here are some of the ways to find a new ob/gyn:

✳ Ask friends or coworkers whose advice you trust for a recommendation.

✳ Ask your internist or general practitioner to recommend someone.

✳ Call the hospital you would like to deliver at and ask for a referral. Our hospital listings (pages 19–23) can help you find a hospital to suit your needs.

✳ Call the American Board of Obstetrics and Gynecology (214-871-1619) or visit them online at www.abog.org.

✳ Call your insurance company for a list of providers.

Once you have narrowed it down to a few candidates, call for a consultation. Any doctor should be willing to sit down with you and discuss what you can expect over the next nine months and during the birth. Be prepared, and bring a list of questions, such as:

✳ Are you part of a group practice? If so, will I be seeing other doctors at my appointments? Is there a chance that another doctor will deliver my baby?

✳ How often do you take vacations? Do you have children of your own? (This is important, because it will give you an idea about what kind of commitments the doctor has other than his or her practice, and how often he or she might be pulled away for family obligations, etc.)

✳ How often will I need prenatal visits?

✳ What prenatal tests do you recommend?

✳ What are your thoughts on natural childbirth, anesthesia, episiotomy, cesarean section, and induction of labor?

✳ What are your cesarean section and episiotomy rates?

✳ What do you consider "high-risk" factors during pregnancy and delivery?

✳ What is the fee for a vaginal birth? What other charges can I expect?

❖ What hospital are you affiliated with? Does this hospital have birthing rooms, labor, delivery and recovery rooms, rooming-in for baby and husband, a neonatal intensive care unit?

❖ Do you have nurses qualified to answer prenatal questions? (Obstetricians often spend half of their day at the hospital checking on patients and delivering babies, so it is important to know if someone else is available to answer questions if your doctor is not.)

Finally, go with your gut instinct when choosing an obstetrician. Check out the waiting room, survey the pregnant women who are there: How long are they usually kept waiting? Does the doctor allow for other opinions in decision-making, or does he or she like to call the shots?

Here are the common prenatal tests given in California:

❖ *Ultrasounds (or Sonograms):* This is basically a machine that is used to see the baby in utero. The doctor (or technician in most cases) will use a probe (internally in the beginning of pregnancy and externally thereafter) to check the baby's development. These are usually given when you first discover you are pregnant to locate the fertilized egg and make sure it is attached to the proper place in your uterus. After that, they will perform a twenty-week extensive "structural" ultrasound (often done at the hospital) to check on the growth and development of the organs of the baby. Finally, you will have another ultrasound in the ninth month to determine the size and position of the baby for birth. Many doctors have in-office machines and may perform other ultrasounds depending on the type of pregnancy you are having (high-risk often requires a closer watch on the uterus and the opening of your cervix).

The newest way to view your child in the womb is with 4-D ultrasounds. They give parents the ability to view three-dimensional images of the baby in motion and are performed by registered ultrasound technologists in doctors' offices, clinics, and hospitals that have the new machinery. They are not meant to take the place of diagnostic ultrasounds performed by your doctor; rather they are more like having a professional photographer take pictures of your baby in the womb. We recommend consulting with your ob/gyn before having an ultrasound performed. The following are a few places that perform 4-D ultrasounds: First Look Sonogram (www.firstlooksonogram.com, 310-543-5152); 3D Sonography Center of Beverly Hills (310-275-6222); Ultrasona (formerly Fetal Fotos, 626-585-9226).

❖ *Triple-Marker/AFP Screening:* This simple blood test is performed on pregnant women in the fourth month (sixteen to eighteen weeks). This test determines the levels of alpha-fetoprotein present in the mother's blood. High or low levels may indicate a problem with the development of the fetus. Be aware that there are many false-positive results.

❖ *Amniocentesis ("Amnio"):* This procedure, performed in the fourth month (sixteen to eighteen weeks) is done in the hospital. Most doctors recommend it for women over thirty-five or those in whom, for one reason or another, genetic or chromosomal abnormalities might be suspected. The procedure is done with a long needle inserted into the abdomen (guided with an ultrasound machine) that withdraws a small amount of amniotic fluid; this fluid is then tested for abnormalities. Many hospitals will offer the option to test for other abnormalities, which your doctor may recommend depending on your family history.

✳ *CVS (Chorionic Villus Sampling):* This relatively painless procedure is done with an ultrasound to guide the doctor in extracting chromosomal tissue from the uterus through a small tube. Like the amnio, it is performed in the hospital, but it is done much earlier than the amnio, between ten and twelve weeks. Many women are opting for this test as it provides them with important genetic and chromosomal information about a pregnancy much earlier. Be aware that this test should only be performed by qualified and experienced doctors who have performed hundreds of these procedures.

The tests and procedures described above are all routine, and the obstetrician you choose will have conducted, ordered, or overseen them for hundreds of pregnant women before you. But remember: This is your pregnancy. You should feel perfectly comfortable asking what you may think are "dumb questions." Ask why you need the tests, and what the results mean.

Midwives and Labor Doulas

Midwives and labor doulas are options for women who want a non-traditional birth. They have become more popular recently, especially among women who are interested in holistic health care, yoga, and the like. Advocates believe that midwives and labor doulas provide a more personal and comforting childbirth experience than doctors with large practices and hundreds of patients. Midwives are most commonly used instead of an ob/gyn during pregnancy and childbirth, while labor doulas are used in conjunction with either an ob/gyn or a midwife.

If you are considering using a midwife, there are a few things you should know. First, very few midwives in L.A. are able to perform their services in hospitals. In fact, very few hospitals allow midwife deliveries at all. If you opt for a midwife who is unaffiliated with a hospital, you will either deliver your baby at a birthing center or at home. Second, many midwives in Los Angeles are not nurses (see descriptions below) and are therefore not equipped to take care of high-risk patients. Third, while not a hard and fast rule, most midwives favor natural childbirth. Finally, midwives expect you to do a good part of your laboring at home alone (without the help of drugs); they appear only when you are good and ready to have your baby!

It is a common misconception that people choose midwives as a less expensive alternative to a hospital birth with an MD. Home births are about the same price as hospital births, and many insurance companies will not cover home births at all, so check with your insurance company before you go any further. Also keep in mind that unforeseen costs may not be included in the midwife's fee; furthermore, if you have a medical emergency that requires transfer to a hospital and a backup doctor, it may not be covered by your midwife fee or your insurance.

If you decide to use a midwife, find out if they are affiliated with a hospital or birthing center, and if they have a physician backup in case of an emergency—in fact, ask them what their emergency plan is in detail, including what drugs they carry with them. You may prefer to deliver in a birthing center or at home, but in the event of a medical complication it is important that your midwife has access to a hospital nearby. If your midwife does not have hospital privileges and a complication forces you to a hospital, your midwife will not be allowed to deliver your baby and may not (depending upon your situation) be allowed in the delivery room at all.

Midwives legally practicing in California are either Certified Nurse Midwives (CNMs) or Licensed Midwives (LMs). CNMs are nurses with advanced degrees in midwifery and are accredited by the American College of Nurse-Midwives (ACNM) based in Washington, D.C., which provides national certification for midwives and sets the standards for the practice of nurse-midwifery. If a hospital in the Los Angeles area allows midwives at all, it will be a CNM. LMs are licensed by the state of California to practice midwifery and are regulated by the North America Registry of Midwives (NARM), but are not accredited by the ACNM.

A midwife provides more or less the same care you receive from an obstetrician: monthly visits during the first three trimesters, every two weeks in the eighth month, and weekly thereafter. A routine midwife appointment consists of checking your vitals (weight, blood pressure, etc.) and listening to the baby's heartbeat, but they may not be equipped to do extensive testing such as those listed above and may send you to an ob/gyn or a hospital to have any such tests performed.

Labor doulas are experienced labor companions who provide both emotional and physical support by teaching you breathing and relaxation techniques to use during labor and childbirth; they can accompany either an ob/gyn birth or a midwife birth. If you choose to use a labor doula, make sure that she is certified by Doulas of North America (DONA), or another qualified doula organization. A labor doula develops a "birth plan" with you and your partner during pregnancy; this is what you would like to happen during labor and childbirth with respect to drugs, IVs, even your choice of music during labor and delivery. Many labor doulas prefer that the birth plan be in writing so that there is no confusion about what you want to happen. Believe it or not, you may be confused and incoherent when you enter labor!

The following is a list of hospital-based independent CNM practices in Los Angeles:

❊ *BECKA Medical Group*
Good Samaritan Hospital
1127 Wilshire Boulevard
Los Angeles
213-241-0901

❊ *California OB/GYN (COGS)*
Daniel Freeman Memorial Hospital
333 North Prarie Avenue
Inglewood
310-673-2647
COGS has four midwives that have hospital privileges. They are also trained in water births.

❉ UCLA Nurse Midwifery Associates

University of California Los Angeles
Medical Center
200 Medical Plaza, Suite 430
Los Angeles
310-825-5172

❉ Westside Family Health Center

1711 Ocean Park Boulevard
Santa Monica
310-450-2191

The following is a list of midwives in L.A. and surrounding areas who assist in home births:

❉ Debbie Frank, RN, CNM

310-659-5810

Debbie Frank has a solo midwife practice, and delivers babies at UCLA in Westwood. She makes house calls as well, and has excellent doctor backup.

❉ Seannie Gibson, LM, CPM

323-394-5332

Seannie is a midwife who performs home births.

❉ Home Birth Service

3959 Laurel Canyon Boulevard, Suite A
Studio City
818-760-6541

Leslie Stewart and Felicia Forrest are CNMs who provide home births for patients seeking natural childbirth. They see patients throughout the entire pregnancy and will provide breast-feeding guidance as well. They have excellent doctor backup in case of an emergency.

❉ Davi K. Kaur, RN, CNM

310-278-6333

Davi is a CNM assisting in home births, and she is also a popular childbirth instructor at Golden Bridge Yoga (see pages 26 and 33).

❉ Mary Lou O'Brien, CNM

310-376-5647

Mary Lou O'Brien is a CNM who assists in home births. Mary Lou is not associated with a hospital, but she has excellent doctor backup, which is chosen based upon your location.

❉ Westside Birth Service

Louanna Seibold, RN, BSN, PHN
2442 Euclid Street
Santa Monica
310-305-4977

Louanna Seibold is an LM who performs home births. Louanna also provides well-woman gynecological services, and will provide a water birth if you wish. She has a backup physician who all of her patients meet prior to delivery and who is on-call for her patients in case of an emergency.

Labor Doulas

❉ A Mother's Touch

805-644-9595
888-644-9595
www.amotherstouch.net

Demaris Rae Bruce has been providing pre- and

post-labor doula support for over thirteen years. She is certified as a postpartum doula by the National Association of Postpartum Care Services and as a birth doula by DONA (Doulas of North America). She is also co-founder of the Doula Institute, an educational organization offering doula-training workshops and seminars for doulas and other childbirth professionals. The professional labor doulas on her staff assist women with conventional and traditional births. They will help you labor at home or at the hospital.

❋ The Chapman Family Center
Judy Chapman
310-453-5144

Judy Chapman is a DONA-certified doula who trains doulas as well. Judy provides a myriad of services through her center, including labor doula referrals. She maintains a registry of excellent doulas and will help you find a doula to assist in your labor.

the birth place
Hospitals

All ob/gyns are associated with a hospital, sometimes two, so once you have selected your ob/gyn, you have also selected a hospital. However, if you haven't yet chosen an ob/gyn, you can work backward: Choose your hospital, and then find an associated obstetrician. Whichever way you do it, we cannot stress enough how important it is to know everything you possibly can about where you will deliver your baby, and who will perform the delivery.

Here's what you must know about the hospital: the number of birthing rooms, cesarean (c-section) rate, level of care provided in the neonatal unit, policies on husbands in the delivery room and rooming-in (so your husband and baby can stay overnight in your room), policy on sibling and family visitors, breastfeeding support, the number of private rooms and their availability.

There are many hospitals in L.A., but not all L.A. hospitals are created equal: Some have newer facilities and are much more comfortable than others. Cedars-Sinai has luxurious VIP recovery suites with room service and your own private nurse and doula that range from $1,200–$1,700 per night (which is not covered by insurance). St. John's Hospital in Santa Monica recently opened a new maternity ward with twelve brand new labor and delivery rooms each outfitted with state-of-the-art features, including plasma televisions (however, they have discontinued their parenting classes). But don't choose your hospital based upon decor: When you are in labor, these details hardly matter. Just about all of the hospitals in Los Angeles allow you to labor, deliver, and recover in one room; and almost all of them have birthing beds, showers, and squatting bars to help your labor and delivery. Please note that some hospitals have started to charge for lactation consultations, so be sure to ask ahead of time.

As far as c-section rates go, this depends on your doctor more than the hospital. If your doctor and/or the hospital have many high-risk patients, the c-section rate tends to be higher. Academic hospitals, which are teaching hospitals, seem to have lower c-section rates; doctors tend to go further in order to teach students what to do in an emergency, using the c-section as a last resort. Also, the level of care in the NICU may not seem important to you right now, but if your child has to spend even one night in the NICU (we both had children who did), it will become very important.

An option many new parents are taking advantage of is storing your baby's cord blood, which is rich in stem cells and can be used in the event a member of your family is ill and requires a blood transfusion. To find out about cord-blood registry, check with your ob/gyn and/or www.cordblood.com, or call 1-800-932-6568 for more information. Be sure to remember to bring the kit when you check in at the hospital, and make one person responsible for reading the instructions regarding when and where it is to be sent.

We have spoken at length to women who have delivered at all of the hospitals in the listings below. Keep in mind an enormous part of what makes for a good hospital and delivery experience is your nurse. Many friends have described wonderful labor nurses who stayed by their bedside with ice chips and a wet cloth. Others describe nurses who helped them feed their baby, and made sure their baby only received breast milk in the nursery. Obviously, a good nurse is the luck of the draw, but more often than not, the hospitals included below have labor nurses who have been on staff for years and are passionate about what they do.

Top Twelve Hospital Tips:

1. Pre-register with your hospital and insurance company, and call your insurance company as soon as possible after the baby is born.
2. Decide whether you want a private room.
3. Bring your favorite pillow with a bright pillowcase (to avoid mix-ups).
4. Bring your own big bath towel, washcloth, robe, slippers, and socks.
5. Be nice to the nurses, they can significantly affect your experience!
6. Make sure someone is always at your side (husband, mother, or friend) to bring you ice chips, get the nurse, and make sure there's film in the camera.
7. Bring your cord-blood kit (if you wish to save your baby's cord blood) and make sure your doctor is aware of this decision.
8. Have key phone numbers handy.
9. Rest as much as you possibly can, because once you get home with your newborn you will get little of it!
10. Be sure to ask about infant-care classes the hospital offers.
11. Validate parking.
12. Bring home sanitary napkins, mesh underwear, numbing spray (if you had an episiotomy), disposable cloths to protect your bed, and anything else that you found handy in the hospital.

Hospital Labor RMS/Other Classes

❖ *Cedars-Sinai Medical Center*
8700 Beverly Boulevard
Los Angeles
310-855-5000 (General)
310-423-5168 (Classes)
310-423-5312 (Lactation)
www.csmc.edu
Visiting Hours: 10 A.M.–9 P.M.; 24 hours in private rooms.

19 LDR/3 Operating
1 Recovery room
MIDWIVES: NO
CESAREAN RATE: 26%
NICU LEVEL: III
This teaching hospital delivers the most babies in California. LDR rooms are spacious with a couch and chairs for guests. Its NICU is known to be one of the best in the world. They have five luxury suites, where nothing is spared. The same nurse takes care of both you and your baby. In-house lactation consultants.
Classes offered:
Early Bird Pregnancy;
Prepared Childbirth;
Cesarean Birth/Vaginal Birth after Cesarean (VBAC);
Anesthesia Forum;
Breastfeeding;
Infant Care;
Infant Massage;
Sibling Class and Tour;
Siblings at Birth;
Prenatal Exercise and Yoga

❉ Encino-Tarzana Regional Medical Center

18321 Clark Street
Tarzana
818-881-0800 (General)
818-609-2280 (Women's Resource Center)
www.encino-tarzana.com
Visiting Hours: 11 A.M.–8 P.M.
Fathers have 24-hour privileges.
6 LDR/2 Operating
2 Recovery rooms

MIDWIVES: NO
CESAREAN RATE: 30%
NICU LEVEL: III
Popular with moms in the Valley; everyone raves about the Women's Pavilion. They have one luxury suite. In-house lactation consultants. They have a virtual nursery online; you can access the names of babies born on specific dates.
Classes offered:
Childbirth Preparation;
Refresher Childbirth;
Parents Expecting Multiples;
Anesthesia and Cesarean Section;
Baby Care;
Infant, Child Safety, and CPR;
The Amazing Newborn;
Breastfeeding;
Sibling Tour;
Childcare for Spanish-Speaking Caregivers

❉ Hospital of Good Samaritan

1225 Wilshire Boulevard
Los Angeles
213-977-2121 (General)
www.goodsam.org
Visiting Hours: 10:30 A.M.–8:30 P.M.
Fathers have 24-hour privileges.
11 LDR/2 Operating
MIDWIVES: YES
CESAREAN RATE: 25%
NICU LEVEL: III
One of the few hospitals in L.A. that allows midwives to deliver babies.
Classes offered:
First Experience;

Baby Care;
Breastfeeding;
Prenatal Yoga;
Childbirth Refresher

❋ *Huntington Memorial Hospital*

100 West California Boulevard
Pasadena
626-397-5000 (General)
626-397-5078 (Maternity Services)
www.huntingtonhospital.com
Visiting Hours: 11 A.M.–8 P.M.
Fathers have 24-hour privileges.
8 LDR suites/3 Operating
MIDWIVES: NO
CESAREAN RATE: 19%
NICU LEVEL: III

In addition to having the only Level III NICU in Pasadena, this hospital also has couplet care, where the same nurse takes care of you and your baby either in your room or in the nursery. In-house lactation consultants.

Classes offered:
Pre- and postnatal exercise;
Breastfeeding Education;
CPR Training;
Childbirth Preparation

❋ *Little Company of Mary Hospital*

4101 Torrance Boulevard
Torrance
310-540-7676 (General)
www.lcmwomen.org
Visiting Hours: 11 A.M.–8 P.M.
Fathers have 24-hour privileges.
22 LDR suites/2 Operating

MIDWIVES: NO
CESAREAN RATE: 30%
NICU LEVEL: II

The new unit has great amenities like CD players, and video and Internet access in the LDRs. There are bathtubs for labor relaxation and birthing balls are available to ease the labor process. In-house lactation consultants.

❋ *Santa Monica UCLA Medical Center*

The Birth Place
1250 Sixteenth Street
Santa Monica
310-319-4000 (General)
310-319-4947 (Birth Place)
www.healthcare.UCLA.edu
Visiting Hours: 8 A.M.–8 P.M.
Fathers have 24-hour privileges.
13 LDR/2 Operating
MIDWIVES: NO
CESAREAN RATE: 28%
NICU LEVEL: II

This teaching hospital is under renovation. It has one VIP suite, so if you want it, you have to reserve it upon arrival. The Pump Station provides in-house lactation consultation.

Classes offered:
Combined Lamaze and Childbirth;
Breastfeeding;
Infant and Child CPR, and Baby Safety;
Sibling Preparation;
Baby Care;
Bradley Method

✻ St. John's Hospital

1328 Twenty-second Street
Santa Monica
310-829-5511 (General)
310-829-8787 (Maternity Floor/Postpartum)
www.StJohns.org
Visiting Hours: 9 A.M.–8 P.M.
Fathers have 24-hour privileges.
12 LDR/2 Operating
MIDWIVES: NO
CESAREAN RATE: 25%
NICU LEVEL: II
The new North Pavilion at St. John's has twelve brand-new birthing suites with the most up-to-date, high-tech labor and delivery ward available. In-house doulas and lactation consultants.

✻ UCLA Medical Center

10833 Le Conte Avenue
Los Angeles
310-825-9111 (General)
310-825-5631 (Maternity)
www.healthcare.UCLA.edu
Visiting Hours: 9 A.M.–9 P.M.
Fathers have 24-hour privileges.
3 LDR/2 Operating
1 Recovery Room
MIDWIVES: YES
CESAREAN RATE: 20%
NICU LEVEL: III
This teaching hospital is the only hospital on the Westside of L.A. that allows midwives to perform deliveries. The LDR rooms are luxurious with everything you could ever need. In-house lactation consultants.

✻ Valley Presbyterian Hospital

15107 Van Owen Street
Van Nuys
818-782-6600 (General)
818-902-2977 (Maternal and Child Health Education)
www.valleypres.org
Visiting Hours: 2 P.M.–8 P.M.
Fathers have 24-hour privileges.
7 LDR/1 Operating
MIDWIVES: NO
CESAREAN RATE: 29%
NICU LEVEL: II
The birthing rooms are standard. It also has two birthing suites that are much more comfortable, with room for your entire family to attend your delivery. The same nurse takes care of both you and your baby. In-house lactation consultants.
Classes offered:
Baby Beginnings;
Heartsaver CPR;
Breastfeeding;
Lamaze;
Grandparenting;
Mommy Shape

✻ West Hills Hospital

7300 Medical Center Drive
West Hills
818-676-4321 (General)
818-676-4155 (Labor and Delivery)
818-676-7325 (Pregnagym)
www.westhillshospital.com
Visiting Hours: 11 A.M.–8 P.M.
4 LDR/2 Operating
MIDWIVES: NO

CESAREAN RATE: based upon individual physicians

NICU LEVEL: II

Pregnagym has workout equipment, yoga, and aerobics classes. Website features NICU Growcam that digitally records your baby in NICU. In-house lactation consultants.

Classes offered:

Baby-sitting Training;

Baby-care Basics;

Breastfeeding Class;

Childbirth Education;

Grandparenting Class;

Maid for Kids (Spanish);

Natural Childbirth;

Nutrition and Pregnancy Class;

Pediatric Class;

Pediatric CPR Class;

Pregnagym Classes

Birthing Centers

A birthing center is the obvious solution for parents who are looking to deliver in a more intimate setting than a hospital, with an affiliated midwife. Family members and friends are allowed to participate, and your pre-delivery labor and labor itself are as relaxed as you can imagine. You can walk around, soak in the tub, and listen to music in the privacy of your intimate birthing room. There won't be any monitors or beepers going off (as happens at the hospital), but on the other hand, you can't opt for an epidural or pain medication either. This is not the place for you unless you are fully committed to natural childbirth. If you are, then go for it! The following is a list of birth centers. Note: Ask detailed questions about what procedures the center follows should a medical emergency arise at the time of delivery.

❖ *Hollywood Birth Center*

1445 Gardner Street

Los Angeles

323-436-7425

www.hollywoodbirthcenterLA.com

Hollywood Birth Center, run by LMs Constance Rock and Diane West, is an exceptional birthing and gynecological center located in the heart of L.A. It has two delivery rooms and two midwives who work as a team delivering babies either at the center or at your home. The center itself is completely non-clinical; it feels like a bed-and-breakfast. They only do six to eight deliveries a month, so the staff can provide personal attention to all of their patients. A specialty is water births, and there are portable tubs for home births as well. The Homebirth Package is $4,800, and includes prenatal, labor, delivery, and up to six weeks of postpartum visits.

❖ *Natural Birth and Women's Center*

14140 Magnolia Boulevard

Sherman Oaks

818-386-1082

www.gr8birth.com

The Natural Birth and Women's Center is a popular birthing center in the Valley run by Tonya Brooks, an LM who has been delivering babies for several years. The center has four midwives and two delivery rooms. They provide childbirth education classes, holistic prenatal care, doulas, water births, and home births as well as augmented care for hospital births.

❊ *Ventura Birth Center*

3110 Loma Vista Road
Ventura
805-667-2229

Dawn Dana and Sue Turner, who run this birthing center together, were two of the first LMs in California. Although located in Ventura, many women from L.A. choose to deliver here or have them assist with water births and home births. About six to ten deliveries per month are performed here. Complete pre- and postnatal care is provided. Although not officially associated with any doctor or hospital, the center has backup physicians in case of emergency.

childbirth methods

Now that the who and the where of your pregnancy and delivery have been settled, you can start to focus on the how of it all. In other words, how is this baby going to enter the world?

As you discuss childbirth with other pregnant women and new mothers, you will hear about every birthing technique under the sun. We are going to describe some of the most popular and well-known birthing techniques first, and then where you can find the people who can teach them to you.

The Bradley Method Husband-Coached Childbirth

This method was developed by Dr. Robert A. Bradley, a Toronto-based obstetrician. The Bradley Method is based on a calming pattern of relaxation, deep abdominal breathing, and close teamwork between husband (or partner) and wife. Bradley's goal is a completely unmedicated pregnancy, labor, and birth: no aspirin or cold remedies while you are pregnant, and no epidural block or Pitocin when you deliver.

With Bradley, the pregnant woman learns various positions for the first, second, and third stages of labor. She is encouraged to approach her entire pregnancy as training for labor and to prepare her muscles for birth and her breasts for nursing.

Very few hospitals offer Bradley instruction for childbirth, but there are many private instructors in L.A. that offer Bradley or some form of unmedicated birth-preparation classes (we have listed some below). You can also call The American Academy of Husband-Coached Childbirth on 800-4A-Birth, or visit the website (www.Bradleybirth.com) to get information on instruction in your area.

The Lamaze Method

This method, named after founder Dr. Fernand Lamaze, head of an obstetrical clinic in Paris in the 1950s, is known as "childbirth without pain." (If only that could be guaranteed!) The method combines breathing techniques (the hoo-hoo-hoo, hee-hee-hee) used during contractions with relaxation exercises designed to help women labor comfortably.

Most hospitals offer Lamaze classes, which you must sign up for in advance. Most labor nurses are trained in Lamaze-type breathing and relaxation methods and can assist you and your coach in the labor room if needed. Couples usually do Lamaze classes in their seventh month, although Linda never made it to her Lamaze class. Her first daughter was born early, so her nurse and doctor had to give her a crash course during labor! There are private instructors around L.A. who will hold classes either in your home or at another venue with other couples in attendance. You can ask your doctor or midwife for some of these names. Judy Chapman of the Chapman Family Institute is quite popular; she currently teaches a variety of classes at the Pump Station (see page 27) and Cedars-Sinai Hospital.

Water Labor and Water Birth

Water birth, a method used in Russia since the 1960s, has become quite popular in L.A. over the last decade. Studies have shown that warm water reduces the hours and stress of labor, provides physical support to the laboring women, and helps relax blood flow, making the baby's journey into the world easier.

Women either rent a water-filled tub, or use their own tub to ease their labor before going to the hospital to deliver. Some choose to deliver in a water-filled tub (either rented or provided by a birthing center). In this scenario, the baby takes his first breaths while most of his body is submerged in water—a gentle and familiar medium from his time in the womb.

The Hollywood Birth Center has tubs available for birth at the center or to rent for home births. Should you wish, you can rent a birthing tub and have a water birth at home with the help of a midwife.

childbirth educators, classes, and other resources

Some practitioners offer more than one type of service; call a few of them and you should be able to find the right match. Class lengths vary, but most meet as a series.

❋ *A Mother's Haven*

15928 Ventura Boulevard, Suite 116
Encino
818-380-3111
www.amothershaven.com
A Mother's Haven, run by Laine Podell-Camino, offers an array of childbirth education classes, including hypnobirthing, supported birth, and the Bradley Method. In addition, you will find infant-care classes, pre- and postnatal yoga, breastfeeding support and supplies, as well as monthly workshops on a variety of topics pertinent to new parents (see page 63).

❋ *Jennifer Altman*

310-480-8855
Jennifer is a labor doula as well as a prenatal massage therapist. She has a background in chiropractic care and physical therapy (see page 38).

❋ *Cheryl Baker*

310-837-5686
Cheryl is a childbirth educator who specializes in the Bradley Method. Baker teaches both privately and at Birth and Beyond (see page 26)

and UCLA/Santa Monica hospital. She is also a lactation specialist and a DONA-certified doula, who assists in home and hospital births.

Birth and Beyond

1810 Fourteenth Street, Suite 208
Santa Monica
310-458-7678
www.birthandbeyond.net

Liz Wade owns this parent-education studio where she teaches infant-care classes based upon her many years of experience as a labor and delivery nurse. Other classes offered: Bradley Method, breastfeeding, infant massage, infant care, infant CPR, and prenatal yoga. Wade also provides in-home support to mothers on bed rest. For more information on Birth and Beyond, see the listing in chapter four, page 64.

The Birth Connection

3459½ North Verdugo Road
Glendale
818-248-0888
www.thebirthconnection.com

The Birth Connection in Glendale has been "mothering the mother" for over ten years. It provides every type of service an expectant parent could need, including exercise classes, and classes in the Bradley Method, Lamaze, prenatal yoga, and pregnancy photography. While you are there, visit the new shop next door, Bellies, Babies & Bosoms, which has products for mother and baby.

Bright Beginnings and Beyond

229 Avenue I
Redondo Beach
310-316-1528
www.brightbeginningsbeyond.com

Bright Beginnings and Beyond is an excellent resource serving the South Bay. A variety of classes are offered from preconception to parenthood. All classes are taught by registered nurses and other health-care professionals. Classes include Preconception, which discusses fertility and the physical and emotional needs of pregnancy, and First Semester Dos and Don'ts, a one-session class focused on first-trimester issues. Courses in Lamaze (including a Lamaze weekend retreat in Arrowhead), hypno-birthing, and VBAC (Vaginal Birth after Cesarean) are also available.

Judy Chapman, RN, CNM

310-453-5144

Judy provides a variety of different services through her Chapman Family Center. Her childbirth classes (a combination of the Lamaze and Bradley methods) currently meet at the Pump Station in Santa Monica and Cedars-Sinai Hospital. She also teaches hypnobirthing.

Golden Bridge Yoga

6322 DeLongpre Avenue
Los Angeles
310-936-4172
www.goldenbridgeyoga.com

Golden Bridge recently relocated to this new space, which is one block south of Sunset in the heart of Hollywood. Gurmukh, who has become one of the most sought-after prenatal yoga instructors in town, teaches here, and offers Kundalini yoga and meditation techniques in her prenatal yoga, pregnancy couples workshops, and Mommy and Me classes. Davi Kaur teaches the childbirth education series of five classes as well.

❋ Octavia Lindlahr
818-645-4692

www.sacredmotherdoula.com

Octavia is a labor doula who also provides pre- and postnatal massage, reflexology inductions, and a myriad of other birth-related services including a "Baby Basics" class.

❋ Maba, Beyond Breastfeeding
9661 Brighton Way

Beverly Hills

310-271-2589

www.atmaba.com

This Beverly Hills store is a relatively new resource for new and expectant mothers. In addition to breastfeeding support, there are monthly classes on topics such as preparing for your labor and delivery, caring for your newborn, and transitioning to fatherhood.

❋ Mommy Care
11606 San Vincente Boulevard (inside Dance Factory)

Brentwood

310-394-6711

Mommy Care offers Bradley Method instruction and is affiliated with the American Academy of Husband-Coached Childbirth. It offers a Bradley Method course that is taught over an eight-week period; you also can opt for private instruction. For more information, see the listing in chapter four, page 66.

❋ Mommy Zone
18399 Ventura Boulevard, #14 & #15

Tarzana

818-345-6060

www.mommyzone.com

This maternity and breastfeeding boutique has become a great resource for new mothers in the Valley. There is a board-certified lactation consultant in the store at all times, who takes appointments or walk-ins. They also offer lactation and childbirth education classes.

❋ Glayol Panbechi, MA, ACCE, CD
310-403-0379

www.spiritoflove.net

Glayol provides doula services for all three stages of the birth process (prenatal, delivery, and postpartum). She can be a coach, a confidante, a teacher, and a friend, and provides continuous emotional and physical support for the couple during the journey into parenthood.

❋ The Pump Station
2415 Wilshire Boulevard

Santa Monica

310-998-1981

1248 North Vine

Hollywood

323-469-5300

www.pumpstation.com

Keep the Pump Station in mind. Along with childbirth preparation courses, it offers information and classes on just about everything else you may need to know about caring for your infant. For a full description, see page 68.

✳ *Alisha Tamburri*

818-775-1868

www.clearmindhypnotherapy.com

Alisha teaches classes in hypnobirthing, which is a childbirth technique that uses self-hypnosis and breathing techniques to assist in labor and reduce pain and need for painkillers. She teaches classes at Women's Physical Therapy (see page 39), A Mother's Haven (see pages 25 and 63), and privately in clients' homes.

✳ *YogaBirth*

310-372-8400

www.yogabirth.com

YogaBirth, created by Lisa Pedersen, is a program that balances exercise, breathing, and guided imagery to moderate the pain of childbirth. Classes are held in Hermosa Beach at Alive and Well and Planet Yoga. She also teaches a labor-prep workshop, holds YogaBirth retreats, and provides birth coaching.

taking care
of you

This chapter is dedicated to you. Now that you've decided how and where you will have your baby, it's time to relax! When you're pregnant, it's important to pamper yourself, both physically and mentally; and since being pregnant in L.A. has become downright chic, there are great options for you to indulge in. Taking advantage of some of the terrific services to relax and refresh the body, mind, and spirit will make the hardships of pregnancy that much easier to bear. Treating yourself to a manicure or a massage in your ninth month may get you through one of those days when you're ready to be done with pregnancy.

This chapter provides information on professionals who offer pre- and postnatal exercise classes, fitness training, yoga, and massage. Everything here is fine-tuned and appropriate for pregnant women, but please always consult with your physician before undertaking any of the activities suggested here. If your doctor allows, we recommend getting involved in a physical fitness program early on in your pregnancy. It will help you feel your best throughout your pregnancy, prepare you for labor, and introduce you to other moms-to-be. Unfortunately, some women (like ourselves) will be forced to spend a large part of their pregnancy on bed rest—we have some tips to make you more comfortable during those long months as well.

exercise

Most experts agree that exercising throughout your pregnancy is safe, healthy, and beneficial to your overall well-being. If your pregnancy is normal and relatively low-risk, you should be able to participate in a moderate exercise program throughout your pregnancy. If you are a serious athlete or have exercised regularly prior to your pregnancy, you should be able to maintain that level of activity, with some modifications, throughout pregnancy and postpartum. However, we cannot stress enough how important it is to check with your obstetrician or midwife before starting or continuing any exercise regimen, whether you are low- or high-risk.

Women in L.A. are obsessed with fitness and looking good, so it is no surprise that there are dozens of health clubs to choose from. They range from the luxurious SportsClub/LA where membership fees can top $1,000 to 24 Hour Fitness, which offers month-to-month memberships for as low as $33 per month (plus enrollment fees). If you are already a member of a health and fitness club, check the class schedule to see if prenatal classes are offered. Check to see if there are personal trainers on staff who are certified to work with pre- and postnatal women.

You can also check with the hospital where you plan to deliver your baby. Some have fitness programs or will refer you to one. Numbers for various hospitals are listed in chapter one.

The following is a list of classes and professionals that specialize in pre- and postnatal exercise programs:

❋ *Baby Boot Camp*
310-968-9433
www.babybootcamp.com
Baby Boot Camp is a national exercise program that started three years ago in San Francisco. It is comprised of seventy-five-minute cardio and strength-training classes that are done with

your baby in a jogging stroller. In Los Angeles, it is run by Brook Klein, who holds classes in Santa Monica, Pacific Palisades, and Manhattan Beach. Classes are $15 each, and there is a discount for purchasing a series.

❄ Camp Technique

Sarah Sventek
Marina del Rey
877-246-CAMP
310-823-1853
www.camptechinque.com

Sarah Sventek runs a one-hour "stroller boot camp" for moms who are serious about getting back in shape. A ten-week session is $350. She also offers private personal-training sessions for prenatal women in her Marina del Rey studio. One-hour sessions are $80. She also provides nutrition counseling.

❄ Birgitta Lauren

310-275-8855
www.expectingfitness.com

Involved in the fitness industry for over twenty-two years, Birgitta is one of the most well-known prenatal fitness experts in L.A. If you are not already motivated to stay in shape during your pregnancy, meeting Birgitta will be your motivation. This former champion body builder is the epitome of fitness. Private training sessions cost $100–$115 per hour. If you can't afford a session with her, check out her book, *Expecting Fitness*, or her informative website, which offers guidelines and suggestions for prenatal health and fitness.

❄ Mommy Care Mothering Center

11606 San Vicente Boulevard (at the Dance Factory)
Los Angeles
310-394-6711

Mommy Care is operated by Nancy Griffin, who has been instructing pre- and postnatal women since 1986. She has a master's degree in child development and special education, is a certified lactation consultant and lactation educator, and a certified Bradley Method childbirth instructor. Exercise classes at Mommy Care were developed by one of the top pregnancy-recovery exercise researchers in the United States. In addition to a pregnancy workout, there is a recovery workout that is designed to get you back in shape after your baby is born. Babies are always welcome at these classes. Mommy Care also offers private personal-training sessions, physical therapy, massage, and bed-rest exercise. A single class costs $15, and there is a discount for purchasing a series. Mommy Care also offers "attachment parenting" and natural childbirth classes.

❄ Lauri Reimer

310-453-2380

Lauri has been involved in the fitness industry for over ten years as an educator, consultant, and group instructor. She conducts group prenatal classes at local health clubs and also has written fitness articles for several publications. Check with her to find out the location of her current classes or speak to her as a consultant for your prenatal fitness program.

❊ Stroller Strides

Santa Monica/Pacific Palisades/
Beverly Hills/Westwood/Century City
800-795-6708

Encino/Tarzana/Woodland Hills
818-723-6898

Hancock Park/Hollywood/Los Feliz
888-233-4071

Calabasas/Agoura/Westlake Village/
Thousand Oaks
888-797-2142

Manhattan Beach
800-571-5722

Pasadena/San Gabriel
888-250-1761
www.strollerstrides.com

Stroller Strides, started in San Diego, is a nationwide exercise program that combines power walking, body toning, and stretching, using a stroller. The group classes are a great way to meet other moms. Stroller Strides also offers other great resources: It helps organize play dates, produces a quarterly newsletter, and hosts a referral network on its website. There are over fifteen locations in the Los Angeles area. Check the website for the location near you.

❊ Universal Wellness

Michelle Hazlewood
805-375-2516
www.universalwellness.us

Michelle Hazlewood, a certified fitness instructor and personal trainer, started her own company about eleven years ago. She works with clients before, during, and after their pregnancies. Sessions cost $80, and there is a discount if you purchase a package. She is located in the West Valley and will train clients at their homes. She will travel for free from Thousand Oaks to Woodland Hills; outside of this area there is a fee. She also does telephone coaching.

❊ YMCA

Various locations
www.ymcala.org

Many of these family-friendly fitness centers offer pre- and postnatal exercise classes including water aerobics. Check your neighborhood location for a listing of classes.

yoga

Yoga has fast become one of the most popular forms of exercise for women, pregnant or not. With its focus on relaxation and breathing techniques, yoga is great for moms-to-be and may help make your pregnancy more comfortable by reducing backaches and other bodily stress during pregnancy.

If you have taken yoga before your pregnancy and want to continue, do so. But it is important to learn the modifications that make it safe during pregnancy. If you have never practiced yoga, pre-natal instructors will guide you through safe exercises at varying stages of your pregnancy. Prenatal classes usually allow more time than traditional yoga for resting and relaxation. You will also learn breathing and postures that are helpful during birth and labor. Almost every yoga studio in the city now offers classes for pregnant women. Below we have listed some favorite private yoga instructors and studios, and the classes that they offer for pregnant women or those who have recently given birth. Many of these studios also offer Mommy and Me yoga classes, Itsy Bitsy Yoga, and other yoga classes for kids. Please see chapter twelve for those listings.

private instructors

❊ Michelle Cassini*
818-906-9717

Michelle is a mother of three and could be the poster woman for prenatal yoga. She offers private lessons, workshops, and classes or parties for an organized group of friends. She charges $100 per hour, and her classes emphasize physical and spiritual strength. One of our friends had Michelle come to her small baby shower and all the women, pregnant or not, enjoyed her class.

❊ Jenny Jamrog
310-387-5902

Jenny teaches private and group prenatal yoga classes in the South Bay.

❊ Shana Meyerson
310-478-2266
www.miniyogis.com
Shana offers private instruction or group classes.

❊ Urban Goddess
Khefri
323-549-5383
www.khefri.net
Urban Goddess provides holistic services including pre- and postnatal yoga. Khefri's classes are held at several locations in Los Angeles, or in the privacy of your home. She is also a labor doula.

studios

❊ A Mother's Haven
15928 Ventura Boulevard, Suite 116
Encino
818-380-3111
www.amothers-haven.com
Pre- and postnatal yoga

❊ Angel City Yoga*
12408 Ventura Boulevard
Studio City
818-762-8211
www.angelcityyoga.com
Pre- and postnatal yoga

❊ Golden Bridge Yoga*
6322 DeLongpre Avenue
Hollywood
323-936-4172
www.goldenbridgeyoga.com
Prenatal yoga

❊ Jiva Yoga
15327 Sunset Boulevard
Pacific Palisades

310-454-7000
www.jivayoga.com
Prenatal yoga

✳ **Karuna Yoga**
19391/2 Hillhurst Avenue
Los Feliz
323-665-6242
www.karunayoga.net
Prenatal yoga

✳ **Mission Street Yoga**
1017 Mission Street
South Pasadena
626-441-1144
www.missionstreetyoga.com
Prenatal yoga

✳ **Planet Yoga**
518 Pier Avenue
Hermosa Beach
310-376-5354
www.planetyoga.com
Prenatal yoga, YogaBirth

✳ **Silver Lake Yoga**
28101/2 Glendale Boulevard
Silver Lake
323-953-0496
www.silverlakeyoga.com
Pre- and postnatal yoga

✳ **Still Yoga**
2395 Glendale Boulevard
Glendale
323-906-8960
www.allstill.com
Prenatal yoga

✳ **Yoga House**
11 West State Street
Pasadena
626-403-3961
www.yogahouse.com
Pre- and postnatal yoga

✳ **Yoga West**
1535 South Robertson
Beverly Hills
310-552-4647
www.yogawestla.com
Prenatal yoga

✳ **Yoga Works***
1256 Westwood Boulevard
Los Angeles
310-324-1200

1426 Montana Avenue, 2nd floor
Santa Monica
310-393-5150

2215 Main Street
Santa Monica
310-664-6470
www.yogaworks.com
Pre- and postnatal yoga

pilates

Pilates is another form of exercise that has become popular for its promise of long and lean bodies. Based on the principles of Joseph Pilates, these exercises focus on developing the core abdominal muscles, which is perfect before, during (modified, of course), and after pregnancy.

❋ *Embodyment Studio/Fusion Pilates*
720 Hampton Drive
Venice
310-581-3822
www.fusionpilates.com
Owner Jennifer Gianni is a fitness instructor with over seventeen years of experience. As a mom, she understands how pregnancy affects the body, and knows how to get it back in shape. At her studio, Embodyment, she offers private and group prenatal classes, which combine Pilates, yoga, and gyrotonics. Private sessions cost $70, and group mat classes are $15. If you cannot make it to her studio, check out her video, Fusion Pilates for Pregnancy.

❋ *Winsor Fitness**
8204 Melrose Avenue
Los Angeles
323-653-8767

12231 Wilshire Boulevard
Santa Monica
310-442-1030
Mari Winsor is a Pilates guru who has trained clients—including celebrities—in both pre- and postnatal Pilates at her West Hollywood and Santa Monica studios. Check out her book, *The*

Pilates Pregnancy: Maintaining Strength, Flexibility, and Your Figure. An introductory one-hour session is $65 and after that sessions are $75 (or more if you book with Mari) with discounts for buying a series of sessions.

nutrition

Good nutrition is a critical part of giving birth to a healthy baby, and there are many books available on the subject. We recommend *What to Expect When You're Expecting* by Arlene Eisenberg, Heidi Murkoff, and Sandee Hathaway. This is the pregnant woman's bible; it has an excellent section titled "Best Odds Diets," which provides guidelines on everyday eating. Also check out their book, *What to Eat When You're Expecting.*

Your ob/gyn or midwife should talk to you about nutrition, but if he or she doesn't, bring it up yourself. If you are underweight, overweight, diabetic, or need extra help managing your diet, we recommend consulting a nutritionist who can set up a program that meets your needs. You might want to keep them in mind for after pregnancy, too!

❋ *American Dietetic Association*
800-366-1655
www.eatright.org
The American Dietetic Association will provide you with the name of a nutritionist in your area who specializes in prenatal diet.

❋ *Elizabeth Baron Cole and Associates*
2121 Wilshire Boulevard
Santa Monica
310-453-5212

There are five registered dieticians at this practice. They are experienced in counseling pre- and postnatal women. Many obstetricians refer patients to this practice. An initial consultation (around one and a half hours) costs about $180. Follow-up appointments are $120 for one hour and $60 for a half hour.

❉ *Creative Nutrition*

Kerri Schwartz, MS, RD

310-312-4888

Kerri is a registered dietician and has a master's degree in nutritional science. She has helped many pregnant women maintain a healthy diet as well as shed those pregnancy pounds postpartum. She charges $175 for a private consultation.

❉ *Susan Dopart*

310-828-4476

www.susandopart.com

Susan is a nutrition and fitness consultant. Many of her clients are pregnant, and her specialty is gestational diabetes.

❉ *Deborah Klein, MS, RD*

435 North Roxbury Drive, Suite 311

Beverly Hills

310-247-0018

www.livetician.com

Deborah has been a nutritionist since 1994 and has her own practice. Her clients are mostly pre- and postnatal women. She works with women on special diets, or those who have developed gestational diabetes. She also counsels women who just want to lose weight post-

partum. The fee is $150 for a ninety-minute consultation. She also offers a thirteen-week program for pre- and postnatal women for $900. Depending on your needs, insurance may cover your visits.

food delivery

Home food delivery may come in handy both before and after your baby is born. These delivery programs offer an easy way to provide nutritious meals for your family, and help you maintain a healthy diet during your pregnancy and shed those postpartum pounds. Their plans are not specifically designed for pregnancies, but while you are eating for two, you can simply choose the higher calorie level and add some à la carte items.

❉ *Bohemian Baby*

800-708-7605

www.bohemian-baby.com

Bohemian Baby delivers fresh, delicious, organic baby food to your home. This food is so tasty, you'll find yourself eating it as well!

❉ *Healthy Gourmet*

17851 Sky Park Circle, Suite G

Irvine

310-829-0111

888-396-3257

626-244-2929

www.susanshealthygourmet.com

Healthy Gourmet offers low-fat, low-cholesterol, and low-sodium meals that still taste good. There are five weeks of rotating menus based on three different calorie levels. The plan is flexible; you can order one meal or a complete day of meals and snacks. There is an à la carte menu, and there are vegetarian options and weekly specials. Meals can be delivered (once or twice a week) or picked up at one of the several locations. The cost for three meals per day starts at $30.

※ *Sunfare**
120 South Anderson Street
Los Angeles
323-780-0888
1-866-SUNFARE
www.sunfare.com
Formerly known as The Delivery Zone, Sunfare prepares and delivers nutritionally balanced meals to those without the time or desire to cook for themselves. There are six programs offered, including the Zone (30-percent protein, 40-percent carbohydrates, and 30-percent fat), high protein, vegetarian, and family style. Personalized meals are based on your likes and dislikes. There are monthly and weekly meal plans or you can select any combination of meals for any duration of time. Three meals and two snacks start at about $45 per day. Meals are delivered to your home or office each morning.

massage

If you have ever seen a picture of what happens to the body of a pregnant woman, you will know exactly why this section is so important! Many women suffer from back and muscle pain, especially during the last trimester. The right set of magic fingers can work wonders with those big-belly aches and pains. When we were on bed rest, we found freelance massage therapists who made house calls, and these appointments quickly became the highlight of our week.

Be sure to find a masseuse who is trained in prenatal massage. A therapist should have massage therapy certification as well as schooling or certification in prenatal massage. There are different therapies for certain aspects of pregnancy such as bed rest and edema (swelling). There are also different types of massage for different periods in your pregnancy. It is especially important that your therapist be aware of the parts of your body thought to be trigger points; according to some, if stimulated enough, they can induce labor. Additionally, there are some essential oils that should be avoided during pregnancy. Always ask your doctor before scheduling a massage.

Communication with your therapist is critical. If you feel light-headed, short of breath, or uncomfortable, let the practitioner know. There are several ways they can make you more comfortable. One of them is the Prego pillow. This pillow has a hole cut out for your belly so you can lie on your stomach; some women love it but some find it makes them nauseous. Another possibility is the contour pillow system. These bolsters are designed so you lie on your side with your head in an anatomically correct alignment. If none of these work for you, just lie on your side and prop yourself up with as many pillows as necessary.

The following therapists will come to your home, and are trained in prenatal massage. If you feel uncomfortable having someone come to your house, many of the day spas offer prenatal massage; just make sure that the therapists have had the proper training.

❋ A Mother's Touch

888-644-9595

www.amotherstouch.net

Demaris Bruce offers a variety of services for the expectant mother, including labor support, prenatal massage, and postpartum doula care. As a mother herself, she knows exactly how uncomfortable the last trimester of pregnancy can be. She uses the Prego pillow or bolsters depending on what is most comfortable for you. She offers aromatherapy and soothing music if you want it. Demaris works with many women who are on bed rest or who are pregnant with multiples. She has even been known to visit clients in the hospital for their massage. Her relaxing ninety-minute massage costs $90.

❋ Jennifer Altman*

310-480-8855

Jennifer is a trained labor doula. She knows all about the aches and pains experienced during pregnancy, and gives a great prenatal massage. She offers a package that includes six one-hour massages and doula services for $1,300. If you are only interested in massage, a one-hour session is $95.

❋ Heather Archer

310-503-1439

Heather is trained in prenatal massage as well as infant massage. A one-hour massage costs $100.

❋ Amanda Bailey

310-822-4504

Amanda has been practicing massage for over fifteen years, and specializes in prenatal massage, including clients who are high risk and on bed rest. A one-hour massage costs between $120 and $125, depending on your location. Many obstetricians refer their patients to Amanda, and in some cases she will take insurance.

❋ Karen Blackmore

310-456-7499

Karen is a certified pregnancy massage therapist and a certified infant massage instructor with over twenty-three years of experience. She brings an assortment of contour pillows and bolsters to make sure that you are as comfortable as possible. She has even lent these pillows to expectant moms on bed rest. Karen gives a good, strong massage that was instrumental in relieving our sore back muscles in the last few weeks of pregnancy. She charges $100 for a one-hour massage and $140 for one and a half hours. Karen also teaches infant massage. These private classes cost $125 and include a book on infant massage.

❋ Alison Lister*

310-281-1975

Alison was referred by friends who warned us that after a massage with her, we wouldn't be able to enjoy a massage from anyone else . . . ever. They were right. Alison has been doing freelance massage for several years and has a large number of clients who are pre- and postnatal. She comes prepared with a pregnancy bolster. Book early: Given her standing appointments, her schedule fills up fast. A one-hour massage costs $90.

Trisha Mohl

818-497-5888

Trisha has been practicing massage for over five years and is trained in prenatal massage. She uses the side-lying technique for her pregnant clients. Trisha does home visits in the Valley and charges $80 for a one-hour massage; outside the Valley is an additional charge.

Jacqui Perle

310-636-5679

Jacqui is trained as a pregnancy doula and has been doing prenatal massage for over five years. She is very knowledgeable about what trigger points to avoid and gives a strong, relaxing massage using the Prego pillow. Prices for a ninety-minute massage are $125–$150 depending on your location.

Rapid Rehab International

13050 San Vicente Boulevard, Suite 119
Los Angeles
310-312-0022
www.rapid-rehab.com

Rapid Rehab is a rehab facility specializing in physical therapy that incorporates Pilates and gyrotonics techniques as well as massage. Be sure to check with both your doctor and insurance company about partial or full reimbursement for many of its services.

Elizabeth Reinstein

310-565-5555

Elizabeth has been practicing pre- and postnatal massage for over ten years. Her prenatal massage includes a bit of stretching, which is helpful if you have not been able to keep up with your normal exercise routine. She is very good at taking care of bed-rest patients, and even makes hospital visits. A seventy-five-minute massage either at her office or in your home costs $120. Elizabeth also does pre- and postnatal exercise training. A ninety-minute session costs $85.

Daneka Soudak

818-448-2725

Daneka is a massage therapist who caters to women, especially pre- and post-pregnancy. She will travel only within the Valley area. A one-hour massage costs $90.

Lisa Swanson

Centre for Life
13323 West Washington Boulevard, #202
Los Angeles
310-712-1691
www.lacentreforlife.com

Lisa is a certified prenatal massage therapist who treats clients at her office located at the Centre for Life, an alternative healing center home to several professionals practicing homeopathy, acupuncture, and hypnotherapy. A one-hour massage costs $95. She also makes house calls for women on bed rest.

Sandie West

310-823-9378
www.creativechakra.com

Sandie has been practicing massage for over thirteen years. She owns a spa in Marina del Rey called Creative Chakra. She also makes house calls. A one-hour massage costs $100 plus a $10 travel fee.

❋ Women's Physical Therapy*

415 North Crescent Drive, Suite 130
Beverly Hills
310-273-0877
900 Wilshire Boulevard, #315
Santa Monica
www.womensphysicaltherapy.com

Gail Pekelis owns Women's Physical Therapy, which offers a ton of different services for women with high-risk pregnancies. Services include physical therapy, massage, yoga, Pilates, and other appropriate exercises, including aqua classes. All of this is provided either at their office or, for those on bed rest, at clients' homes. For the most part, their clients are referred by doctors and charges are covered by insurance. Look for an office in the South Bay soon.

beauty services and alternative medicine

❋ Golden Cabinet

Drew Francis
310-575-1955
www.goldencabinet.com

Dr. Drew Francis is the founder of the Golden Cabinet, a herbal store and rejuvenation center, which offers a holistic approach to healthcare. Our friends rave about the acupuncture they received, which helped relieve nausea, headaches, and sciatica. Many women visit Dr. Francis to increase fertility. Massage is also available, as are a wide variety of herbal products.

❋ Ocean Oasis Medical Spa

1333 Ocean Avenue
Santa Monica
310-458-8190
www.mastersonmd.net

Dr. Lisa Masterson's ob/gyn office has changed the way L.A. women think about going to the doctor. The second floor is a spa dedicated to pampering pregnant and new mothers. Spa services include: On My Way Labor-Inducing Massage, TLC Postpartum Massage, Pre-Baby Bliss Facials, and the Ready for My Close-up Bikini Wax. The rest of the space hosts exercise classes like Pilates and yoga (including a mommy and baby yoga class), as well as support and classes on breastfeeding, childbirth training, a Journey to Motherhood class, and parenting classes. There is also a talk series for women, and appointments with a nutritionist are available.

bed rest

Unfortunately, many pregnant women experience complications that require them to be on either partial or full bed rest. Both Linda and Lisa were on bed rest for some part of their pregnancies so they know how hard it can be. You don't realize until you've been on bed rest how sore you can become just from lying in the same position for hours on end. (They don't call them "bed sores" for nothing!) There are many things that you can do to make bed rest easier; one of these is to talk to anyone you know who has been through it. If you don't have any friends who have been on bed rest, there is a national support organization called Sidelines (1-888-447-4754 or www.sidelines.org) that will pair you with a local "partner." Your ob/gyn will have a list of resources as well (including hospital bed rentals, physical therapists, nutritionists, and masseuses) and will work with you and your insurance company to determine what is covered. Linda used Women's Physical Therapy during her pregnancy; the staff worked very hard with both her doctor and her insurance company so that Linda had to pay as little as possible for physical therapy and massages at home.

from healthcare
to day care

Around the third trimester of your pregnancy you should begin searching for the people who will help care for your little one. This is a toughie! The very idea of entrusting your baby to another person's care can be terrifying. You'll feel more comfortable with the idea if you take the time to do some important research: scout around, ask questions, get on the phone, and make visits.

First, you will need to find a pediatrician. Your goal here is to find someone who you connect with and who will provide your baby with the best possible medical care. But this is just the beginning. You may wish to hire a baby nurse or doula to help out in your home for the first few days or weeks after your baby is born. After that, your childcare needs depend on what else is going on in your life. If you are returning to work after a maternity leave, you will probably require full-time help either in your home or elsewhere. If you work at home or are involved in activities that will take you away from your child during the day, you will need some part-time childcare. If you simply want to get out of the house now and then sans baby, you should have one or two reliable baby-sitters to call upon. If you are one of the lucky L.A. moms with family nearby, you may have access to free baby-sitting!

You may be fortunate to find a nanny that stays with you for a while. Transitioning childcare providers can be tough on both you and your children. That said, the most important person in your child's life is you, the parent. Kids eventually adjust to a new nanny or caregiver. So try to find the best nanny or caregiver you can, and be persistent until you are comfortable with your choice.

This chapter lists resources that will help you find reliable childcare. But as with everything, make sure to trust your instincts!

selecting a pediatrician

One of the many benefits of living in L.A. is the abundance of good medical care, including pediatricians. Selecting a pediatrician can be a challenge, and it is a popular topic of conversation among new mothers. Begin looking for a pediatrician during the last few months of your pregnancy. Your newborn's doctor will be noted on the hospital registration sent to the hospital prior to your due date, and he or she will examine your baby in the hospital before the two of you are released.

Here are some guidelines to help you select a pediatrician:

❋ Ask your ob/gyn for a recommendation. Often they can give you several names of doctors their patients are happy with.

❋ Ask relatives, friends, and neighbors.

❋ Call any of the hospitals in the city and ask for a referral from the pediatric department.

❋ Consider location. You may visit the doctor often with a newborn and having a doctor near your home is practical, especially in an emergency.

❋ Consider whether you place importance on the doctor's age: Several of our friends chose the pediatrician they had as children! Consider the type of practice: group, partnership, or solo practitioner. What about gender? Some parents prefer to have a pediatrician the same sex as their baby.

❋ Check with your insurance to determine which pediatricians are included in your plan.

Once you have the names of two or three promising pediatricians, set up a consultation. Lisa felt somewhat uncomfortable about setting up an appointment strictly to interview a doctor, and was surprised to learn that this is actually a common practice. Most pediatricians will set aside time each week to meet with the parents of prospective patients. This is a great chance to see the doctor's office and what type of environment you can expect; for example, Lisa set up interviews with three pediatricians: Two of them kept her waiting for over one hour. In the end, she selected the pediatrician who saw her in a timely manner and has found this to be indicative of the way he runs his practice. If your pediatrician is part of a group practice, try to meet with as many of the other doctors as you can; chances are a few of them will be treating your child at one time or another.

While you are waiting, take a look around the waiting room.

❋ Is it child friendly, with enough toys, pictures, and books to keep a baby or toddler busy during the wait to see the doctor?

❋ Is the receptionist friendly, or does he or she seem curt and hurried?

❋ If you are visiting during office hours, ask parents in the waiting room about their experiences with the doctor; have these been positive? Find out how long they typically wait to see the doctor.

❋ Do sick and healthy children wait in the same waiting room? Some pediatricians schedule healthy and sick children at different times of the day, and will let patients know what the situation is in the waiting room when they call in with an emergency.

❋ Is there an on-site lab for quick blood and urine tests, ear wave sonograms, etc.?

Prepare a list of questions in advance and write down the doctor's answers. When you sit down with the doctor, ask:

❋ How does the doctor answer parents' non-emergency calls throughout the day? Is there a call-in hour, or does the doctor take calls all day and return them intermittently between patients? Is there a nurse who can answer questions? Linda loves the fact that her pediatrician answers his own phone and asks that his patients call him by his first name.

❋ Ask the doctor how many patients he or she sees on a normal day. This will give you some indication of how busy the office is and what you can expect in the waiting room. A doctor who sees between forty and sixty children a day will have less time for you than one who sees thirty a day.

❋ Ask about the schedule for newborn visits. One of us had a doctor who saw the children once a month for the first year, while another had a doctor who saw the children at ages two weeks, two months, four months, six months, nine months, and one year.

✳ How does the pediatrician feel about breast-feeding? Whether or not you choose to breast-feed, you will want a pediatrician who is supportive and encouraging of your decision.

✳ What are the pediatrician's views on circumcision, homeopathic remedies, antibiotics, nutrition, immunizations, and preventative medicine? Living in a progressive city like L.A., you will find doctors on both ends of the spectrum. It is important that you and your doctor are in sync.

✳ If the doctor is a solo practitioner, who handles phone calls when he or she is on vacation?

If you don't feel rushed during the consultation and the pediatrician is patient with you, these are good indicators of how he or she will be with your baby. Again, don't be afraid to ask questions. And even if you are unhappy with your pediatrician after you select one, don't worry about changing doctors. There are many pediatricians in the city, so just keep looking; the right one is out there.

baby nurses/doulas

Many mothers decide to have a baby nurse or doula assist them at home after the birth of the baby. It can be a big expense, but they can really help make the transition easier.

"Baby nurse" is a general term used for someone who will assist you with all aspects of the baby's care. Some are registered and licensed nurses while others have just been trained in infant care. Many have passed the British certification of the Nursery Nursing Examination Board (NNEB). You can find nurses to live at your home and work twenty-four hours, or night nurses who generally come to your house in the early evening and leave in the morning. Having a nurse help out with the nighttime feedings is a big advantage for new mothers. The nurse will get up in the middle of the night with the baby and either bring him to you for breastfeeding or feed him a bottle. This allows new mothers to get as much rest as possible during this time. Nurses can be a reassuring presence as well, especially for first-time moms. It is nice to have an experienced hand around to help bathe, calm, or feed the baby.

The name "doula" is a Greek word for server. Thus, postpartum doulas give you any non-medical support in any way you need, from caring for the baby to running errands and preparing dinner. They usually come to your home for a few hours a day. Unfortunately, there is no recognized licensing for doulas.

Of course, your mother, mother-in-law, or other family member may offer to come stay with you. If you feel comfortable with a family member helping out, great. However, we've found that many new parents prefer to hire short-term professional help, which allows them to get the rest they need without having to impose on a relative. A word of caution, though: Nurses and doulas can be a mixed blessing. It is important to interview them beforehand to find out if you are compatible. There is a tendency for these professionals to be set in their ways—and their ideas on child rearing may not fit with your ideas on childcare. Plus, this is another person in your home during what can be a stressful time.

Having professional help is a luxury that does not come cheap; prices range from $15–$35 per hour for part-time help and anywhere from

$225–$400 a day for 24-hour care (more for multiples). If you plan to hire a baby nurse or a doula, it is best to book ahead of time. Many will be booked far in advance. In L.A., there is a large network of baby nurses, many of whom are trained in Britain; they have their own informal networking system, referring one another if they can't take jobs rather than working through agencies. The key is getting the name of a few good nurses. You can do this either through friends, your pediatrician, or at the referral board at the Pump Station (see entry in chapter four, page 68). Keep in mind that just because your friend loved her baby nurse, it does not mean that this person is right for you. And if your nurse is not working out, don't be afraid to find another one—it happens all the time!

If you are unable to find a nurse through referrals, below are a few agencies that place baby nurses and doulas. Some hospitals also offer doula services or can give you a referral.

※ *A Mother's Touch*
805-644-9595
888-644-9595
www.amotherstouch.net
Run by Demaris Rae Bruce, this agency has been providing services to new mothers since 1996. Services include labor support, postpartum doula care, and pre- and postnatal massage. Demaris is a doula trainer and all doulas registered with the agency have completed a training program. For postpartum care, there is a six-hour minimum shift and rates start at $25 per hour.

※ *American Childcare/Rose's Domestic Agency*
323-937-3169
323-939-9861
Rose's Domestic Agency primarily places nannies and the occasional baby nurse.

※ *Fox Agency*
212-753-2686
Yes, this agency is located in New York! But we decided that it had to be included as so many of our friends in L.A. have used them. The Fox Agency places New York–based nurses all over the United States. You pay for the nurse to fly here, but the cost per day (approximately $225) is cheaper than what you will find in L.A. We used frequent flier miles to book our nurses' tickets, which gave us the advantage of flexibility with unpredictable due dates.

※ *The Help Company*
310-828-4111
888-435-7880
212-366-4111
www.thehelpcompany.com
Specializing in full-time, trained, and referenced employees, this high-profile agency offers full-time domestic help. With the recently opened New York office, they are placing more and more baby nurses. The agency **fee** is 20 percent of the nurse's fee.

※ *Sweet P Baby*
818-999-9005
888-744-4347
www.sweetpbaby.com

Started in 1994, Sweet P provides mother and baby-care support as well as other services such as sibling care, breastfeeding support, nighttime care, light meal preparations, layette shopping, and nursery organization. The agency's owner, Dana Klitzer, personally meets with each client and remains involved in care. Each doula from Sweet P completes a National Association of Postpartum Care (NAPCS) class and is trained in infant CPR; doulas also undergo background checks and TB testing.

❋ *Tender Care Doulas**

661-253-2100

www.tendercareMC.com

Tender Care Doulas was the first doula agency in California and one of the first three in the country. It remains one of the premier doula agencies in L.A. Run by Chris Morley, Tender Care is the only doula program used by hospitals for their patients. If your hospital does not participate in this program, you can still call for a referral. All doulas from this agency have extensive training, background checks, and annual TB testing. Tender Care now has a Mother Center in Valencia, which is a full resource for the new and expectant mother. They offer prenatal education, postpartum support, lactation counseling, and breastfeeding supplies such as pumps. There is even a gym staffed by a fitness trainer. Even if you are not in need of a doula, Tender Care is a good resource.

nannies

Hiring someone to look after your child while you are at work or away can be nerve-racking. You want a good, kind, smart, honest, flexible, reliable, sober, kid-loving caretaker who knows infant CPR, bakes cookies, and is going to think your baby is the most adorable child she or he has ever laid eyes on. Basically, you want another you.

Of course, this is impossible to find. But if you are determined and patient, you can find someone who will meet most of your requirements. Between the two of us, over five years, we have interviewed countless prospective nannies, so we have lots to say on the subject! We also recommend *The Nanny Book: The Smart Parent's Guide to Hiring, Firing, and Every Sticky Situation in Between* by Susan Carlton and Coco Myers. This step-by-step guide can help you through the nanny search and almost any scenario you might encounter along the way.

A professional nanny will usually be responsible for all child-related tasks, including laundry, meal preparation, and child-related cleaning. Some nannies will also perform light or heavy housecleaning, errands, and cooking. You should have a clear definition of what you expect your nanny's responsibilities to be. Decide whether you want a live-in or live-out nanny. Live-in nannies are harder to find and must be a good match with your family. Live-in nannies will have a starting or ending time and usually work twelve-hour days, but tend to be flexible with their schedules. If you prefer a live-out nanny, decide what hours you want her or him to work and what the overtime policy will be. How much are you willing to pay? What will your vacation policy be?

Full-time live-out nannies with little experience usually start at around $350 a week. For an experienced, educated caregiver who speaks fluent English and drives, you can pay as much as $1,000 a week. Live-in nannies, for whom you provide room and board, start at $300 per week. Prices vary according to experience, education, checkable references, and legal status.

There are several ways to go about finding a nanny. Most of our friends have found them either through agencies or word-of-mouth referrals. There are advantages and disadvantages to both approaches.

Agencies

An agency will send you several different people who match the criteria you provide. Depending on the agency, you may get the person's application, work history, DMV background check, and letters of referral. All employment agencies in California are required by law to register their caregivers with TrustLine, the California registry of in-home childcare providers who have passed a background screening. Most agencies will do their own background checks as well. We recommend using several agencies to increase your applicant pool. Keep in mind, though, that most nannies will register with several different agencies, so don't be surprised if two agencies send you the same person.

Even though an agency does some of the preliminary legwork for you, we cannot stress enough the importance of checking references and thoroughly questioning candidates. While checking the references of one candidate, Lisa discovered that the previous employer had recently fired her and gave her a horrible reference. It turns out that the agency had not done a recent reference check.

If you hire a nanny through an agency, you will pay an agency fee (thus, high turnover is actually good for their business). This is the opposite of what you are looking for—a reliable caregiver who will stay with your family for a long time. The most common fee is 12–15 percent of the nanny's annual salary. Most agencies will give you a one- or two-week trial period. After this, some agencies will offer what is called a "replacement guarantee," for anywhere from three months to one year. During this period, if the nanny leaves or is fired, the agency will begin another search without charging an additional fee. Be sure to ask the agency what the policy is at the beginning.

Referrals

Word-of-mouth referrals are an excellent way to find a caregiver without having to pay a fee. Ask friends who have childcare whether their nannies have friends looking for work. Ask nannies in the park and look at bulletin boards in child related and religious institutions, as well as in your pediatrician's office. Families that are relocating and employ beloved nannies will usually try very hard to find good replacement situations for them. But remember: If you find a nanny through a referral, it is up to you to do a complete background check.

Newspaper Ads

If you get nowhere by word of mouth, try placing an ad in the newspaper. (We have found that this is a more suitable technique for finding a college-age student for baby-sitting needs rather than full-time childcare.) When you place an ad, be as specific as possible. Here is an example of a detailed ad:

Live-out nanny needed for a two-year-old boy in Westwood. Light housekeeping, shopping, and errands. Must have two years' experience with toddlers and excellent local references. Nonsmoker. Must speak fluent English, drive, and cook. Must have legal working papers and be willing to travel with family. Hours are Tuesday–Saturday, 10 A.M.–7 P.M. Call 555-5555.

Interview candidates on the phone before you have them come to your home. Screen them carefully; it will save you time later. When you call newspapers, check their deadlines. Most will let you fax your ad and pay by credit card.

Below are some of the local daily and weekly newspapers in the city.

❋ The Argonaut
310-822-1629
www.marinadelreyargonaut.com
Weekly paper for Marina del Rey and surrounding areas, including Playa del Rey, Venice, Westchester, and Santa Monica.

❋ The Beach Reporter
310-372-0388
Weekly publication servicing the beach cities, including Redondo Beach, Manhattan Beach, Hermosa Beach, and El Segundo.

❋ Beverly Hills 213
310-275-8850
Weekly magazine for the Westside, including Bel-Air, Beverly Hills, Holmby Hills, Westwood, and Brentwood.

❋ Daily Breeze
310-540-5511
www.dailybreeze.com
Daily newspaper servicing south Los Angeles, including Santa Monica, Culver City, and Mar Vista.

❋ Daily News
818-713-3000
www.dailynewslosangeles.com
Daily publication for the San Fernando Valley and surrounding areas.

❋ La Opinión
213-622-8332
www.laopinion.com
The city's largest Spanish newspaper.

❋ Los Angeles Times
213-237-5000
www.latimes.com
The largest daily newspaper serving all areas of Los Angeles.

❋ Malibu Times
310-456-5507
www.malibutimes.com
Weekly publication for the Malibu community.

❋ Palisadian-Post
310-454-1321
www.palisadespost.com
Weekly newspaper for the Pacific Palisades community.

The Interview

Nothing is as important as the interview to determine whether a candidate is the right person to take care of your little one. Are you looking for someone to join the family, or will this person be more of an employee with formal working arrangements? It may be a good idea to have your child nearby so you can see how potential candidates interact with her or him. Most importantly, trust your instincts! Here is a suggested list of interview questions:

❋ Why are you looking for a job now? Why did you leave your previous job?

❋ Why do you like being a nanny?

❋ What previous childcare experiences do you have? Tell me about these jobs.

❋ What was a typical day like in your previous job? What were your duties? Did you drive, prepare meals, host play dates, bathe the children, and perform light housekeeping?

❋ How many children did you take care of in your previous positions? What were their ages? Did your responsibilities change as the children got older?

❋ Do you have children of your own? Who cares for them while you are at work?

❋ What did you like best about your previous jobs? What did you like least?

❋ Did your previous employer work? (If you are not working full-time or are working from home, be sure to ask how they feel about having you around the house.)

❋ Do you smoke?

❋ Do you have CPR or first-aid training?

❋ Ask about gaps in employment or a history of high turnover.

❋ Can you stay late during the week or work weekends if necessary?

❋ Describe an emergency or stressful situation and how you handled it.

❋ What are your child-rearing philosophies and how do you feel about discipline? Do you believe in spanking or time-outs?

❋ What are your interests? What do you do in your spare time?

❋ What are you looking for in a family?

❋ Do you know your way around the city? Do you drive? Do you own a car?

❋ Can you travel with the family if needed?

❋ Do you have any health restrictions or dietary preferences?

✻ Do you swim? (Think about what else might be important to you; for example, do you like to be outside?)

✻ Do you like to read? What is your favorite children's book?

✻ When can you start? What are your salary requirements?

Checking References and Background Checks

Checking references with previous employers can be one of the more challenging parts of the nanny search. Who are you calling? Can you be sure the name you have been given is not a candidate's friend or relative? Some tip-offs for a fake reference are if a nanny's previous employer has moved and now has an unlisted phone number "somewhere in Florida," or if the applicant gives you a questionable handwritten letter of reference. When calling to verify references, be prepared to be frustrated; some people just aren't very talkative on the phone and will not provide the information you are looking for.

Use your common sense and intuition. Be open and friendly and identify yourself in detail. Tell the reference about your family. This will help break the ice and allow you to ask about her family and the work conditions; for example, "Hello Mrs. X, this is Mrs. Y and I am calling to check a reference on Susan Jones, who told me she worked for you. I live in Z neighborhood and I have a three-year-old daughter." It is important to know the kind of household your potential nanny has worked in, as it may be very different from yours. Be realistic: If Mrs. X

had a staff of three and Susan had no household duties, she may not be happy in your home if you ask her to cook, clean, and do the laundry.

TrustLine is the only background check authorized by the state that uses three databases that the general public (including private investigators) cannot access. These databases include fingerprint records from the California Department of Justice Criminal History System, the Child Abuse Central Index of California, and fingerprint records of the FBI Criminal History system. Since its formation in 1987, TrustLine has cleared more than 97,000 childcare providers and disqualified more than 11,000. If you want to perform your own background check, you can either use TrustLine or an investigative firm that provides this service. You can perform a variety of searches, including a social security trace, criminal records search, a DMV search, credit report, education and employment verification, professional license verification, and sex offender registration. Our experience is that the most expensive search does not necessarily yield the most information. A friend of ours had two searches done: one for $300 and one for $100. Ironically, the less expensive search provided the more important information. Please note that some of these reports require a signed release by the applicant.

We cannot stress enough the importance of doing your own background check, in addition to the one the agency does. In one instance, an agency came back with a clean report, while a private investigator discovered some discrepancies, such as a social security number that did not match and a civil file. Agencies usually only check for criminal files. In this case, the civil file was a restraining order—information we certainly found pertinent to our consideration.

❋ The Amherst Group

800-521-0237

This nationwide company will perform various background checks, including criminal, legal, and credit. A criminal check that goes back seven years will cost $25; Social Security, DMV, and credit checks are $15; and sex offender checks are $25. Their turnaround time is twenty-four to seventy-two hours.

❋ 4Nannies.com

www.4nannies.com

This online recruiting site offers a variety of services, including a nanny search, background checks, and payroll services (including tax remittance), as well as a ton of information on employing a nanny. As a subscriber you have access to all of this information, or you can just pay to have a background search.

❋ TrustLine

1-800-822-8490

www.trustline.org

Please see the description above. TrustLine is a useful tool parents can use to check the background of a potential domestic employee. You can call the 800 number and check if an applicant you are interviewing is registered. If not, applicants complete a one-page form that requires submitting fingerprints. A background check with TrustLine costs approximately $125, which is payable to the Department of Social Services, and may take up to twelve weeks or longer to complete.

Agencies

California law requires that employment agencies personally interview the job seeker and make a reasonable effort to verify her or his experience or training. Additionally, California is the only state that currently requires all agencies to register their candidates with TrustLine. Consequently, many agencies don't perform this background check or do it only at the client's request and expense. If you decide to use an agency, ask if candidates are registered. If not, you can do it yourself. Please see the information for TrustLine above.

There are dozens of agencies in L.A. Rather than list them all, we have included only those that our friends or we have had personal experience with and recommend.

❋ A Woman's Touch

310-277-5749

Simone Davis has been running this domestic placement agency for approximately twenty-five years. She charges a flat fee of $1,200 but offers a three-month guarantee and will return your fee if she can't find a suitable replacement.

❋ American Childcare/Rose's Domestic Agency/Domestic Data Line

323-937-3169

323-939-9861

This agency has been placing all types of domestic employees for over eighteen years. There are three divisions for every type of domestic need. Nannies hired through American Childcare are college-educated and usually start at around $800 per week. The fee is 18 percent of the annual salary. Housekeepers and nannies hired through Rose's typically start at $500 per week and the fee is 15 percent of the annual salary. Domestic Data Line places employees whose salary is around $400 per week. The fee is usually one month's salary or 12 percent of the annual salary, depending on the job. American Childcare offers a six-month guarantee, while Rose's and DDL offer a three-month guarantee. Baby nurse services are also offered.

❋ Buckingham Nannies
818-784-6504
800-200-7161
310-247-1877
www.buckinghamnannies.com

Buckingham Nannies is a nationwide agency that has been around for over fourteen years. The company prides itself on its extensive background checks. All nannies are English-speaking, have childcare experience, and are CPR certified. Upon employment, they are registered with TrustLine. The agency fee is 12 percent of the employee's annual salary and comes with a four-month guarantee. It also offers on-call baby-sitting services (see entry in baby-sitting section later in this chapter).

❋ Choices—The Nanny Agency*
310-459-2841
www.choicesnannies.com

Lisa was impressed by the amount of information this agency provided on its applicants. Each candidate completes a ten-page questionnaire dealing with his or her background, experience, child-rearing philosophy, and "what if" scenarios. The fee is 15 percent of the

annual salary and comes with a full guarantee for six months. If after six months you decide you are not satisfied with your nanny or she or he leaves, the agency will credit you 25 percent of the fee toward another nanny up to nine months, 10 percent for one year.

❋ Domestic Connections
818-784-8102
www.domesticconnections.com

Domestic Connections has been placing domestic help for approximately sixteen years. For a six-month guarantee, you pay 10 percent of the annual salary. The owner, Marta Perrone, has written a very helpful guide, called HELP, How to Find, Hire, and Train Your Household Employee.

❋ The Help Company*
310-828-4111
212-366-4111
888-435-7880
www.thehelpcompany.com

This agency places all types of domestic employees and does a thorough reference check on its candidates. The agency has a large celebrity clientele that is willing to pay top dollar for a top-quality nanny, so nannies tend to be on the expensive end, starting at $650 per week. The fee is 15 percent of the annual salary with a six-month replacement guarantee.

❋ Nakeya Hurd and Associates
310-617-9363

Nakeya is a local preschool teacher who started a nanny agency from her large network of child-care providers. Her nannies must have at least two years experience working with children, be fluent in English, and be registered with TrustLine. She also provides baby-sitters.

The Nanny Source
323-930-1101

The Nanny Source has been placing all types of domestic employees for over twelve years. We found that the staff really try to get to know the clients and focus on making a good match with families. The fee is 12 percent for a weekly salary of less than $500 and 15 percent for weekly salaries greater than $500. They offer a one-year replacement guarantee for new clients.

Rosario's Nannies
310-645-7633

This agency has two levels of fees: a flat fee of $800 comes with an eight-month replacement guarantee, and a fee of $1,200 has a one-year guarantee.

Sandra Taylor Agency*
310-205-2810
818-788-7599
www.sandratayloragency.com

This agency has been in business for over thirty-eight years and places all types of domestic employees. The agency has a tiered fee based on the length of the guarantee. For a three-month guarantee, the fee is one month's salary; for a six-month guarantee, the fee is 10 percent of the annual salary, and for a one-year guarantee, the fee is 15 percent of the annual salary.

S'il Vous Plaît
310-395-8812
www.silvousplaitagency.com

The owner of this agency, Marina, came to L.A. from France as a nanny over ten years ago. She started this agency to fill the demand she saw for European domestic help, though she places American nannies as well. The fee is 12 percent of the annual salary (with no less than $1,000) with a replacement guarantee for three months. After three months there is a fee credit of 50 percent for up to six months, 25 percent for up to nine months, and 10 percent up to twelve months.

Valley Domestics Agency
818-996-9782

Cristina Guzman has owned this agency for over thirty years. Her fee is 70 percent of the first month's salary and she offers a nine-month replacement guarantee.

When the Nanny Starts

After you have found the right person, it is important to watch how she or he interacts with your baby and/or children in order to make sure everyone is comfortable. It is a good idea to prepare a list of duties as well as what is expected of the nanny on a daily basis aside from childcare. Again, be specific. Sit down and go over everything a second time within the first few days to make sure he or she understands and accepts the responsibilities of the job. Set a date for a follow-up meeting in two weeks to discuss how things are going. What's working? What isn't?

We are big on giving the nanny a "trial" period. We wait a week or so to see if it is a match before hiring the nanny full-time. This is especially important with a live-in nanny. Lisa made this mistake when her new nanny moved into her home with everything she owned—only to pack it up a week later when it was obvious the relationship was not going to work.

You may also want your nanny to have a physical examination. Certainly, inquire abut her or his health and vaccinations. Depending on where your nanny is from she or he may not be vaccinated against measles, mumps, rubella, or tuberculosis. If not, arrange with your doctor for him or her to get these shots.

Once a nanny is on the job, you may want to monitor her or his activities in your absence. Parents who have had to hire a caregiver very quickly and have little time to train and supervise a new nanny may find that a "nanny-cam" provides peace of mind. Personally, we only know of one person who used surveillance cameras. It was to confirm what they already suspected; the child was being neglected during the day. Most security and investigative firms can provide surveillance cameras.

Taxes and Insurance

Remember, once you hire a nanny you have become an employer. The Internal Revenue Service publishes a helpful guide detailing your responsibilities as a household employer called "Household Employer's Tax Guide" (publication 926). This publication helps you determine if you are responsible for paying employment taxes as well as a checklist of documents and obligations as an employer. To receive this helpful guide, visit the website www.irs.gov or call 1-800-829-3676.

The IRS requires payroll tax filings by a domestic employer who pays a household employee more than $1,400 cash wages in a calendar year. These may include Social Security, Medicare, federal unemployment tax, state unemployment, and disability insurance. Other areas of concern are compensation and disability policies. If you employ a childcare provider for more than forty hours a week, you should buy a workers' compensation and disability policy.

The following companies offer tax- and insurance-related services for household employers:

❊ *Breedlove and Associates*
888-273-3356
www.breedlove-online.com
Breedlove provides payroll and tax services as well as insurance plans for domestic employees. The website has a paycheck calculator if you want to determine how much tax must be withheld for different salary levels.

❊ *Essentia Software*
888-999-1722
www.essentia-soft.com
Essentia Software offers a Windows-based payroll program for household employers called NannyPay. This service will calculate all federal and state withholding taxes and also provides an employer guide for tax compliance. Compared to other services, this program is reasonably priced and is upgradeable every tax year.

✳ *Home/Work Solutions*

www.4nannytaxes.com

This company offers services such as NaniPay, which features payroll and tax remittance through electronic funds transferred from your bank account or credit card. NaniTax prepares quarterly and annual payroll taxes.

au pairs

The au pair program is a government-regulated educational and cultural exchange program with an extensive childcare component. It is a childcare option that some parents find practical and economical. Au pairs come to the United States from various countries, although they are usually European. They can remain in this country legally for one year and work a forty-five-hour week. Generally, an au pair has a weeklong orientation after she arrives in this country and takes one academic course during her or his stay. In addition, she or he is provided with support counselors and a health plan by the umbrella organization.

An au pair lives with you and is paid a weekly stipend (approximately $140) which is established by the government based upon the minimum wage, less an allowance for room and board. In addition, there is an application fee and a program fee. Most agencies provide background information on several candidates. Always interview a prospective au pair over the phone or, when possible, in person.

Some things to think about: Au pairs tend to be inexperienced. They often work in homes with stay-at-home moms. They are not allowed to remain alone with children overnight, so an au pair is not a good option for parents who travel. Another hitch is that they are young, so many will want to have an active social life. There are six sponsoring organizations that place au pairs in the United States. We have listed three below. For a complete list, as well as detailed information on the au pair program, visit the website http://exchanges.state.gov.

✳ *Au Pair America*

800-9AU-PAIR (800-928-7247)

www.aupairinamerica.com

✳ *Au PairUSA/Interexchange*

800-AU-PAIRS (800-287-2477)

www.interexchange.org

✳ *go Au Pair*

800-574-8889

www.childcrest.com

day-care centers

Los Angeles has more than 1,300 licensed day-care centers and large family (up to fourteen children) childcare homes. Licensing is overseen by the California Department of Social Services Community Care Licensing Division. For a list of licensed providers, call 916-445-6951. The Los Angeles County Childcare Directory also provides a list at http://childcare.co.la.ca.us. Centers must meet strict requirements in order to be licensed by the state. The highest accreditation a day-care center can receive is by the National Association for the Education of Young Children (NAEYC). There are over seventy-five centers in Los Angeles with this accreditation. For a list of these day-care centers, you may check the organization's website at www.naeyc.org. This site also lists guidelines and what to look for when selecting a day-care center.

Investigate options offered by your employer. More and more companies are offering onsite day care or are willing to contribute to day-care costs.

For other referrals and/or references for childcare facilities check with the services listed below:

✳ **California Resource and Referral Network**
800-543-7793
www.rrnetwork.org

✳ **Child Care Resource Center**
818-756-3360
www.ccrcla.org

✳ **Crystal Stairs**
Child Care Services, Research, and Advocacy
323-299-8998
www.crystalstairs.org

✳ **Pathways**
213-427-2700
www.cfsla.org

baby-sitting

If you are a stay-at-home mom who needs a little childcare on a Saturday night or a few afternoons a week, the solution is a baby-sitter. You can find a sitter like you find a nanny: through word of mouth, agencies, and newspaper ads. We have some friends who have had luck posting job offers in local college newspapers or on job placement boards. The following are services for finding a baby-sitter:

✳ **Baby Sitter's Guild**
310-837-1800
The Baby Sitter's Guild has been around since 1948 and is the largest on-call agency in town, with approximately fifty baby-sitters on staff. All baby-sitters are required to speak fluent English and have verifiable childcare licensing or experience. This is the service the major hotels in town use for their guests. There is no fee to use the service. Rates range between $10 and $15 an hour depending on the number of children. There is a $5 gas fee and a four-hour minimum. While they often fill last-minute requests, they recommend calling at least one day in advance; call two days in advance for a Saturday night.

✳ **Babysitting Agency of West Los Angeles (formerly Santa Monica Babysitting Agency)**
310-306-KIDS (5437)
This agency has been providing baby-sitting services for Los Angeles families for more than forty-five years. Rates start at around $13 per hour, with a four-hour minimum and a transportation fee based on your location. Calling twenty-four hours in advance is recommended.

If you require a shift of six hours or longer, the price per hour is negotiable.

✲ Buckingham Nannies
818-784-6504
310-247-1877
800-200-7161
www.buckinghamnannies.com

This employment agency provides on-call baby-sitting services. Sitters are usually qualified nannies who are looking for a job, or employed nannies looking for more work. There is a $75 fee to use the service for three months or $50 fee for a year.

✲ Craigslist
www.craigslist.org

Use this website to either post a job or view postings from job seekers. We know many moms and babysitters that use this free service.

✲ MonsterTrak
www.monstertrak.com

This website is the easiest way to reach a large job-seeking audience of college students and, compared to agencies, is relatively inexpensive ($25 per school). After you select which schools you want to access (almost every college and university in and around L.A. has an agreement with the site), MonsterTrak posts your job listing. Lisa placed an ad for a weekend baby-sitter and got at least ten phone calls in the first two days.

adjusting to new motherhood

Once you bring your newborn home, it won't be long before you realize that life as you have known it has changed. Don't get us wrong, the change is great, but it still takes time to adjust to life as a mom.

Without a doubt, the first weeks at home will be turbulent. Don't forget that having a baby is an emotionally draining experience—plus postpartum, those hormones really kick in, which complicates things further. Life may seem to be reduced to baby feedings, diaper changing, and laundry, laundry, laundry. The state of your house will deteriorate before your eyes. If you are an organized person, as both of us are, your new baby will bring a new standard of organization to your life. If we didn't get everything done on our "To Do" list, we thought the day was wasted. One of the best pieces of advice we received after having a baby was to realize that some days you won't get anything done at all—and this is okay! This is a special time in your life; you should enjoy it as much as possible. Allow willing friends and grandparents to throw a load of laundry in or help prepare a dinner. We can't say enough about how important it is to form or join a playgroup with moms who have babies the same age as your own. These groups aren't just for the kids, as you'll see. In this chapter, we suggest dozens of places to meet other new mothers and to learn from the experts. Join a breastfeeding support group, sign up for an infant-care class, take your baby to the park—and before you know it you and your baby will have a new set of friends! These get-togethers are vital to a new mother's sanity, and will become one of the highlights of your week.

Ten Tips For Keeping Sane With a Newborn

❊ Stock the freezer before the baby is born.

❊ Don't be a martyr. Accept help from your friends and family. If possible, hire a baby-sitter. Remember: You are a better mom if you can take care of yourself.

❊ Sleep when the baby sleeps.

❊ Set reasonable expectations for yourself.

❊ Buy diapers and formula in bulk.

❊ Let the house get messy.

❊ Make friends with other new moms and call them often.

❊ Try to get out of your pajamas before noon and get outside every day.

❊ Get help from a support group or professional if you need it.

❊ Order what you need online from a grocery store that delivers, like www.homegrocer.com, Albertsons (www.Albertsons.com), or Vons (www.Vons.com).

new mother classes and resources

There are an abundance of classes for new mothers all over L.A. One of the best resources we found was the Pump Station. While moms from all over L.A. have traveled to the Santa Monica location, many are relieved to hear about its new Hollywood location. Aside from everything you need to breastfeed your baby, they offer infant-care classes, classes in CPR (which every parent and caregiver should take), infant massage, and more. Additionally, they have large resource boards, where flyers are posted for everything from nannies to child development specialists.

Hospitals are another good resource (see chapter one for a complete listing of classes at each hospital). Offerings vary, so ask about resources and/or referrals the hospital can provide while you are there. Also, you don't necessarily have to deliver at a particular hospital to take their classes. Your pediatrician's office is also a good place for resources and referrals.

Below we have listed citywide support and discussion groups that are not hospital-affiliated. Schedules and fees are always subject to change, so call for the most up-to-date information.

❊ A License 2 Parent

Kaela Austin

310-996-7564

www.alicensetoparent.com

Kaela is a licensed marriage and family therapist who has been teaching parenting classes for over thirty years. Her book, *License to Parent*, teaches "simple, specific parenting communication skills, techniques and methods that enhance and improve relationships between parents and their children." Her classes, based on this book, are held in West Los Angeles and Hollywood.

❊ A Mother's Haven

15928 Ventura Boulevard, Suite 116

Encino

818-380-3111

www.amothers-haven.com

A Mother's Haven is exactly that—a haven for expectant and new mothers. Run by Laine Podell-Camino, A Mother's Haven offers everything from breastfeeding supplies and support to pre- and postnatal massage and Kindermusik classes. It also has a boutique that sells clothing, nursing bras, and other baby-related products. During your pregnancy, you can take birthing classes, infant care, and prenatal yoga. After your baby is born, you may want to attend a new mother support group. Additional classes offered include: infant massage, sign language for babies, mommy and baby yoga, Daddy and Me, and Kindermusik. Monthly workshops address topics such as finding a nanny or how to wear your baby in a sling. The store will soon start offering baby announcements and stationery as well.

❊ American Red Cross

Greater Los Angeles Chapter

213-739-5200

www.acrossla.org

Santa Monica Chapter

310-394-3773

www.redcrossofsantamonica.org

The Red Cross offers infant and child CPR training, as well as first-aid basics, and baby-sitting training (for young adults).

❊ Kathrin Auger, Doula, RN

310-430-1113

Kathrin is a DONA-certified postpartum doula and trainer.

Babies Advantage

2461C Santa Monica Boulevard, #128
Santa Monica
310-850-8880
www.babiesadvantage.com

Babies Advantage was started by Kathy Sinclair, a doula, baby nurse, and certified lactation consultant. She provides in-home consultations for parents of newborns on issues such as sleep and breastfeeding. She charges $75 for a one-hour lactation consultation and $100 for a sleep consultation. Her website offers a wide variety of products for a new mother and baby.

Birth and Beyond

Lizabeth Baker-Wade
1810 Fourteenth Street, Suite 208
Santa Monica
310-458-7678
www.birthandbeyond.net

Birth and Beyond is a childbirth education studio that provides support and informational programs for expectant and new mothers. They offer breastfeeding classes as well as private consultation, postpartum "re-education classes," infant-care classes, and infant CPR.

The Birth Connection

34591/2 Verdugo Road
Glendale
818-248-0888
www.thebirthconnection.com

The Birth Connection in Glendale has been "mothering the mother" for over ten years. They offer yoga, Mommy and Me, infant CPR, and breastfeeding support classes.

Breakthrough Parenting Services

12405 Venice Boulevard, #172
Los Angeles
310-823-7846
www.bpinaction.org

These classes are designed for parents of children with discipline problems or divorce/custody issues. Classes are offered in Westchester and West Los Angeles, and cost between $30 and $40 per class plus a $40 materials fee.

Bright Beginnings and Beyond

229 Avenue I
Redondo Beach
310-316-1528
www.brightbeginningsbeyond.com

Bright Beginnings and Beyond is an excellent resource for moms in the South Bay. In addition to breastfeeding supplies, nursing bras, and gift items, this center offers a variety of classes to meet a new parent's every need. The Scoop on Babies class gives every new mom the knowledge to handle everyday situations with her newborn. Other specialty classes include Fatherhood and Preparing for Your Adopted Baby, as well as infant CPR, infant massage, Mommy and Me, and a mother's support group. The center hosts special events periodically. You can also find information on domestic help, massage, and exercise.

Center for Improvement of Child Caring

818-980-0903
www.ciccparenting.org

The Center for Improvement of Child Caring

has developed programs designed to teach parenting skills and strategies. These programs are offered without cost to parents and almost anyone else involved in childcare. You can either take a class that meets once a week for ten to twelve sessions or take a one-day seminar.

❖ Center for Postpartum Health
20700 Ventura Boulevard, Suite 203
Woodland Hills (also has offices in Tarzana)
818-887-1312
www.postpartumhealth.com
Dr. Diana Lynn Barnes, PsyD, MFT, started the Center for Postpartum Health in 1995 to focus on women's mental health issues, particularly pregnancy and postpartum health. As a mom and author, she is a true expert and speaks frequently on the subject. She offers private and group consultations. Call for fee information.

❖ Childsleep*
11645 Wilshire Boulevard, Suite 1100
Los Angeles
310-230-1823
www.childsleep.com
Childsleep is run by Jill Spivak, Tracy Smolin, and Jennifer Waldburger, all of whom hold master's degrees in social work and have experience in support-education groups for mothers and families. Aside from their Mommy and Me groups (see listing in chapter twelve, page 169), they run mother-infant and mother-toddler groups for ages two to eighteen months and offer private parent education sessions on issues such as toilet training, siblings, behav-

ioral issues, and so on. They are probably best known for dealing with sleep issues, from setting a nap schedule to adjusting to different time zones when traveling. Thanks to much local and national press, these gals have become well known as child experts in L.A.!

❖ CoMamas
Crispen Williams, MA
10350 Santa Monica Boulevard
Los Angeles
310-843-2700
www.comamas.com
CoMamas is based on the book *Stepwives* by Lynne Oxhorn-Ringwood and Louise Oxhorn, with Dr. Marjorie Vego Krausz, which was written to assist children and families of divorce. The program is designed to help mothers and stepmothers learn to get along. Email and phone consultations are available.

❖ Cynthia Epps, MS, IBCLC/Motherwork
310-458-6430
Cynthia is an expert in infant nutrition and provides an excellent in-home breastfeeding management service to new parents. She also provides instruction in transition to solids at six months, and, when needed, a gentle weaning plan.

❖ How to Baby
17401 Ventura Boulevard, #B-18
Encino
818-907-0272
www.howtobabyclasses.com

These classes were started by Dr. Jill Campbell, a psychologist trained at Cedars-Sinai who specializes in early child development. The classes provide support to new mothers and involve age-appropriate discussion, singing, and other stimulating activities. A series of eight one-hour classes is $168.

❋ Allison LaJona, MA, MFI
310-636-6989

Allison, a mother of two, runs a parenting group called Partners . . . Now Parents. Her seminars cover topics such as the art of compromise, remembering how we were parented, and acknowledging the marital friendship. Call for a current schedule of workshops. The cost is $45 per couple and is limited to six couples.

❋ Amy Ma
310-339-8631

www.mothernaturebaby.com

Amy is a board-certified lactation consultant and offers private classes in the South Bay. She also offers a Chinese support group in the San Gabriel Valley.

❋ Maba Beyond Breastfeeding
9661 Brighton Way
Beverly Hills
310-271-2589
www.atmaba.com

In addition to carrying baby clothes, supplies, and gifts, this Beverly Hills store offers a variety of services, including pump rentals and sales, breastfeeding support, a weekly Mommy and Me class, and classes in infant CPR and massage.

❋ Maple Counseling Center
9107 Wilshire Boulevard
Beverly Hills
310-271-9999
www.tmcc.org

The Maple Counseling Center is a private nonprofit mental health center that also has a popular parenting lecture series that attracts some of the city's best speakers on various parenting issues. One of the most popular is the education series, which teaches parents about different educational philosophies, and provides tips on selecting the best schools for their children. Visit the website or call for a current schedule. Each session costs $25 per person or $35 per couple.

❋ Mommy Care
11606 San Vicente Boulevard
Los Angeles
310-394-6711

Mommy Care teaches a New Mother Healthy Beginning series that is held in a pediatrician's office in Santa Monica. You can enroll for the entire series ($230) or for an individual class ($50). Classes include breastfeeding basics, mommy care, starting solids, early childhood nutrition and weaning, nutrition for pregnancy and breastfeeding, and your baby's brain. They also offer private in-home educational therapy for children with learning disabilities.

Mommy Zone

18399 Ventura Boulevard, #14 & #15

Tarzana

818-345-6060

www.mommyzone.com

Mommy Zone has fast become a favorite spot for moms in the Valley. The owner, Linda Hanna, is an RN and a board-certified lactation consultant, who formerly ran the lactation program at Cedars-Sinai. In addition to the boutique, which carries everything a new mother or baby needs, there are support groups, lactation counseling, and classes in infant care, infant CPR, and infant massage. It has also become a favorite place for moms to just drop in and hang out!

Mothercare

Lori Sunkin and Susan Satzman-Toczek

310-335-2791

Mothercare provides help and support to women and family members suffering from postpartum depression, miscarriage, and infertility. Lori and Susan work in both the Westside and Valley areas, consult with obstetricians and pediatricians, and provide community resources for help with the above issues.

National Parenting Center

818-225-8990

www.tnpc.com

The National Parenting Center is known for its review of children's products and services. The Seal of Approval is awarded in the fall and spring and during the holiday season to those products that passed independent quality test-

ing. The center also publishes parenting articles written by experts on a variety of topics and has a list of product recalls.

Karol Darsa Nechushtan, PsyD

Attachment Parenting Class

310-451-8880

www.akashacenter.com

Attachment Parenting is a popular parenting philosophy that teaches parents how to develop healthy attachment between babies and their caregivers. Karol teaches an ongoing class on this subject, and provides a support group for parents of babies up to one year old. Call for a current schedule of classes.

Lynn Oyama, RN

310-395-7220

Lynn has been teaching infant CPR and safety, as well as infant massage, for over ten years. Her massage technique is wonderful, and many mothers swear it got them through colic.

Parent Magic

Patricia Zomber

310-459-7464

Patricia has graduate degrees in child development, education, and psychology, and has been teaching parenting techniques for over twenty years. She is a frequent speaker at L.A.-area schools and holds private consultations with parents. Topics include the transition to parenthood, raising a secure child in an insecure world, and managing marriages.

Parenting Pathways*

310-459-9209

www.parentingpathways.com

Betsy Brown Braun is a well-known parenting expert in L.A. with over thirty years of experience as a director of preschools. She has a master's degree in human development and is a mother of triplets—so she speaks from experience! Through support groups and private consultations, Betsy can help you navigate any challenge encountered in parenthood. We can't say enough good things about her! In addition to parenting groups (for parents of both single children and multiple children), she conducts seminars such as "Keeping Your Child Safe," "Learning About Death," and "Nursery School Know-How." Her most popular class right now is "Affluenza: The Perils of Over-Privilege," which she teaches in small groups and at many of the local private schools. Her seminars are $30–$40 per person and she also offers private consultations for $125 for a fifty-minute session. Parenting groups are based on children's ages, and cost $150 per person or $275 per couple for five sessions.

Sarah Petrie

310-235-2739

Sarah is a parent and child consultant specializing in all areas of child development issues such as sleep, breastfeeding, and separation anxiety. Her focus is on teaching lifelong problem-solving skills, and empowering parents to resolve their child's behavioral development issues. Her uniquely evolved method is influenced by the teachings of Magda Gerber and the RIE (Resources for Infant Educarers) philosophy. With over fifteen years of practical experience, Sarah's observational approach offers behavioral solutions for all types of families. Available for in-home consultations, groups, and classes.

The Pump Station*

2415 Wilshire Boulevard
Santa Monica
310-998-1981

1248 North Vine
Hollywood
323-469-5300

www.pumpstation.com

The Pump Station should be the first stop for every new mom in L.A. The owners, Corky Harvey and Wendy Halderman (both RNs), are lactation specialists who got their start at Santa Monica Hospital. The Pump Station's newest location in Hollywood is a welcome addition for moms who had been attending Wendy's makeshift classes at a restaurant in Hollywood. Anyone who has been to the Pump Station in Santa Monica knows the myriad classes offered aren't the only reason this place is great; it is a place to meet other new moms, get support, and raid the bulletin board for everything from nannies to photographers. One of the most popular classes is the breastfeeding and baby-care class taught by Corky and Wendy. There are also new parent classes, Mommy and Me, working mothers' support groups, childbirth preparation series, infant massage, music, movement and development—all taught by some of the best teachers in L.A., who are handpicked by Corky and Wendy. (Donna Holloran of Babygroup originally held her groups at the Pump Station.) There is also a popular four-part series of "Hot Topics for Moms," which features noted specialists in their respective fields (everything from "Coping with Preschool Panic" to "Toxic Avenger, Reducing Exposure in Your Baby's Environment"). Memorize these phone numbers and addresses—you'll need them!

❋ RIE (Resources for Infant Educarers)

1550 Murray Circle
Los Angeles
323-663-5330
www.rie.org

The RIE philosophy of child development has grown in popularity, especially in L.A., where author and founder Magda Gerber is based. The RIE philosophy is based on respect for children, with the goal of raising a confident child. We have several friends who swear by this approach to parenting. Classes are taught by certified RIE instructors at various locations throughout the city. While you attend the class with your infant, the class is generally structured so that most of your time is spent observing your child play and act independently. If you are interested in reading about RIE, check out Magda's books, *Dear Parent* and *Your Self Confident Baby*. Call Karen Ziskin at 310-372-5137 for a current schedule and locations.

❋ Save a Little Life*

Richard Pass
818-344-1442
www.savealittlelife.com

Richard Pass is certified with the American Heart Association and has been teaching CPR and first-aid training for parents and caregivers in both Spanish and English since 1988. He teaches at the Pump Station in Santa Monica, A Mother's Haven in the Valley, and several Gymboree locations. Be sure to check his website, as he is always adding new locations. Richard will also teach courses in the comfort of your own home to a group of parents.

❋ Sign with Your Baby

Laine Podell-Camino
818-601-5381
www.sign2me.com

Many experts believe that teaching your baby sign language before he or she can speak eases the frustration often encountered during the verbal learning period. Babies should be at least nine months of age to participate. Laine offers classes and workshops in Sherman Oaks. A series of eight classes costs $120 and a two-hour workshop costs $80 per couple. Check the website for new class locations.

❋ Kathleen Sullivan

Soft Slumbers
310-276-1605

Kathleen Sullivan is a postpartum doula, who provides emotional and breastfeeding support, along with practical newborn care tips that help ease the transition into new parenthood. She also provides help with sleep training, nutrition, and baby massage.

❉ *Louise Tellalian, RN*
310-274-2272
Louise is a certified lactation consultant teaching breastfeeding preparation classes for couples.

❉ *Julie Wiebe*
310-466-3470
Julie, a physical therapist, teaches "Restore," a pregnancy recovery class that focuses on getting you fit from the inside out and "restoring" the muscular imbalance created by pregnancy. Sessions consist of four weekly classes that help new moms identify and strengthen muscles weakened during pregnancy and childbirth, and teach them how to safely lift their babies using these muscles and correct posture. Classes are held in Santa Monica and Tarzana.

hotlines, websites, and other support groups

There may be times during your baby's first few weeks or months when you will need help and support far more specific than your pediatrician, mother, or friend can provide. It is a good idea to keep telephone numbers of the nursery at the hospital where you delivered and your pediatrician's office handy. Some hospitals have special telephone numbers set up to assist new moms. Inquire about your hospital's policy for new mother call-ins. The following are a variety of additional support groups and referral programs, as well as some important numbers to have in case of an emergency.

Adoption

❉ *Los Angeles Adoptive Parents Support Group*
310-215-3180
www.adoptionhelp.org

At-Home Moms

❉ *International MOMS Club*
www.momsclub.org
A nationwide organization that provides neighborhood support groups for at-home mothers. Check out the website for a club near you.

Breastfeeding

❉ *A Mother's Haven*
15928 Ventura Boulevard, Suite 116
Encino
818-380-3111
www.amothers-haven.com
See description in previous section

❉ *Babies Advantage*
2461C Santa Monica Boulevard, #128
Santa Monica
310-850-8880
www.babiesadvantage.com
See description in previous section

Birth and Beyond

Lizabeth Baker-Wade

1810 Fourteenth Street, Suite 208

Santa Monica

310-458-7678

www.birthandbeyond.net

See description in previous section

The Birth Connection

34591/2 Verdugo Road

Glendale

818-248-0888

www.thebirthconnection.com

See description in previous section

Breastfeeding National Network

800-TELL-YOU

www.medela.com

This network will put you in touch with Medela breastfeeding products and specialists in your area.

Bright Beginnings and Beyond

229 Avenue I

Redondo Beach

310-316-1728

www.brightbeginningsbeyond.com

See description in previous section

La Leche League

www.lalecheleague.org

La Leche League is the premier support organization for breastfeeding mothers. It is a worldwide volunteer organization founded by a group of mothers to assist other moms who choose to breastfeed their babies. La Leche's services are free, nonsectarian, and supported by membership fees ($36 per year). La Leche has trained group leaders in various locations throughout L.A. They run monthly meetings to discuss breastfeeding and provide a valuable telephone help service. To find a leader in your area, call the numbers below.

Hollywood/Silver Lake

323-669-3366

San Fernando Valley

818-377-4474

South Bay

310-545-9600

Torrance

310-538-8953

West Los Angeles

310-538-8953

Mommy Zone

18399 Ventura Boulevard, #14 and #15

Tarzana

818-345-6060

www.mommyzone.com

See description in previous section

Pump Connection

22554 Ventura Boulevard, Suite 112

Woodland Hills

818-225-8822

www.thepumpconnection.com

The Pump Connection offers breastfeeding

pumps for sale and rental, as well as support classes. They also carry nursing wear and supplies.

❋ *The Pump Station**
2415 Wilshire Boulevard
Santa Monica
310-826-5774

1248 North Vine
Hollywood
323-469-5300
www.pumpstation.com
See description in previous section

Concierge and Organizational Services

❋ *All Clear*
310-239-4023
Caitlin Phillips, a former labor doula and massage therapist, recently started All Clear to help people clear their lives of clutter and help them reorganize. She has found that many new mothers benefit from (and appreciate!) this service.

❋ *FeathersSmoothers Baby*
Lisa Gache
310-276-9078
FeathersSmoothers Baby helps moms find, do, or arrange anything. Whether you need help furnishing your nursery, finding a nanny, or organizing a playgroup or birthday party, Lisa is your resource. Rates vary according to the service.

❋ *Live, Love, Organize*
Kimberly Schwarz
310-666-2878
www.liveloveorganize.com
If you are feeling overwhelmed and disorganized, Live, Love, Organize can help. Whether it is rearranging a playroom, designing a storage place, or organizing your kids' rooms, Kimberly can help you get your life in order.

Diaper Supplies

❋ *Dy-Dee Diaper Service*
800-80-DY-DEE
www.dy-dee.com
Aside from being a cloth diaper and supply service, this company publishes a bimonthly newsletter, the *Wet Set Gazette*; it features informative articles and resource information for parents.

General Medical

❋ *American Academy of Pediatrics*
847-434-4000
www.aap.org

❋ *Los Angeles County Health Department*
213-351-7800
The County Health Department will provide you with information on the nearest facility administering free immunizations.

Hotline Help

* ❊ *California Poison Control*
800-876-4766
This hotline is staffed by pharmacists, nurses, and technicians ready to answer any questions in case of a poison emergency.

* ❊ *Child Protection Hotline*
800-540-4000
This number is provided by the Los Angeles Department of Family Services to report suspected cases of child abuse.

* ❊ *Domestic Violence Hotline—Los Angeles County*
800-978-3600

* ❊ *Family Crisis Center*
310-379-3620
213-745-6434
This 24-hour hotline provides counseling and referrals for battered women and children.

* ❊ *Parents Anonymous*
800-339-6993
www.parentsanonymous.org
A 24-hour hotline providing immediate responses to parents seeking help. They also run local support groups. Call or check the website for a location near you.

Multiples

There are many associations for families of multiples in the L.A. area. We have listed some below, but you can also check the following websites for links to local clubs: Southern California Mothers of Twins Clubs, Inc. (www.scmotc.org) and the National Organization of Mothers of Twins Clubs, Inc. (www.nomotc.org).

* ❊ *Beach Cities Parents of Multiples Association*
www.twinsclub.org
This club serves families with multiples from El Segundo to San Pedro. The club organizes playgroups and other family activities for its members. Monthly meetings with alternating support groups are offered, and experts will lecture on "double dilemmas," tackling topics such as traveling with twins, or sleeping and school issues for multiples.

* ❊ *Mothers of Multiples Club—San Fernando Valley*
818-713-8747
This group provides support and education for parents of multiples in the San Fernando Valley. In addition to monthly support groups, parents arrange playgroups.

* ❊ *Twinsight*
1137 Second Street, Suite 109
Santa Monica
310-458-1373
www.twinsight.com
Specifically related to multiples, this organization offers counseling, workshops, and consultations in person, on the telephone, or through email. There is also a workshop for parents expecting multiples.

❋ West Los Angeles Parents of Multiples

www.wlapom.org

Our friends found this support group really helped them through their first year as parents of twins. For a $30 annual membership, you can attend monthly meetings, which alternate between speakers and support groups. The website, which has an active chat room, includes a popular buy/sell section.

Postpartum Depression

❋ Depression After Delivery, Inc.

www.depressionafterdelivery.com

This website offers support and referrals for women suffering from postpartum depression.

Single Parents

❋ Parents without Partners

San Fernando Valley Chapter
818-775-3895

South Bay/West Los Angeles Chapter
310-784-9153
www.parentswithoutpartners.com

PWP is an international organization that provides support for parents who are either divorced, widowed, or have decided to parent alone. The South Bay chapter serves every community from West L.A. to Palos Verdes. In addition to support groups, there are many adult and family activities offered.

Special Needs Groups

❋ American Heart Association

213-580-1408
www.heartsource.org

❋ Asthma and Allergy Foundation of America-Southern California Chapter

323-937-7859
www.aafasocal.com

❋ Autism Society of Los Angeles

562-804-5556
www.unitedautismalliance.org

❋ Blind Children's Center

323-664-2153
www.blindcntr.org

❋ Compassionate Friends

310-474-3407
www.compassionatefriends.org

This group offers support to bereaved parents, grandparents, and siblings.

❋ Down Syndrome Association of Los Angeles

818-242-7871
www.dsala.org

Referral, counseling, and support for parents of children with Down syndrome.

❋ Exceptional Children's Foundation

310-204-3300
www.ecf-la.org

Serves children with developmental disabilities and acquired brain injuries.

❋ *Father's Network*
310-829-6395
www.fathersnetwork.org
Support network for fathers of children with disabilities.

❋ *House Ear Institute*
213-353-7005
www.hei.org

❋ *Juvenile Diabetes Research Foundation—Los Angeles Chapter*
626-403-1480
www.jdrf.org

❋ *Leukemia and Lymphoma Society—Los Angeles Chapter*
310-216-7600
www.leukemia-lymphoma.org

❋ *March of Dimes—Southern California Chapter*
213-637-5050
www.marchofdimes.com

❋ *Muscular Dystrophy Association*
310-450-9032
www.mdausa.org

❋ *Parents and Friends of Lesbians and Gays*
310-472-8952

❋ *SIDS Foundation of Southern California*
800-9-SIDS-LA (974-3752)
www.sidsfoundationofsoutherncalifornia.org

❋ *John Tracy Clinic*
213-748-5481
www.jtc.org
Provides free services to children with hearing loss.

❋ *United Cerebral Palsy of Los Angeles*
818-782-2211
www.ucpla.com

Websites

The Internet has revolutionized the lives of parents. When we were first-time moms, we used to order everything from groceries to diapers online. (Although, now that our kids are a bit older, we actually like taking them to the market. It's a little excursion!)

When shopping over the Internet, beware of shipping and return policies. Some stores offer free or discounted shipping, but keep in mind that such costs can add up and you have to weigh the price of convenience. Returns may be a hassle if you have to repackage items and go to the post office.

What we really use the Internet for is information: finding places, people, and things. It is a great resource when you don't know where to begin looking for something—like a diagnosis for your infant's rash. We even use it to get driving directions before we embark on a long car trip—it is a lifesaver!

As you have likely noticed, we have printed the websites for many of the entries in our book, so there is no need to duplicate all of them here. But here is a list of websites that we use for general information quite often. We hope that you find them useful too.

General Information

www.babycenter.com

www.geoparent.com

www.ivillage.com

L.A.-related Sites

www.babyzone.com

www.citysearch.com

www.dailycandykids.com

www.dy-dee.com

www.gocitykids.com

www.lakidsdirectory.com

www.lapregnancy.com

www.urbanbaby.com

www.whatsupforkids.com

Chapter Five

maternity
clothes

Whatever clothing your lifestyle demands during your pregnancy, you can find it in L.A.'s maternity stores. Between trendy stores such as Naissance and Liz Lange, and affordable chains introducing maternity lines such as the Gap and Old Navy, it is possible to be both stylish and comfortable while you are pregnant. In fact, Liz Lange even designs a maternity line specifically for Target. From cashmere twin sets to Michael Stars T-shirts, you can pretty much find whatever you want to wear during your pregnancy.

Between our six pregnancies, we've shopped in every maternity store in L.A. With each pregnancy, we were amazed at how many new stores and designers had jumped on the maternity bandwagon.

If you are not a shopper, or are sticking to a budget, the Belly Basics Pregnancy Survival Kit (available at many maternity and department stores) provides staple items for your wardrobe from day one of your pregnancy. The kit includes pants, a shirt, a skirt, and a dress, and comes in either short or long sleeves. You can mix and match the pieces or wear them with non-maternity clothes. Another smart alternative is the Bella Band (www.bella-band.com), which is a stretch tube that can cover the unbuttoned waistband of old pants or cinches the waist of new ones.

Keep in mind that you can go all out shopping for maternity clothes or get by with just a few pieces. We have friends who spent a fortune and literally created an entirely new wardrobe with maternity clothes, and other friends who only bought a few maternity pieces. Another trend is to have your clothes "maternitized"; i.e. taking your designer duds to a tailor and having them sew elastic fabric or stretch panels to waistbands and hip seams.

shopping tips

Before you shop, here's some advice from two women who have learned by trial and error.

✳ Hold off on buying maternity clothes for as long as you can. Remember, nine months is a long time, and as you grow larger, you'll need different things.

✳ In the first and second trimester, shop in regular clothing stores for larger sizes and items with elastic waists. The Gap, Old Navy, and Banana Republic often carry inexpensive, machine-washable items with elastic waists. Buy one or two sizes larger than normal.

✳ Buy online. There are many websites that specialize in maternity clothes. Also, many of the stores listed below have websites where you can purchase clothes online. While you might not feel comfortable buying maternity clothes without trying them on, most online retailers have very liberal return policies. In fact, we found that the return policy online can be more liberal than the one at the actual stores; for example, at Liz Lange, clothes bought online or through the catalog can be returned for a full refund or store credit; if purchased at the store, you can only receive store credit or exchange.

✳ Most maternity stores have stuffed pillows that you wear like a belt to mimic your growing belly when you are trying on clothes. While awkward to put on, they will give you a good idea of whether or not an item will still fit a few more months into your pregnancy.

❋ Be careful when buying shoes while pregnant—your feet may expand.

❋ Buy new bras, pantyhose, and maternity panties. You may go up as many as three cup sizes during your pregnancy. Maternity pantyhose by Hue and underwear by Japanese Weekend are some of our favorites.

❋ Don't be afraid to wear fitted clothes. As more and more fashion models and celebrities pose while pregnant, it has become trendy to wear form-fitting clothes. You can feel sexy and be pregnant at the same time. Liz Lange Maternity and Naissance Maternity specialize in that sophisticated pregnancy look.

the stores

❋ *A Pea in the Pod**

352 North Beverly Drive
Beverly Hills
310-273-3522
www.maternitymall.com
Return Policy: Exchange and store credit within 10 days only. Special occasion, intimates, swimwear, and sale items are final sale.

If you want a large selection of fashionable maternity clothes and are not opposed to spending a pretty penny, A Pea in the Pod is for you. We found quality, fashionable clothes from designers such as Chaiken, 7 for All Mankind,

Citizens of Humanity, Joie, Three Dot, Juicy, and many more. While it carries a variety of basics, such as T-shirts and jeans, you can also find a large variety of clothes to wear to work, out on the town, and to a dressy occasion. The store carries exercise clothes, nursing bras, and underwear as well. It also has a small selection of clothing upstairs from Mimi Maternity, which is not as trendy and more moderately priced.

❋ *Babystyle**

1324 Montana Avenue
Santa Monica
310-434-9590

3200 Sepulveda Boulevard (Manhattan Village Shopping Center)
Manhattan Beach
310-802-0224

14006 Riverside Drive (Westfield Fashion Square)
Sherman Oaks
818-986-1588
www.babystyle.com
Return Policy: Full refund within 30 days with receipt. Sale, holiday, and some furniture items are final sale.

Babystyle offers stylish maternity clothes from both its private label as well as designer labels. The private label is very well priced and is a favorite among many expectant moms. Items are available online, in the stores, or through the company's catalogs. The stores also carry clothes for newborns and toddlers.

❋ Cadeau Maternity

8113 Melrose Avenue
Los Angeles
323-297-2000
www.cadeaumaternity.com
Return Policy: Refund within 14 days; after that store credit.

This maternity store was started by Emilia Fabricant, who designed Procreation, the former maternity line of Barneys. It's located on Melrose, just across the street from Fred Segal, so it's not surprising that the store carries stylish, quality maternity wear. Though a bit pricey, the pieces are designed to take you through all stages of your pregnancy. The store also hosts monthly seminars for new mothers and carries a small selection of children's clothes.

❋ Fred Segal Fun

500 Broadway, Suite G
Santa Monica
310-458-9940
Return Policy: Store credit or exchange within 5 days of purchase.

This stylish store carries only a few maternity items but it carries our favorite jeans by Juicy. These jeans fit below the waist and have an elastic panel that allows you to grow into them. The store also carries Michael Stars T-shirts.

❋ GapMaternity

189 The Grove Drive
Los Angeles
323-857-7234
www.gap.com
Return Policy: You can return any item that has not been washed or worn for a full refund if you have your receipt, and for store credit if you don't. Items washed and worn must be returned within 14 days.

GapMaternity is currently available in only a few locations, though you can also place orders online. (If an item doesn't fit, you can return it at any Gap store.) The maternity items here tend to run big but are reasonably priced.

❋ Generations Maternity Shoppe

5658 West Third Street
Los Angeles
www.generationsmaternity.com
Return Policy: Exchange or store credit within 7 days; no return on sale items.

This small store boasts a large collection of classic and stylish maternity clothes that are perfect for the career woman. The store carries some European brands not found elsewhere, plus popular brands such as Childish, Earl, Atessa, and Olian. The owner, Claudia Roberts, gives great personal service, and is planning to open a children's store next door.

❋ Liz Lange Maternity*

346 North Beverly Drive
Beverly Hills
310-273-0099
www.lizlange.com
Return Policy: Exchange or store credit within 2 weeks of purchase; sale items are final. If you order online or through the catalog, you can get a full refund. Sale items are final sale.

Liz Lange, a former fashion editor for *Vogue*, believes that pregnant women should be able to dress just as well as they did before they became pregnant. The store offers chic, trim, and sophisticated clothing for hip and well-to-do moms. Lange's innovation was to do away with traditional maternity panels and instead make her clothes out of stretch fabrics. We love these clothes, but the sizes tend to run small. Still, most of Liz's separates mix and match very well, and are good for both office and casual wear. These clothes do tend to be on the expensive end, but Lange recently launched a less expensive, yet still stylish, line for Target. She also created a workout line for Nike. The store also carries diaper bags, bathing suits, and hand-knit baby blankets. Check out her book, *Liz Lange Maternity Style*.

❊ Michael Stars*

1114 Manhattan Avenue
Manhattan Beach
310-376-8700

1233 Montana Avenue
Santa Monica
310-260-5558
www.michaelstars.com
Return Policy: Store credit or exchange only within 10 days.
This popular T-shirt store carries a small selection of maternity shirts. The comfy tees are designed to stretch with you throughout your pregnancy.

❊ Mimi Maternity

10250 Santa Monica Boulevard, Suite 102
Century City
310-201-0655

6600 Topanga Canyon Boulevard
Canoga Park
818-348-4064

2148 Glendale Galleria
Glendale
818-291-0435

750 West Seventh Street
Los Angeles
213-628-9311

380 East Colorado Boulevard
Pasadena
626-683-9352

3525 Carson Street (Del Amo Fashion Square)
Torrance
310-542-1938
www.maternitymall.com
Return Policy: Store credit or exchange within 10 days of purchase. Sale items are final sale.
Mimi Maternity carries a large selection of reasonably priced clothes for work, casual, and evening wear. Check out the Mimi Essentials line, which offers inexpensive active wear such as tanks, T-shirts, shorts, and jeans. The stores also carry a good selection of lingerie, sleepwear, nursing wear, books, skincare products, and diaper bags. Most of the salespeople are very helpful.

❊ Mom's the Word*

910 Montana Avenue
Santa Monica
310-451-9604

121821/2 Ventura Boulevard
Studio City
818-760-7192
877-452-MOMS
www.momstheword.com
Return Policy: Exchange or store credit within 10 days of purchase. Sale items, lingerie, swimwear, and evening wear are final sale.
This store offers a good selection of maternity clothes, both style- and price-wise, ranging form everyday casual to leather and sequins for special occasions. Brands offered include L'Attesa, Japanese Weekend, Three Dot, and Michael Stars. You can also find nursing bras, underwear, and diaper bags. The sales people are always helpful and will order a size for you if they do not have it.

❊ Motherhood Maternity

128 Fox Hills Mall
Culver City
310-397-4310

10800 West Pico Boulevard (Westside Pavilion)
Los Angeles
310-441-2309

9301 Tampa Avenue (Northridge Fashion Center)
Northridge
818-701-0556

1815 Hawthorne Boulevard (South Bay Galleria)
Redondo Beach
310-370-2827
315 Santa Monica Place

Santa Monica
310-451-1850

Janss Marketplace
275 North Moorpark Road
Thousand Oaks
805-778-0973

3525 Carson Street (Del Amo Fashion Square)
Torrance
310-371-6061

7100 Santa Monica Boulevard
West Hollywood
323-874-2738
www.maternitymall.com
Return Policy: Store credit or exchange within 10 days of purchase. Sale items are final.
Motherhood Maternity carries inexpensive, decent-looking maternity clothes. In our final trimesters of pregnancy, we picked up some comfortable T-shirts and pants that got us through those last weeks without having to spend a lot of money. The stores also carry nursing bras, breast pumps, diaper bags, and books.

❊ Naissance on Melrose (NOM)*

8254 Melrose Avenue
Los Angeles
323-653-8850
www.naissancematernity.com
Return Policy: Exchange or store credit within 2 weeks of purchase.
Naissance Maternity is the place to go for the most hip and trendy maternity clothes. While it does carry other brands, most pieces are made

specifically for NOM. Prices range from moderate to expensive. The salespeople are very helpful.

❊ *Old Navy Maternity**

3369 East Foothill Boulevard
Pasadena
626-351-5946

1232 Third Street Promenade
Santa Monica
310-214-2997
www.oldnavy.com
Return Policy: Within 90 days, full refund with receipt; without receipt, store credit.
Old Navy has a good selection of well-priced maternity clothes, available online or at these locations.

❊ *Sweet Pea and Me*

3758 Sepulveda Boulevard
Torrance
310-373-4800
www.swt-pea.com
Return Policy: Full refund within 14 days with original receipt; sale items are final.
This maternity and baby boutique carries clothes and supplies for both mother and baby. Maternity brands include Japanese Weekend and Olian. There is a large selection of children's clothes from layette through toddler boys and girls. The store also hosts weekly Music 'n' Motion classes.

❊ *Target*

1800 Empire Avenue
Burbank
818-238-0132

10820 Jefferson Boulevard
Culver City
310-839-5200

3535 South La Cienega Boulevard
Los Angeles
310-895-1131

5600 East Whittier Boulevard
Los Angeles
323-725-1121

11051 Victory Boulevard
North Hollywood
818-761-3083

9725 Laurel Canyon Boulevard
Pacoima
818-896-8214
www.target.com
Return Policy: Refund or exchange within 90 days.
Target has its own line of maternity clothes, In Due Time, as well as a line designed by Liz Lange. In Due Time has fairly basic pieces such as shirts, shorts, pants, and even athletic clothes, while the clothes designed by Liz Lange offer fashion and affordability. All of the maternity wear at Target is reasonably priced—most pieces are under $20. Based on our experience, clothes here run big.

*Note: A Pea in the Pod, Mimi Maternity, and Motherhood Maternity are all owned by the same company and can all be found online together at www.maternitymall.com.

baby furniture
and accessories

The world of nurseries and baby accessories can be foreign territory to a first-time mom. Most moms feel pressure to become an expert on everything from cribs to car seats long before their little ones arrive. Don't worry; we're here to help. So slow down, relax, and read on!

The first rule is, don't run out and buy everything the day the pregnancy test is positive. Your needs change as your baby does; for example, you won't need a high chair until your baby is actually sitting up and eating. You will, however, need a car seat and place for your baby to sleep (either a bassinet or a crib) immediately, but you can wait until after the baby is born to buy just about everything else. If you are having a baby shower and have registered somewhere, wait and see what you get. When you are ready to shop, read through our listings. Baby "superstores" carry almost everything you will need; the information here will give you an idea of what you should look for when you go. Keep in mind that it is easy to go overboard when buying for your baby—everything is so adorable! If you like to shop, you may want to bring someone who will help rein you in.

A few other bits of advice. First, order your furniture at least ten weeks in advance to be on the safe side. Also, we recommend purchasing the *Consumer Reports Guide to Baby Products*. This comprehensive guide covers the pros and cons of basic products. Also, double check recent product recalls, especially if you are a second-time parent, as certain car seats and toys have been recalled in the last few years. The Juvenile Products Manufacturers Association (JPMA) has a website (www.jpma.org) that is updated daily, with recall information supplied by the Consumer Product Safety Commission

(CPSC) on everything from strollers to playpens. You can also call the CPSC at 800-638-2772.

Ten Tips for Baby's Room

* Good overhead lighting is key for convenience and safety.
* Have a humidifier on hand for the dry L.A. air and to help prevent colds.
* Have as many dressers, drawers, or shelves as possible—you'll need them.
* Have the room baby-proofed. We've listed several baby-proofing companies on page 106.
* Do not put toys or pillows in a newborn's crib.
* Keep your diaper disposal system and all other changing needs within arm's reach of the changing table.
* Do not hang anything on the wall over your baby's sleeping area.
* A glider or rocker can save the day (or night).
* Curtains and blackout shades may help the baby sleep.
* If possible, leave a play space in the middle of the room.

the necessities
Bassinets/Co-sleepers

A bassinet is a small basket for a newborn to sleep in. It is used for approximately three months, sometimes longer. It can be handy if you want your baby to sleep in your bedroom, or if a full-size crib seems too big for your tiny infant. Also, if you need to raise the mattress for health reasons it is easier to do so with a bassinet than a crib. Styles range from bassinets with wheels, to bassinets that rock, to those that lift off the stand. Some come with full bedding ensembles. Prices generally range from $50 to $150, though you can pay up to $700 for a top-of-the-line bassinet at some of the more expensive boutiques around town.

Co-sleepers are a relatively new phenomenon. They enable babies to sleep next to parents, but in their own bassinet-size bed that has an opening on one side and attaches to your bed. Arm's Reach Original Co-sleeper and Baby Style's Baby Delight "Snuggle Nest" also make the padding separate from the bassinet for parents who want their infant to sleep in their bed but in their own cocoonlike padding. Arm's Reach has patented its Original Co-sleeper plus Bassinet, which actually attaches to the side of your bed, allowing your baby to sleep at "arm's reach" but not in your bed with you; it also converts into a freestanding bassinet. Prices start at $50 for the padding alone, and $179 for the Original Co-sleeper with Bassinet. There is also a Mini Co-sleeper from Arm's Reach that doesn't take up as much room and is perfect for smaller bedrooms and apartments. It also converts into a freestanding bassinet and a changing table. Prices start at $139.

Here are popular bassinet and co-sleeper brands sold in L.A.:

* *Arm's Reach*
* *Badger*
* *Century*
* *J Mason*
* *Kids Line**

Cribs

You can find cribs to fit just about any design style you may want for your baby's room. All cribs sold today should be certified by the JPMA. Its safety specifications require that the space between the crib bars be no more than two-and-three-eighths inches apart; that the mattress fits snugly in the crib; and that all cribs have a locking drop side with a childproof lock-release mechanism.

Here are the questions to ask when you shop for a crib:

* Do both sides of the crib drop, or just one side?

* Can you raise or lower the crib's sides with one hand while holding the baby, or do you need both hands?

* Is the crib stable when you shake it?

* Does the crib include stabilizer bars (metal rods fastening the end boards and located underneath the crib)?

* Do the wheels have locks to prevent the crib from "walking"?

* Can the crib be converted into a youth bed?

The crib you bring home should have a mattress that fits snugly (a gap of no more than one-and-a-half inches between the mattress and the crib's sides and ends). Bumpers should be securely tied on with at least six ties or snaps. Keep the crib clear of any items—mobiles, clothing, and toys—that have strings longer than seven inches. Don't place the crib near any potential hazards in the room, such as a heater, window, or cords from blinds.

Below are the crib manufacturers whose products are widely available in L.A. You should know that because of the strict JPMA regulations, many boutique furniture stores do not actually manufacture their own cribs, rather they buy them from JPMA-approved manufacturers and paint them to match their own furniture lines. Most of these manufacturers are well-known and established in the baby market and some lines, like Legacy and Renaissance, are exclusive divisions of established lines (Childcraft and Simmons, respectively). The choice comes down to what you like and how much you want to spend. Prices range from less than $200 for a Cosco to more than $1,000 for a crib from an exclusive boutique. Cribs from companies like Nurseryworks (www.nurseryworks.net, available at La La Ling—see page 118) and Netto Collection (www.nettocollection.com) have become popular with parents who are looking for something more modern and sleek. Be sure to ask whether the store charges for delivery and assembly. While you can assemble the furniture yourself (Linda's husband insists on doing this), the stores generally send delivery people who know what they are doing.

Here are popular crib brands sold in L.A.:

* *Bassett*
* *Bellini**
* *Childcraft*
* *Cosco*
* *Legacy*
* *Morigeau Lépine**

* *Million Dollar Baby*
* *Ragazzi**
* *Simmons*

Changing Tables

Today's most popular changing tables are the flip-top dresser models. The top of the dresser becomes a changing area when you place the flip top, fitted with a pad, on top of the dresser. Once you are beyond the diaper stage, just remove the flip top and you will have a standard chest of drawers perfect for a toddler's room. Most of the major baby furniture companies manufacture flip tops, coordinated with the cribs they sell. Some changing tables have shelving above the table. At first this may seem ideal, but once your baby starts moving around he or she might hit his or her head if it is too low. Costs run about $120 and up. Another option is to have a flip top made for your own dresser or built in. Or, even more reasonable, you can simply buy a contoured changing pad to fit any plain dresser or tabletop you already have. These are available at most baby stores and cost about $25.

Conventional changing tables have a small pad on top with a guardrail that goes all the way around the top (in a rectangular shape) so your baby can't roll off easily. However, you should never leave your baby unattended, as you never know when he or she is going to roll over for the first time. Popular brands include Gerry, Simmons, Childcraft, and Pottery Barn. Prices range from $99 and up.

Gliders

If you have the space, you'll love having a glider or a rocking chair when you're feeding your baby or trying to get him or her to sleep. Dutailier gliders are the most readily available, and retail for about $250 to $450 depending on the finish and fabric you choose. They are available at Nationwide Baby, Tiny World, Bellini, Fun Furniture, and other superstores. The only difference among the stores is how customized you want the glider to be. But be careful: We know plenty of moms who can't break the habit of putting the child to sleep this way, and they are stuck rocking their two-year-olds to sleep every night.

Strollers

When choosing a stroller, keep in mind your lifestyle and your neighborhood's geography. There are four basic types of strollers: lightweight, umbrella, full-size, and jogger. However, since the Bugaboo Frog was introduced, we have noticed the popularity of the "hybrid" stroller around L.A. The hybrid is a combination of a full-size and jogger stroller. The baby can relax in a bassinet while absorbing the shocks and turning the tight corners in these sporty new strollers. The Bugaboo Frog is the most well-known, but there are many others on the market these days.

We can't stress enough how important it is to determine what you need before buying your stroller. If you are going to take long walks, you may want a full-size stroller with handles that switch from front to back depending upon the direction of the sun. If you live in the hills or have no sidewalk (like many L.A. neighborhoods), you may want a light-

weight, easy-to-fold stroller that you can throw in your trunk. Unfortunately, we both have more than three strollers in our possession. Many moms find that once their child can sit upright, they use inexpensive and lightweight umbrella strollers such as the Chicco or the ultra-lightweight Maclaren Volo most while their full-size or jogger stroller sits in the garage gathering dust.

Other desirable features include a stroller seat that reclines (a must for newborns to three-month-olds), storage space underneath, brakes on all four wheels, and a handle that reverses to allow the baby to face you or face out. Most brands now come with a conversion kit of some kind that allows you to fit a car seat into the stroller. If not, you can buy a Snap 'N Go, which is a stroller frame that you can snap a car seat into, and which ranges in price from $50–$120. As far as umbrella strollers go, Combi and Maclaren are the most popular brands used by parents in L.A. The Combi is one of the lightest (fifteen pounds for the Combi Ultra Savvy PM), but the Maclaren is much sturdier. They are both fairly easy to fold up and throw in your trunk. The Combi Ultra Savvy PM ($279) and the Maclaren Global Buggy ($299) both have conversion kits and fit most major car seat brands.

For a full carriage-type stroller, the hottest is the Bugaboo Frog. It boasts a three-in-one system that can accommodate most popular infant car seats, a bassinet, and an upright seat, so it can serve all your needs from infant to about four years of age. Retailing for around $729, it is truly the Rolls Royce of strollers. Stokke, known for its unique Kinder Seat, has recently come out with the XPlory stroller ($749). The seat is set higher than other strollers. You can pull it right up to a table at a restaurant, which enables your baby to join you for a meal. Combi, Maclaren, Peg Perego, Graco, and Britax all make full-size strollers with conversion kits that hold most popular car seats, and are less expensive than either the Bugaboo or the XPlory. (Our favorites are the Combi and Maclaren.) Again, remember that these strollers can be heavy and cumbersome to carry and transport, so they're really best for strolling around in your neighborhood.

Jogging strollers are a great option for active parents. The large wheels are easy to maneuver up and down curbs and around tight corners. But before you buy one, there are a few things you should keep in mind. First, they have little support, so they are not for infants. Your baby should be sitting up on his or her own before using a jogging stroller. Second, they do not fold up easily; some even require disassembling the wheels to get them in your car. Third, jogging strollers are fairly heavy, and with an added fifteen to forty pounds of baby, it may not be the easiest run. The current top brands are Baby Jogger, BOB*, InStep, Kool Stop, Kelty, and Zooper*. Prices range from $150 for a regular jogging stroller to $500 for a double (side-by-side) jogger.

If you are a parent of twins, side-by-side strollers are really the best solution. However, side-by-sides don't have enough support for infants, so they're not good for parents with a toddler and infant. Instead, a toddler and infant should be in a tandem (front and back) stroller. Moreover, side-by-sides do not hold a car seat, and it may not be a good idea for the toddler to have the infant within arm's reach.

Another option for two children is an attachment that looks like a skateboard, called a Junior Rider Deluxe, available at Tiny World (page 101), that you can attach to the back of just about any stroller. It has fast become Linda's daughter Sarah's favorite mode of transportation.

Here is a list of popular strollers sold in L.A.:

* Aprica
* Baby Trend
* Bugaboo
* Century
* Combi*
* Evenflo
* Graco
* Kolcraft*
* Maclaren*
* Peg Perego*

Car Seats

An infant car seat is one of the most important items to buy before your baby's arrival. State law requires that all babies (including newborns straight from the hospital) must be in a car seat when in an automobile. Hospitals won't let you leave without seeing you put your child in one. Further, the American Academy of Pediatrics has reported that the highest rates of serious infant injuries are due to automobile accidents.

The number one consideration in an infant seat purchase is safety. The first step in car seat shopping is to check the latest recalls. Besides the JPMA website, you can find information on recalls at the Consumer Product Safety Commission's website (www.cpsc.gov) or by calling the Department of Transportation Automobile Safety Hotline (888-327-

4236). Next, remember that all infant car seats must be rear-facing until your child is both one year old and twenty pounds. Last, it is safest to install the car seat in the rear center seat.

One of the most important recommendations we can make is to have your car seat professionally installed. This can be done either at your home by an independent NHTSA-certified installer such as Car Seat Savvy (323-664-7458), at some superstores (such as Tiny World, Traveling Tikes, and Wonderland), and at car dealers who have experts that know how to install car seats correctly in just about any type of car. There may be a nominal fee, depending on whether or not you purchased the car seat from them.

to buy an infant car seat (good for babies up to twenty pounds) and later a full-size toddler seat. The alternative is a convertible car seat that can be used from birth through the toddler years. However, we recommend buying an infant car seat, as they're portable and can be easily carried in and out of the car without disturbing a sleeping baby. Check out the website www.elitecarseats.com; it is a great resource for car seat shopping.

As of September 1, 2002, all car seats have been equipped with the LATCH system (Lower Anchors and Tethers for Children), which makes using car seats easier and safer. The LATCH system allows you to secure your car seat with tethers located in all cars manufactured after September 1, 1999. Most cars can be retrofitted for the LATCH system as well. The LATCH is not required by law, but if you are buying a new car and/or car seat be sure it is equipped with LATCH.

Three designs of restraining straps or harnesses are available in car seats: the five-point harness, the T-shield, and the bar shield. While all designs are considered safe, most experts agree that the five-point harness is the best. The best sellers are Britax, Century, and Evenflo. They retail for $70–$300 and are available at just about every superstore, including Babystyle, Traveling Tikes, Tiny World, Nationwide Baby, Toys "R" Us, and Right Start.

Booster seats and high-back boosters are designed for kids over forty pounds (when a child is too big for a convertible seat), but the law requires them to be in a booster until they are six years old, or sixty pounds. Boosters have a raised, rigid base

General Car Seat Tips

❋ Infants under twenty-six inches tall, less than twenty pounds, and under one year must be in a rear-facing seat. Also, the backseat is safest.

❋ Never put a car seat in front of or next to a front seat air bag.

❋ As of January 1, 2002, California law requires that children must be secured in a booster seat until they are at least six years of age or weigh at least sixty pounds.

❋ Buy a new car seat if you can. If you do borrow one, check to make sure it hasn't been recalled or in an accident.

❋ Buy a car seat that is easy to use. Try it out in the store, and be sure you can maneuver the harness fasteners yourself. Some of the "puzzle" locks are difficult for most people to use, and you will be hooking and unhooking this gadget many times a day. Experts advise you that allows children to use an adult seat belt. Britax and Graco are the most popular models. Prices range from $25–$150. Another option is to buy a car with a built-in booster seat. Most Volvos and Chrysler/Dodge minivans offer this as a factory option. This certainly makes life easier, especially when you have more then two children to fit in your backseat. Be sure to check carefully with the car manufacturer to see what weight, age, and height limitations exist.

Baby Swings

A baby swing may—or may not—be your lifesaver during your baby's first few months. We have friends who swear by them, but neither Jack nor Sarah ever really got into the whole swing-to-sleep idea. We recommend you borrow one before making the investment. The most popular swings are made by Graco and Fisher-Price, and each comes with a variety of features, including different speeds, reclining seats, and musical tunes and timers. Prices range from $40–$120.

Bouncy Seats

The bouncy seat is another potential lifesaver. We know many moms who would not have been able to shower for six months if they had not been able to put the baby in this safe spot. They are portable and can be moved from room to room. Most bouncy seats have a vibrating feature that can lull a fussy baby right to sleep. The bouncy seat is also great for feeding your baby when she or he's starting to eat solid food but is still too small for a high chair. The most popular bouncy seats are Kids II, Summer,

Oeuf, and Combi. They retail from $35–$105 and are available at the superstores and many specialty baby stores in L.A.

Here's a list of bouncy seats available in L.A.:

* *Chicco*
* *Combi**
* *Evenflo*
* *Kids II*
* *Oeuf*
* *Summer*

High Chairs

When you are buying a high chair, it is advisable to:

1. Buy a chair with a wide base to limit chances of the chair tipping over.

2. Find a chair with a one-hand tray-release mechanism, which makes taking your baby in and out a snap.

3. Look for a wraparound tray; it is easier to eat from and keep clean.

4. High chairs get really dirty, so be sure to find one with a detachable seat cushion.

Most high-chair accidents occur (usually with children under one year) when a child has not been strapped in properly and falls out. Don't rely on the chair's tray to keep your baby enclosed; use the safety belt. Also, do not place the chair too close to a surface that the baby could push off of, tipping the chair over.

By far, the most popular high chair on the market is the Peg Perego Prima Pappa, which has a one-handed tray-release mechanism and adjustable reclining and height features. The newest version has a removable seat cover that is machine washable. It also has a dinner tray with a cup holder that sits on top of the tray attached to the high chair. It is an expensive model, at $170. While most old-fashioned wooden, hand-painted high chairs are beautiful, generally they're not very practical. If you want a modern non-plastic look, try the Svan infant high chair, which costs $225 (available at www.babystyle.com). This Scandinavian-designed wooden high chair is both aesthetically pleasing and easy to clean. It also converts to a toddler seat once your child has outgrown the high chair.

Here are some popular brands sold in L.A.:

- *Chicca*
- *First Years*
- *Million Dollar Baby*
- *Peg Perego**
- *Rochelle*

Booster Seats/Hook-On Seats

You may want to buy a portable chair to use when you take your baby or toddler to a restaurant or to other places where high chairs are not available. Hook-on seats have a short life. These seats have also caused many accidents with children under the age of one, occurring when the seat was incorrectly hooked to the table or when the child detached the seat from under the table with his foot. If you do use a hook-on seat, always place a chair under it.

We have found booster seats to be safer and more practical than hook-on seats. They can be used for children up to preschool age, and our favorite, Safety 1st ($30) is easy to fold and store in the trunk of your car for when you are going to a restaurant without a high chair. The Kinderseat by Stokke is another option; it adjusts to different heights as your child grows and is available in different finishes to match your furniture ($199).

Playpens/Portable Cribs

Playpens are a great place to park your baby when you need five minutes to yourself to shower, answer the door, talk on the phone, or make dinner. Some babies can amuse themselves in a playpen for up to thirty minutes at a time, while others will stand at the side and cry as if they are in jail! As helpful as they can be, playpens are big and difficult to store and transport, so you might want to go for a portable crib instead. Portable cribs have thin mattresses and sheets, so they can be used as a crib when you are traveling. The most popular brand is Graco Pack 'n' Play*, which offers several different models; some even have a bassinet that attaches to the top for newborns, a built-in musical mobile, and a vibrating mattress. Prices range from $80-$189.

Bathtubs

Before your baby's umbilical cord falls off, you will be giving your baby a sponge bath in the kitchen or bathroom sink. After this, however, it is safest to use a baby tub or large sponge as it can be dangerous to bathe your baby in the sink—he can easily hit his head on the faucet. Furthermore, you don't want any part of your baby's body accidentally touching a hot faucet.

Most baby tubs are similar; they come either with or without a sponge insert. The Cuddletub by Graco ($25) is a great bathtub, with an adjustable foam cushion and mesh underneath for newborns to rest on and that can be removed later once your baby can sit up on her own. The Rite Temp Infant Bath ($20) has a color-changing pad that indicates when the water is too hot. Once your baby can sit up, try the Safety 1st Bath Seat ($20), which attaches to the tub with suction cups. (Note that if you have slip-proof tubs, the seat does not stay totally secure.)

Baby Carriers

Most people now refer to baby carriers as a "Bjorn," after Baby Bjorn, the most popular brand (the Baby Bjorn retails for about $75). Linda used her Bjorn to carry Eve when she was a baby, leaving her hands free to push Sarah in her stroller. Newborns love being close to your body and sleep quite soundly in the Bjorn. Keep in mind that many experts do not recommend using the carrier until a baby is old enough to hold his head up. Once your baby is older and more alert, she will love to face out in the carrier.

The baby carrier is another item that you'll only use for a short time. We recommend that you borrow one from a friend and test it with your baby to make sure you are comfortable with it. Prices range from $25 for a Snugli to $75 for the best-selling Baby Bjorn. Nojo and Maya make popular slings (about $40 each), which allow you to hold your baby horizontally (so your baby is able to sleep more comfortably). These are wonderful for breastfeeding,

because you simply pull the fabric up over the baby's head and you are guarded from exposure.

Baby Monitors

A good baby monitor will allow you to hear your baby's every movement when you are in another room or even outside—but consider borrowing one from a friend who no longer uses hers. Most baby monitors are A/C or battery operated, and easy to move throughout your home. Newer models allow you to hear and see your baby through a video monitor. Linda swears by this innovation; it saved her from going to investigate every peep she heard in the baby's room. Save your receipt though; you may experience static interference from other household electronics. This can also occur if you have two monitors in your house. We recommend buying two different brands to avoid interference or finding an interference-free monitor. Here are the most popular types of monitors:

900 Megahertz (MHz) monitors: For the best range and clarity we recommend either First Years Everywhere Rechargeable Monitor ($60) or Phillips Read and Rest ($65). Be careful if you have a portable telephone that is also 900 MHz; we found it causes static when they are next to each other.

Monitors with two receivers: A great choice for the upstairs-downstairs house; leave one monitor on each floor. Graco and Fisher-Price make popular models ($50).

Visual monitors: These work with a wireless camera and are far easier to operate than they may sound. Just about every company is making them these days, but be careful: Many people experience interference in their homes and are not able to use them. Mobicam Wireless Color Video Monitoring System ($188) is one of the most popular, with 2.4 Gigahertz (GHz) for added clarity. Less expensive alternatives are available from Summer Infant ($99) and Safety 1st ($129).

BebeSounds Angelcare Movement Sensor and Sound Monitor ($75) is an ultra-sensitive sensor pad, which is placed under the baby's mattress; if the pad does not sense motion for twenty seconds, including heartbeat and breath, an alarm sounds to alert you. Beware: This has the potential to drive you crazy and keep you up all night—even when your baby is safe and sound asleep.

Diaper Bags

Diaper bags come in so many styles you will be tempted to change them as often as you do your handbags! Be careful if you are the type that goes crazy over the newest bags each season: Snacks and sippy cups might not make extravagant purchases worth it. We have friends who have spent a fortune on a diaper bag from their favorite designer, only to have a bottle of milk spill inside it right away!

Beyond that, some advice: You won't believe how much stuff you will carry for your baby. Find a roomy bag with lots of pockets for bottles, wipes, and the like. Look for a bag with a plastic lining and straps long enough to fit over the handles of your stroller— Bugaboo's custom-made bag fits perfectly on the handles of its stroller. A changing pad is yet another great feature. Some of our newest favorites are Fleurville, Petunia Pickle Bottom, Diaper Dude (meant

for dads, but really easy to use for moms), and Paulina Quintana. The superstores also have terrific selections by Baby Bjorn, Babystyle, and Belly Basics, and babyGap carries a seasonal selection of bags that are good-looking and relatively inexpensive.

The last tip: When you have family or friends with children coming for a visit, check www.babydelish.com for baby rentals of all types. They carry everything from cribs to strollers. The company also does baby-proofing at local hotels and grandma's house! (See entry in chapter fifteen.)

the stores

Superstores

The superstores we list aren't necessarily large in size, but they are guaranteed to make your life easier. You can buy all the furniture you need as well as sheets, towels, diapers, nipples, bottles, layettes, clothing for newborns, strollers, high chairs, playpens, baby carriers/backpacks, and much, much more in one easy trip. While most sell toys, their selections tend to be limited and the prices are often higher than those online at Toys "R" Us. Some stores are ritzier then others, some more value oriented. Try to find a store close to your home; you will find yourself going back often, whether it's to buy more bottles or get your stroller fixed. Also, buy in bulk. Most stores won't discount "officially," but they may give you a better price if you are placing a large order. Most will match a better price that you have seen somewhere else. One last tip: Check out each store's delivery policy.

Baby Ant*

18561 Ventura Boulevard
Tarzana
818-609-0410
www.babyant.com
Return Policy: Full refund within 30 days with receipt.

Baby Ant, the popular online retailer, has opened its first store in Tarzana. Carrying everything from diaper bags to strollers and furniture, from brands including Aprica, Childesigns, Million Dollar Baby, Maclaren, and Inglesina. Car seat installations are available with Tamara from Car Seat Savvy (323-664-7458); by appointment only.

Baby Town

18725 Sherman Way
Reseda
818-881-4441
www.babytownLLC.com
Return Policy: Full refund with receipt within 7 days (except on special orders). Without a receipt, store credit within 7 to 10 days. If you pay cash, the store will mail you a check as your full refund. Items must be unopened and unused.

This huge, stand-alone store has a large staff on hand to answer any and all questions. If you're looking for good products at low prices, it is definitely worth a visit. Be prepared to spend a lot of time here. The store carries at least a dozen different cribs and changing tables (including Ragazzi and Legacy), and strollers (including Combi, Maclaren, and Peg Perego), so it helps if you know what you want.

Everything is marked with the retail price and Baby Town's discounted price. They also have floor-model specials and sales. We found the prices on strollers to be about the same as other stores, but the furniture prices are lower. Baby Town also carries a large selection of top-of-the-line bedding (such as Blue Moon) at discounted prices.

Babystyle*

3208 Sepulveda Boulevard (Manhattan Beach Mall)
Manhattan Beach
310-802-0224

1324 Montana Avenue
Santa Monica
310-434-9590

14006 Riverside Drive
Sherman Oaks 818-986-1588
www.babystyle.com
Return Policy: Full refund within 30 days with receipt.

With stores being added monthly, a Babystyle is sure to pop up in your neighborhood if it hasn't already. These stores carry great cribs, changing tables, and bedding at reasonable prices. They also carry car seats, high chairs, and strollers from the most popular companies, including Combi, Graco, Britax, Chicco, Stokke, Maclaren, Bugaboo, Combi, and Peg Perego. Some merchandise must be specially ordered for pick-up in the stores.

Bellini

114 South Beverly Drive
Beverly Hills
310-859-7133

900 Wilshire Boulevard
Santa Monica
310-394-6420

165 South Fair Oaks Avenue
Pasadena
626-449-8113

14514 Ventura Boulevard
Sherman Oaks
818-990-0860
www.bellini.com
Return Policy: Store credit or exchange only.
Before there were so many boutique baby stores, Bellini was the place for baby furniture. You can still find quality furniture and accessories here. We found the staff to be very helpful and knowledgeable, and they can work within your budget. Be aware that depending on the stock situation, it may take eight to ten weeks for furniture to arrive. The company custom makes bedding sets and has a library of fabrics to choose from. Bellini stores also carry strollers, toys, clothes, and other baby accessories, so it's a great place to register for gifts. There is a charge of about $95 for delivery and setup of a crib.

BKI Baby's Room

204 South Sepulveda Boulevard
Manhattan Beach

310-798-6433
Return Policy: Exchange or store credit.
BKI is the place for well-priced furniture and baby gear in the South Bay. Do not let the store's appearance deceive you; they carry just about every brand that the upscale stores carry, but at better prices. Stroller brands include Combi, Maclaren, and Peg Perego. They also have a ton of furniture at great prices, including Ragazzi, Legacy, Childcraft, and Baby's Dream. This store is definitely a find.

Juvenile Shop

13356 Ventura Boulevard
Sherman Oaks
818-986-6214
www.juvenileshop.com
Return Policy: Full refund with receipt within 14 days.
This popular store in the Valley carries furniture, strollers, accessories, clothes, and just about everything you need for your baby. The salespeople are extremely knowledgeable about baby gear. You will find just about every brand of stroller, pack 'n' play, and car seat here. Gift registry is available.

Kid's Land

3807 Wilshire Boulevard, #100
Los Angeles
213-487-9090
www.kidslandusa.com
Return Policy: Store credit or exchange only.
Kid's Land is a great place to find bargains. Located just west of downtown L.A., Kid's Land carries thousands of brands of items for

babies and kids, so you can compare prices on items you've seen elsewhere. If you are looking to save some money, be sure to visit this store.

❈ Nationwide Baby

1911 Lincoln Boulevard
Santa Monica
310-452-3805
www.nationwidebabyshops.com
Return Policy: Full refund with receipt within 30 days.

Widely considered the best prices in town, Nationwide Baby is a family-run business that carries just about every brand you can imagine. From cribs (Pali, Childcraft, and Legacy) to strollers (Combi, Maclaren, and Aprica), car seats (Britax and Evenflo), and high chairs (Peg Perego and Combi), they have it all, at some of the lowest prices around. While not the most glamorous shopping experience, the discounts and helpful staff make it well worth the trip. Gift registry is available.

❈ Right Start

10800 West Pico Boulevard
West Side Pavilion
Los Angeles
310-446-4770

2001 North Sepulveda Boulevard
Manhattan Beach
310-939-1147

2212 Wilshire Boulevard
Santa Monica
310-829-5135

13413 Ventura Boulevard
Sherman Oaks
818-817-6550
www.rightstart.com
Return Policy: Full refund with receipt.

Now under new ownership, Right Start is still good for one-stop shopping for just about every stage in your baby's development. The stores have a large stroller and car seat selection, including Peg Perego, Combi, and Maclaren. The feeding section carries everything from pumps to nipples, forks, and spoons. But beware: The stores are not large and they rotate their selection frequently, so what you may have seen in January may no longer be carried in the store come October. The website stocks just about everything, whether it's in the stores or not. There is a great gift registry and a liberal return policy (except on strollers and car seats; once they've been used you can't return them).

❈ Sid & Me

8338 Lincoln Boulevard
Los Angeles
310-670-5550
www.sidandme.com
Return Policy: Full refund with receipt within 14 days. Furniture is final sale.

This super warehouse near LAX carries furniture, strollers, gliders, bassinets, high chairs, and bouncy seats, all at low prices. It has a huge selection of Pali and Morigeau furniture. Prices on Combi, Peg Perego, and Maclaren are some of the lowest we've seen, but if you find something somewhere else for a lower price, Sid & Me will match it. A large selection of fabrics is available to choose from, so you can personalize your glider and bedding.

❋ Target

10820 Jefferson Boulevard
Culver City
310-839-5200

3535 South La Cienega Boulevard
Los Angeles
310-895-1131

5711 Sepulveda Boulevard
Van Nuys
818-779-0163

14929 Raymer Street
Van Nuys
818-922-1001

7100 Santa Monica Boulevard
West Hollywood
323-603-0004
www.target.com
Return Policy: Full refund with receipt.

Target has great prices on clothing and shoes for toddlers. Brands include Graco, Evenflo, and Cosco, but it's hit-or-miss, so not a good bet if you're looking for something specific. The drawback to this inexpensive chain is that the sales staff is few and far between. The West

Hollywood store, located on the corner of LaBrea and Santa Monica, is a welcome addition to the neighborhood: It is sleek and cavernous, and you could spend all day in the children's department buying everything from pull-ups to Dora the Explorer pajamas.

❋ Tiny World

2356 Cotner Avenue
Los Angeles
310-444-9763
Return Policy: Full refund with receipt within 30 days (excluding furniture and special orders).

For superstores on the Westside, Tiny World is it. Resembling a large warehouse, the store has a large selection of the most popular brands of baby gear. Brands include Combi, Maclaren, Martinelli, Century, and Britax. The large furniture selection includes custom pieces and brands such as Bonavita, C&T, Sorelle, and Mondi. Tiny World is best known for its car seat installation program: It's $26.99 if you buy your car seat from them; otherwise it's $34.99. Be sure to get there early on the weekends, because by noon there can be quite a wait to get your car seat installed.

❋ Toys "R" Us & Babies "R" Us

683 North Victory Boulevard
Burbank
818-841-5037

11136 Jefferson Boulevard
Studio City
310-398-5775

1833 South La Cienega
Los Angeles
310-558-1831

16040 Sherman Way
Van Nuys
818-780-5115
www.toysrus.com
Return Policy: Full refund with receipt, otherwise store credit only.

As anyone who has ever shopped at Toys "R" Us or Babies "R" Us will tell you, these stores have everything and at the best prices in town. Don't expect service, because that's not what they're known for. They carry just about every mass-market brand you can think of, including Peg Perego, Kolcraft, Graco, Cosco, Safety 1st, and Evenflo. You can choose to pay an extra fee and have them assemble items for you, but they don't deliver and you may have to wait twenty-four hours for assembly. They have some of the best prices on diapers and formula (which you can buy by the case) in L.A.

❖ Wonderland

11726 Barrington Court
Los Angeles
310-440-9970
www.childrenswonderland.com
Return Policy: Store credit or exchange only within 7 days.

This baby-gear boutique in Brentwood carries strollers, toys, baby monitors, and diaper bags from top brands like Bugaboo, Maclaren, Britax, and Paulina Quintana. They also provide car seat installation. There are story times and an area where children can play while parents shop.

Specialty Stores

❖ Auntie Barbara's Antiques

238 South Beverly Drive
Beverly Hills
310-276-2864
www.auntiebarbaraskids.com
Return Policy: Store credit or exchange only.

Barbara Bartman has owned this Beverly Hills store for years. She sells a variety of hand-painted furniture, including cribs, changing tables, and Maclaren strollers. She will help you coordinate everything with adorable accessories, linens, and bedding. Design services and a gift registry are available.

❖ Bassinets and Blueberries

369 East Seventeenth Street
Costa Mesa
949-650-2244
www.bassinetsandblueberries.com
Return Policy: Full refund with receipt within 30 days.

Bassinets and Blueberries specializes in hand-painted cribs, changing tables, bassinets, and bumpers. We found the store to have one of the largest selections of bedding, as well as custom-made and ready-made bumpers, complete with matching tissue holders. The clothing and gift selection is also quite impressive. If you want to splurge, the store carries an amazing wicker bassinet on wheels by Michael's Wicker. Other brands include

Carey More and Corsican brass cribs. Gift registry is available.

❋ Fun Furniture

8451 Beverly Boulevard
Los Angeles
323-655-2711
www.efunfurniture.com
Return Policy: Store credit or exchange only.
If you want to be creative and go all out in your child's room, this is the place to go. Known for their decorative beds and playhouses, they will custom make just about any piece of furniture you want. For a fee of $450 (which is credited toward any purchases of $2,000 or more) they will come to your house and personally design your room. Most items take between eight to ten weeks, depending on what is in stock and the intricacy of the painting.

❋ House Boutique

1603 Montana Avenue
Santa Monica
310-451-1321
www.houseinc.com
Return Policy: Store credit or exchange only within 10 days.
The popular House Boutique line has opened a retail store, which carries bumpers, crib sheets, and pajamas. The basic set includes a bumper, crib sheet, and crib skirt and starts at $330, and the patterns are some of the cutest we've seen. You can also buy fabric by the yard here.

❋ Jenny Bec's*

927 Montana Avenue
Santa Monica
310-395-9505
www.jennybecs.com
Return Policy: Store credit or exchange only.
Jenny Bec's carries everything from cribs to Bugaboos. The spacious store has models of various crib styles on the floor, all of which are custom made. It also has a large selection of bedding for older kids, fun furniture, and toys.

❋ Joseph Wahl Arts

5305 Topanga Canyon Road
Woodland Hills
818-340-9245
www.josephwahlarts.com
Return Policy: Store credit or exchange only.
Joseph Wahl manufactures hand-painted furniture in just about every style and color you can imagine. He will design anything you can dream up and his prices are competitive.

❋ La Bella Cosa Kids

3240 Helms Avenue
Los Angeles
310-559-5142
La Bella Cosa manufactures its own line of wood and iron beds, armoires, dressers, and bookcases. They carry cribs from Pacific Rim, Corsican, and Status (starting at $750), which are finished in beautiful colors with coordinated bedding. They also make a great wooden bed with railings for toddlers recently out of a crib; it starts at about $900. This is a great place to find gifts.

Little Red Barn*

23504 Calabasas Road
Calabasas
818-591-2007
Return Policy: Store credit or exchange only within 7 days.
We bet moms from all over L.A. will travel to Calabasas once they find this hidden gem! Carrying unique custom cribs, beds, and bedding. In addition, the store has a great selection of vintage toys and gifts.

Mortise and Tenon

446 South La Brea
Los Angeles
323-937-7654
www.mortiseandtenon.com
Return Policy: No returns.
This upscale furniture store devotes its entire second floor to children's furniture. All of the furniture is made by the store, except the cribs, which are hand-painted and start at $500. The store will custom make just about anything you have in mind, but the best-seller is a wooden bed with a headboard that resembles a picket fence. They also make beautiful cradles, changing tables, and dressers.

Petit Tresor

6341/2 North Robertson Boulevard
Los Angeles
310-659-3970
ww.petittresor.com
This European-style boutique carries high-end furniture, clothing, and accessories, and carries hard-to-find brands such as Gordonsbury, Trousselier, Larucci, and Kaloo. They carry Bugaboo strollers and a small selection of durable handmade toys from Haba.

Pottery Barn Kids*

South Coast Plaza
3333 Bristol Street, Suite 1821
Costa Mesa
714-427-0813

189 Grove Drive (The Grove)
Los Angeles
323-549-9344

3200 North Sepulveda
Manhattan Beach
310-939-7703

511 South Lake Avenue
Pasadena
626-405-1743
www.potterybarnkids.com
Return Policy: Full refund with receipt.
The opening of Pottery Barn Kids stores around L.A. is a blessing for those of us who were stuck ordering from the catalog and website. The stores are popular destinations due to their good-looking furniture and great prices. They also have a great selection of furnishings for older children, and are helpful and accommodating about returns. Just remember: They don't assemble cribs (because of potential liability) so be sure you're ready for the challenge!

❋ Room with a View

1600 Montana Avenue
Santa Monica
310-998-5858
www.roomview.com
Return Policy: Store credit only; returns must be made within 10 days.

Room with a View carries a small selection of high-quality cribs, baby furniture, and accessories. If you have money to burn, be sure to make this your first stop. Cribs start at $1,000. Brands include Simon Horn, Million Dollar Baby, and Michael's Wicker, as well as hand-painted and custom-made furniture. Design services are available.

❋ Thea Segal Designs*

11740 San Vicente Boulevard, #115
Los Angeles
310-207-2577

13327 Ventura Boulevard
Sherman Oaks
818-789-6465
www.theasegaldesigns.com
Return Policy: Store credit or exchange only.

Before starting her own business Thea Segal designed furniture for stores such as Auntie Barbara's. Her hand-painted furniture (for the whole family) has an antique wash look to it, but there is a large selection of colors and coats sure to suit every taste. She also makes matching accessories and sells folk art pieces painted by her family. Design services and a gift registry are available.

❋ Traveling Tikes*

10461 Santa Monica Boulevard
Los Angeles
310-234-9550
www.travelingtikes.com
Return Policy: Full refund with receipt within 30 days.

This great baby store specializes in everything you need for your "traveling tike," including strollers and car seats. The owner, Bryan Pulice, stocks only brands that he has personally picked for their durability and ease (Bugaboo, Maclaren, Inglesina, Maxi-Cosi, and Peg Perego). If you are not sure what you need, Bryan will listen and give his advice so that you don't end up with too many strollers. There is a twins and triplets program, which allows a 5-percent discount on anything bought in multiples.

interior design and decoration

Depending on your time and budget, you can really be creative with a nursery. If you are too busy to shop on your own, and you can afford it, many of the boutique stores listed in this section have design services available. You can also hire an interior designer, but keep in mind that he or she will likely charge a commission on everything you purchase. Some retailers give a small designer discount, but it is usually nominal. Unlike interior design for homes, you won't find any baby furniture wholesale showrooms at the Pacific Design Center. Unfortunately, there are really no secret supplies other than the furniture resources listed in this book.

Muralists

❋ Angelika's Dream Murals
818-446-0643

Angelika will paint "whatever your heart desires" in your child's room. Prices depend on the artistry but start at $250 per wall.

❋ Irina Chelypapov
310-289-5915

www.irinasmurals.com

Irina is extremely talented, with an eye for detail and color. She can paint anything you fancy— from vintage airplanes to animated animals. Her prices are reasonable (about $30 per hour) and she will work with your time frame.

❋ Monica Donoso
310-391-1789

www.dontknowso.com

Monica is a talented artist who will meet with you to come up with a theme or color scheme for your nursery. She can do just about anything you can imagine with a paintbrush and her prices reflect her creativity, at $325 per day. Some of her work can take over a week to complete, but be prepared to be astounded! She did a Peter Rabbit room and when she finished, there wasn't an inch of wall or ceiling space without artwork on it!

❋ Eric James Neiman Studio
310-837-4664

Eric paints fabulous murals of a broad spectrum of subjects, including scenes of car races and characters from Winnie the Pooh. He charges $15–$55 per square foot depending on the complexity of your project. A Winnie the Pooh scene will cost between $300 and $400.

Baby Proofing

Now that you have a baby, what once seemed like a nice, safe home has revealed itself as a safety hazard! Once your baby is on the move—which is not as far off as it may seem—every corner, doorway, and staircase is where they will be heading. If you are like us, you'd like to keep use of the word "no" to a minimum. The only way to do this is to remove as many of the dangerous temptations as you can from your home. You can't guard against everything, and many of us learn by trial and error, but there are certain things that you can easily do to baby proof your home:

❋ Hire a baby-proofing expert to come out to your house and assess the situation. Both Lisa and Linda used Rick Palmer at Family First (310-390-0210; www.ibabyproof.com), an excellent baby-proofing company and store. He will come out to your house and provide you with a free estimate and, if you choose, will return to install everything. Family First will take the time to discuss why you need certain things and how you can make an area secure for your child to play. Call well before you really need the company, as it may take a while to get an appointment. Other popular baby-proofing companies are Safer Baby in Studio City (818-784-6628), Total Child Safety in Thousand Oaks (805-230-1100), and Boo Boo Busters in Manhattan Beach (310-546-4714).

✳ Ask advice at baby stores such as Right Start. Much of the baby-proofing equipment you'll need is sold here and can be installed easily. The important thing is to determine what the potential hazards are in your home.

✳ If you have a pool, install a fence—not just for your own children, but for neighborhood children as well. There are numerous pool fence companies in L.A.; Linda used Guardian Pool Fence Company to install a mesh fence around her pool, which can be removed easily: 818-767-7233; www.guardianpoolfence.com. These mesh fences are not as obtrusive or expensive as the old-fashioned iron gates.

✳ Fill one bottom kitchen drawer that your child can reach with Tupperware and other unbreakable plastics; your child will enjoy playing with them.

Many people baby proof their homes themselves. If you choose to do this, here are some tips from Rick Palmer at Family First:

✳ Choking hazards are the hardest to protect against. Crawl around your house and look at what you can reach at your child's level. Is anything small enough to fit in a child's mouth? If so, remove it.

✳ A closed door is not a barrier to a toddler. Use gates and/or door latches at the top of the door to protect against entry into rooms that you can't otherwise baby proof (like laundry rooms, offices, and gyms).

✳ All cabinets and drawers containing cutlery, dishware, and small items should be locked with childproof latches. All cleansers and chemicals should be moved out of reach altogether. Get in the habit of latching the dishwasher, oven, and trash compactor closed.

✳ Keep an "ABC"-rated fire extinguisher in your kitchen and install a smoke alarm just outside of your cooking area. Use dual-sensor smoke alarms in bedrooms and common hallways.

✳ Have a fire escape ladder for two- and three-story structures. Develop an evacuation plan with two escape routes from every room in your house and practice it.

✳ Install carbon monoxide detectors in the baby's room to protect against gas leaks and heater emissions.

✳ Electric hazards within your child's reach should be removed.

✳ Shorten or clean up all hanging blind cords.

✳ Secure all freestanding furniture, such as bookcases, entertainment units, and TVs, to the frame of the house.

❊ All railings that have openings between the bars greater than four inches or lower than thirty-six inches in height should have a pane of Plexiglas, netting, or another protective device covering them.

❊ Install gates at both the bottom and top of staircases.

❊ Upstairs halls and balconies should not have anything (furniture, planters, and so on) that a child can use to climb up and over a railing.

❊ Low tables with sharp edges and corners should be padded with foam edging or corner guards. Removable coffee-table pads can help as well.

❊ To keep your child from closing her or his fingers in doors, secure them so that they remain open or shut at all times.

❊ All toilets accessible to babies should have toilet locks.

❊ Secure the perimeter of your house. Window screens do not stop babies or toddlers from going through them. All windows should be locked or barred. Pay particular attention to doors that have access to swimming pools.

❊ Many household plants are poisonous; get a list of all such poisonous plants from California Poison Control System (800-876-4766).

❊ Emergency night-lights should turn on automatically when the power goes out.

❊ Keep a well-stocked first aid kit, and become certified in CPR (see chapter three).

❊ Keep a list of emergency phone numbers next to your telephones.

clothes for babies, toddlers, and kids

When you are a parent, buying baby clothes is probably the most fun you can have with a credit card. L.A. is one of the most fashion-forward areas of the country, so it should be of no surprise that you can find some pretty fashionable—and pricey—attire for your tots! In this chapter we're going to help you navigate these stores, whether it is finding that extra-special gift for your best friend's baby, or finding the stores that you'll visit so often your son or daughter will be on a first-name basis with the salespeople!

Before we begin, we want to point out a big difference we discovered between shopping for our first and second children. The first time around we bought every adorable outfit we saw. Jack and Sarah have clothes that they wore once or twice before they outgrew them. The second time around we were smarter shoppers. Now, we tend to buy more things on sale and stock up on staples at stores like Target and Old Navy.

shopping tips

✳ Be sure to save the receipts from your purchases and baby gifts. Once you stash the clothes away in a drawer you may very well forget about them until they are either too small or you have missed the season altogether. If you don't save the receipt, you will end up with either the final sale price for credit or worse, nothing; some stores won't accept returns at all after a certain amount of time. We recommend buying clothes from stores with liberal return policies, and have noted them in the listings in this chapter.

✳ Keep up on the sales around town. Many stores have annual or semiannual sales where everything is marked down 50 percent or more. Fred Segal and 98% Angel are two stores that have big sales you won't want to miss.

✳ Shop at department stores whenever possible. Their return policies are the most liberal, which is useful because often children grow out of clothes before they get to wear them. Even if you don't have a receipt, if you don't cut the tags off you can usually get a full refund or credit.

✳ When buying baby gifts try to shop at stores in the new baby's neighborhood. The last thing a new mom wants to do is schlep all over town returning gifts.

✳ Don't go crazy buying dresses and pants for babies under six months of age. They sleep most of the day, and cotton, terry cloth, and velvet onesies are much more comfortable than "outfits" and dresses.

✳ Infants grow like weeds! So don't buy too much at any one time. If you do your laundry as often as we do, your child can seriously get by with two pairs of pajamas worn on alternating nights!

Layette

Only what you really need!

* 5 onesies (infants tend to poop and spit up often)
* 5 sleeper onesies with feet (infants kick socks off all the time)
* 2 side-snap shirts (until umbilical cord falls off)
* 2 hats (for the visits to the doctor and the walk around the block)
* 4 pairs of socks
* 4 bibs
* 10 burp cloths
* 2 hooded towels and washcloths
* 1 heavier sweater and/or velour onesie
* 4 receiving blankets
* 1 kit containing nail scissors, thermometer, aspirator, and hairbrush
* 1 baby bathtub

the stores

Since L.A. is so spread out, it can be overwhelming trying to find the best place to shop. We have started the list with stores that have multiple locations, and then divided them by neighborhood, providing a brief description of the area and a more detailed account of the baby stores you will find there. Our listings include a mix of stores that vary in price and selection, so you can decide what best suits your needs. Whether you are looking for fuzzy cashmere booties for your newborn's trip home from the hospital or the perfect cotton pants for your three-year-old to wear to preschool, we'll tell you where to find it.

Chains and Stores with Multiple Locations

* *babyGap**

Locations throughout Los Angeles
www.babygap.com
Return Policy: Full refund with receipt. Store credit for amount paid with gift receipt. Store credit for last sale price without receipt.

What can we say about babyGap that you don't already know? Fashionable clothes for good prices, decent quality, great sales, and a solid return policy make babyGap the number one place to shop for your child (just be prepared to see other babies at the playgroup in the exact same ensembles). But don't be fooled into thinking that all babyGaps are created equal; they don't all stock the same items, and service varies among locations. All babyGaps have great rest rooms, and some even have large individual baby changing rooms where you can have privacy while you nurse and change your baby.

* *Babystyle**

Manhattan Beach Mall
3208 Sepulveda Boulevard
Manhattan Beach
310-802-0224

1324 Montana Avenue
Santa Monica
310-434-9590

14006 Riverside Drive (Fashion Square)
Sherman Oaks
818-986-1588
www.babystyle.com

Return Policy: Full refund within 30 days with receipt.

Babystyle has quickly become everyone's favorite store for both everyday staples and unique gifts. The Montana Avenue store is the meeting place for just about every mom pushing a stroller along the street. The stores carry a large selection of Babystyle's well-priced private-label clothing along with many other brands. There is also a great selection of toys, blankets, and maternity clothes. The stores have ample room for strollers, and they also have weekly story times. They stock their most popular strollers and monitors in the store, but you can order whatever you like from the website and you can pick it up at the store for no extra shipping charge. You can also return items purchased on the website at the stores. Brands carried: Babystyle, Barefoot Dreams, Mad Sky, and Ralph Lauren.

❋ Bloomingdale's

Century City Mall
10250 Santa Monica Boulevard
Los Angeles
310-772-2100

Beverly Center
8500 Beverly Boulevard
Los Angeles
310-360-2700

Sherman Oaks Fashion Square
14060 Riverside Drive
Sherman Oaks
818-325-2200
www.bloomingdales.com

Return Policy: Full refund with receipt.

Bloomingdale's has a huge children's department, and the largest layette section that we have ever seen (with some of the best prices). You'll find accessories, toys, and gifts, as well as the fantastic end-of-season sales. We come to these stores for their huge Ralph Lauren sections. But be aware that the Century City location does not have a rest room nearby, so plan ahead! Brands carried: Carters, Little Me, Baby Dior, Absorba, Ralph Lauren Baby, Esprit, Flapdoodles, Baby B'Gosh, Baby Guess, and their private label, Next Generation.

❋ Gymboree

421 North Beverly Drive
Beverly Hills
310-278-0312

Beverly Center
8522 Beverly Boulevard
Los Angeles
310-289-5206

Westside Pavilion
10800 West Pico Boulevard
Los Angeles
310-474-8404

240 Santa Monica Place
Santa Monica
310-393-7798

Sherman Oaks Fashion Square
14006 Riverside Drive
Sherman Oaks

818-783-6821

www.gymboree.com

Return Policy: Full refund with receipt; without a receipt, store credit only for the final sale price.

Gymboree stores specialize in play clothes and activewear for newborn to eight-year-old boys and girls. Their clothes are moderately priced, and there are always sales. They also carry extremely soft, double-thick receiving blankets.

❋ Janie and Jack

189 The Grove Drive (The Grove)

Los Angeles

323-938-9528

1311 Montana Avenue

Santa Monica

310-458-0167

14006 Riverside Drive (Fashion Square)

Sherman Oaks

818-728-1175

www.janieandjack.com

Return Policy: Full refund with receipt.

Janie and Jack is the perfect place to buy your baby's layette. They carry their own line, for sizes newborn to 4T. It is reminiscent of the more expensive European boutiques in Beverly Hills, but half the price.

❋ Life Size at Fred Segal*

8118 Melrose Avenue

Los Angeles

323-651-3698

500 Broadway

Santa Monica

310-458-1160

Return Policy: Store credit or exchange only within 5 days (more lenient with gift returns).

This is the mecca of baby clothes! If you are looking to dress your child (or a friend's child) in something unique and money is no object, Life Size is the place for you! They carry their own wonderful line of dyed cotton pieces in every color of the rainbow, as well as an array of European designers that you can't find elsewhere, like Replay for toddlers. They have a great shoe section as well. The beauty of Life Size is that it always seems to be one step ahead of the trends. Brands carried: Rocky T's, Juicy, Petit Bateau, Miniman, Diesel, Charabia, and Levi's.

❋ M. Fredric Kids

4751 Commons Way

Calabasas

818-222-1699

16101 Ventura Boulevard, Suite 120

Encino

818-981-1261

Brentwood Gardens

11677 San Vicente Boulevard

Los Angeles

310-207-4140

12128 Ventura Boulevard

Studio City

818-985-9445

160 East Promenade Way, Suite C
Westlake Village
805-777-3434
Return Policy: Store credit or exchange only.
M. Fredric, a women's and children's boutique, has multiple locations in Los Angeles and the Valley. There is a small newborn to twenty-four-month section and a much larger toddler section, carrying all of the latest styles and a great selection of raincoats, boots, and pajamas as well. Brands carried: Sister Sam, Flowers by Zoe, Quicksilver, DaNang, Billabong, and Hard Tail.

✳ Macy's

315 Colorado Avenue
Santa Monica
310-393-1441

Century City Mall
10250 Santa Monica Boulevard
Los Angeles
310-556-1611

Beverly Center
8500 Beverly Boulevard
Los Angeles
310-854-6655
www.macys.com
Return Policy: Full refund with receipt.
The children's department at Macy's sells everything from baby skin cream to Stride Rite shoes and offers changing rooms for babies. The stores carry a huge variety of clothing for newborns and older children. The prices are generally moderate, and you can always find something on sale. Brands carried: Oshkosh B'Gosh, Esprit, Disney, Mickey & Co, Sam & Libby, Tommy Hilfiger Kids, and Ralph Lauren.

✳ Nordstrom

Westside Pavilion
10830 West Pico Boulevard
Los Angeles
310-470-6155

189 The Grove Drive
Los Angeles
323-930-2230
www.nordstrom.com
Return Policy: Full refund with receipt.
Nordstrom has just about everything you could ever need for your child, age newborn and up. The huge shoe selection puts others to shame. The stores carry their own well-priced layette line (Nordstrom Baby) and toddler line (Pine Peak Blues) priced from $10–$28. There is a large women's rest room with chairs and couches if you need to feed your baby. Brands carried: Tommy Hilfiger, Ralph Lauren, Little Me, Carters, Skechers, Elefanten, Aster, Nike, Adidas, and their own private label shoes.

✳ Old Navy Clothing Co*

Locations throughout Los Angeles
www.oldnavy.com
Return Policy: Full refund with receipt. Store credit for amount paid with gift receipt. Store credit for last sale price without receipt.
Old Navy, owned by the Gap, is a less expensive (and often more interesting) alternative. Although there are not as many locations as the Gap, it is definitely worth putting Old Navy on

your shopping rotation. There are adorable overalls for $10–$16, and onesies for $5.50, in addition to sunglasses, socks, hats, bathing suits, and whatever else is currently in vogue. And believe us, the sale prices are even better!

❋ *Ragg Tattoo*
199 South Beverly Drive
Beverly Hills
310-271-5423

17245 Ventura Boulevard
Encino
818-990-7244

133 South Barrington Place
Los Angeles
310-440-2989
Return Policy: Store credit or exchange only.
This popular mini-chain carries sizes newborn to 14, but the newborn section is small compared to the 2–6x and 7–14 sections. With cutting edge style, Ragg Tattoo caters to shoppers who aren't afraid to spend a bit of money. You can find bathing suits here year-round. Brands carried: Roxy, Juicy, Rocky T's, At Home, Flowers by Zoe, and Monkey Wear.

Beverly Hills

Beverly Hills is one of the shopping capitals of the world, so it is no surprise that some of the best—and most expensive—children's stores are located within Beverly Hills. Aside from the department stores like Saks, Barneys, and Neiman Marcus, there are baby stores dotted along Beverly and Rodeo drives as well as many of the side streets. Whether your wallet is burning a hole in your pocket or not, these are fun streets on which to stroll and window shop with your baby. There is metered parking on both sides of the street as well as several parking lots with free parking for two hours. To save you time (and money) we've listed a couple of the best baby places to find that extra something special for your child.

❋ *Barneys New York*
9570 Wilshire Boulevard
Beverly Hills
310-276-4400
Return Policy: Full refund with receipt within 30 days. Gifts returned for store credit or exchange only.
At Barneys you can find it all under one roof, and the return policy is better than at most boutiques. Barneys has the latest designer diaper bags, jewelry, and gifts for those looking for unique (and pricey) presents. Brands carried: Juicy, Paper Denim and Cloth, Lilly Pulitzer, Charabia, Petit Bateau, and Barneys private label.

❋ *Bonpoint*
9521 Brighton Way
Beverly Hills
310-278-1161
Return Policy: Store credit only. No returns on sale items.
Bonpoint carries its own label, imported from France. The girls' clothing is fairly feminine, while the boys' clothing is surprisingly "rugged" for a French label. Although it is a bit pricey, this is the place to go if you're looking

for a special outfit for a birthday, christening, or baby naming.

Childhood

8950 Olympic Boulevard
Beverly Hills
310-860-9550
Return Policy: Store credit or exchange only.

This new children's store on Olympic has a good selection of clothing, ranging in price from moderate to high. Brands carried: Flowers by Zoe, Hannah Banana, JM Originals, and Kiddo.

My Little Dimples

201 South Beverly Drive
Beverly Hills
310-276-1501
Return Policy: Store credit or exchange only.

Located on South Beverly Drive, My Little Dimples carries its own brand of party dresses and clothing for children. Brands carried: My Little Dimples, Chevignon, and JM Originals.

Neiman Marcus*

9700 Wilshire Boulevard
Beverly Hills
310-550-5900
Return Policy: Full refund with receipt. Gifts (with gift receipt) can be returned for cash, credit to your Neiman Marcus credit card, or store credit.

The once-cramped children's department has been expanded and relocated to the basement. It still has a great layette section and the best party clothes in town, including christening gowns by Posies and dresses by Helena and Florence Eiseman. The store now has much more in the six- to ten-year-old range as well. Additionally, Neiman Marcus is one of the only places in town that stocks "resort wear" at Christmas. Brands carried: Petit Bateau, Juicy, Dior, Absorba, DKNY, and Burberry.

Oilily

9520 Brighton Way
Beverly Hills
310-859-9145
www.oililyusa.com
Return Policy: Full refund with receipt within 14 days; thereafter store credit or exchange only.

This Dutch import carries its own line exclusively. Although it is a bit pricey for play clothes, if you're looking for something really different and colorful for your child, Oilily is the place to go! They also have bedding, crib bumpers, and diaper bags.

Pixie Town

400 North Beverly Drive
Beverly Hills
323-272-6415
Return Policy: Full refund (on full-priced items) with receipt within 7 days; thereafter store credit or exchange only.

The selection at this Beverly Hills institution is comparable to any department store in town. Carrying just about every brand (in every price range) that you can imagine, it is well-organized by sizes and clothes are easy to find. There is a large shoe store upstairs, rivaling Harry Harris in selection. Brands carried: Baby Dior, Florence

Johnston, JM Originals, Rosette Millington, Naturino, and Stride Rite.

❋ Ralph Lauren*

444 North Rodeo Drive
Beverly Hills
310-281-1500
www.ralphlauren.com
Return Policy: Full refund with receipt.
Ralph Lauren's children's department has everything you need to outfit your baby for play or dress-up occasions. The clothing makes great hand-me-downs. Many of our friends dress their boys in Ralph Lauren, but their girls' clothes are just as cute. It is also one of the few places where we found dress-up clothes for boys.

❋ Saks Fifth Avenue

9600 Wilshire Boulevard
Beverly Hills
310-275-4211
Return Policy: Full refund with receipt. Gifts (with gift receipt) can be returned for cash, credit to your Saks credit card, or store credit.
Saks is known for its layette department (we call it a "department" because the selection is enormous). You can find everything your newborn needs—and then some. The staff is extremely helpful and will even wrap your gift in a bassinet, making for a great shower gift. The sales at Saks are terrific—all the best for less! Brands carried include Ralph Lauren, Florence Eiseman, Absorba, Flowers by Zoe, Heartstrings Baby, and DKNY.

> ### Trendiest Kid's Clothes (They're Sooo L.A.!)
> ❋ Cranky Pants
> ❋ Entertaining Elephants
> ❋ Fred Segal Life Size
> ❋ La La Ling
> ❋ Mini Market

Brentwood/West L.A.

We have listed Brentwood and West L.A. together, because if you are in the car you can easily visit these stores in one trip. Although Brentwood Gardens has historically been considered the shopping hub, Brentwood Country Mart on San Vicente has recently been revived with new stores for kids, so now you can pair children's clothes shopping with lunch at Reddi-Chick (everybody's favorite). There is a shopping area in Brentwood at Barrington and Sunset as well. Aside from the malls (Century City and Westside Pavilion), the stores in West L.A. are spread out. We've highlighted the stores worth visiting below.

❋ Baby Nay

200A 26th Street
Los Angeles
310-260-9949
Return Policy: Store credit or exchange only within 7 days.
Baby Nay, located across the street from the Brentwood Country Mart and around the corner from Harry Harris, carries its own line of clothing, priced between $10 (a bib) and $60 (an outfit).

Baby Sacks

2318 South Westwood Boulevard
Los Angeles
310-470-0987
www.babysacks.com
Return Policy: Full refund with receipt.

This small storefront located in the heart of Westwood carries the owner's line exclusively. Paula Sacks designs everything from the booties to the bedding, and everything is made with 100-percent cotton, chenille, or vintage-looking fabrics. The prices reflect the uniqueness of the pieces, making it a great place for that extra-special gift.

Flora and Henri

Brentwood Country Mart
225 26th Street
Santa Monica
310-587-1188
www.florahenri.com
Return Policy: Full refund with receipt within 21 days.

Flora and Henri's first California store sells its own simple cotton clothing, sizes newborn through 12. The prices are high, but many believe the quality is the best of any baby brand out there, starting at $18 for a T-shirt and up to $150 for a patterned summer dress.

Glen Kids

2944 Beverly Glen Circle
Los Angeles
310-474-9966
Return Policy: Store credit or exchange only within 2 weeks.

Located at the top of Beverly Glen, this store attracts moms from the Valley and the Westside. The store itself is nothing spectacular, but it has a sizable Petit Bateau section, and a smattering of other trendy brands making it a good place to shop on your way to and from the Valley. Brands carried: Petit Bateau, Le Tout Petits, and Flowers by Zoe.

Jigsaw Junior

Brentwood Country Mart
225 26th Street
Santa Monica
310-395-8883
Return Policy: Store credit or exchange only within 14 days.

The popular British clothing designer has opened an outpost in the Brentwood Country Mart that sells size 2–12 girls' clothes. Jigsaw is known for their floral flowing skirts and tops, but they also carry pants, jackets, and accessories. The store is relatively well-priced for an imported European clothing line, and you can find really special dresses, skirts, and tops here for under $60.

Mini Market*

11724 Barrington Court
Los Angeles
310-471-5166
Return Policy: Store credit or exchange only within 14 days.

The offshoot of Market, the popular women's store located across Barrington, Mini Market has fast become a favorite of Brentwood moms looking for the same high-quality, hip-yet-comfortable merchandise for their kids. The owner, Jen, is known for scouting all the newest clothing lines, from both local and European designers, and has such a following that many designers start out their kids' lines at Mini Market before marketing them across the country. Brands include: Woo, Paper Denim, Splendid, C&C, and Entertaining Elephants.

✳ *Rebelette*

Brentwood Gardens
11677 San Vicente Boulevard
Los Angeles
310-826-6600
Return Policy: Full refund with receipt within 5 days; thereafter store credit or exchange only.
This children's store is exclusively for girls up to size 14. The owner really knows her stuff and stocks the hottest brands and styles that every Westside girl wants to wear! Brands carried: Giggle Moon, Lemon, Tiki, and At Home.

✳ *Riginals*

Century City Mall
10250 Santa Monica Boulevard
Los Angeles
310-557-2532

✳ *Peanut Butter Playground*

2042 Westwood Boulevard
Los Angeles
310-475-5354
Return Policy: Returns for exchange only within 30 days.
Both Riginals and Peanut Butter Playground (same owner) have a dedicated and loyal customer base as they are great for finding both reasonably priced staples and unique gifts. Peanut Butter Playground has more of an emphasis on boys' clothes, with a huge selection of T-shirts housed in old-fashioned lockers. They also carry a ton of books, toys, blankets, and even bassinets. The staff is friendly and helpful. Brands carried: One Kid, Charlie Rocket, Cotton Caboodles, and CC Clothing.

Hollywood/Los Feliz/Silver Lake/Echo Park/Eagle Rock

Areas like Silver Lake and Eagle Rock are bursting with babies, and retailers are taking notice. Since our first edition of *City Baby L.A.* came out in 2003, tons of really great baby stores have popped up on the Eastside. Here are some of the best we found:

✳ *Dragonfly Dulou**

2066 Hillhurst Avenue
Los Angeles
323-665-8448
www.dragonflydulou.com
Return Policy: Full refund with receipt within 30 days.
The owner of this new children's boutique in Silver Lake had her store Feng Shui-ed to create an optimal shopping environment, complete with a giant fish tank in the middle of the store that kids love. The store carries the latest clothes for newborns through children age twelve, as well as toys, gifts, diaper bags, and Bugaboo strollers. Brands carried: Flora and Henri, Entertaining Elephants, Diaper Dudes, Converse, Luna Luna, and Robeez.

Grometville

2876 Rowena Avenue

Los Angeles

323-665-5524

www.grometville.com

Return Policy: Store credit or exchange only within 14 days.

Many parents in Silver Lake view Grometville as the store that started it all for families in the area. Owner Lyvonne Klingler left her career in the entertainment industry in 2002 to open this small store, which is stocked with a constantly replenished selection of baby clothes, toys, bath products, and gear for parents and baby. Brands carried: Wee Rock, Baby Lucky, I Can Fly, Claude, and Icky Baby.

La La Ling*

1810 North Vermont Avenue

Los Angeles

323-664-4400

www.lalaling.com

Return Policy: Store credit or exchange only within 14 days.

Located in Los Feliz, Ling Chan's store is a haven for the latest fashion finds for tots. She also carries custom stationery, a selection of unusual toys, and, rounding out the boutique's lifestyle concept, the modern furniture line by new nursery company Nursery Works. The store also holds children's classes in the back room. (Sign-ups are in advance; see entry in chapter twelve, page 180.) Brands carried: Paper Denim and Cloth, Puma, Diesel Kids, DaNang, and Claude.

Paulina Quintana

1519 Griffith Park Boulevard

Los Angeles

323-662-4010

www.paulinaquintana.com

Return Policy: Store credit or exchange only within 14 days.

Paulina Quintana, a children's clothing designer, has opened her first boutique in Silver Lake at the Sunset Junction, carrying her own line of clothes, including tops, bottoms, dresses, and accessories for newborns to size 6. She also carries a few toys from Sweden and Chile (her birthplace).

Rockin' Baby Shop

5048 Eagle Rock Boulevard

Eagle Rock

323-257-8644

Return Policy: Store credit or exchange only within 14 days.

The two Mt. Washington moms who design the popular Rockin' Baby Sling now have their own boutique in Eagle Rock, which carries children's clothes for newborns through size 4. The store also has a play area and hosts special events.

Sugar Baby

7523 West Sunset

Los Angeles

323-969-9143

www.sugarbabyonsunset.com

Return Policy: Store credit or exchange only within 14 days.

The motto of this new baby store on Sunset is "rocker moms not soccer moms." The owners take pains to make their store special and it shows, with touches like the racks of kid-size tutus and leather jackets alongside the clothing, toys, and diaper bags. Brands carried: O'Keefe, Oinkbaby, Claude, Kid Rascal, and At Home.

Malibu

If you want to get away to the beach without actually going to the beach, visit Malibu Country Mart. There are a lot of stores and restaurants, so you can shop without getting in and out of your car. The shopping area surrounds a large park, which is a nice place to have lunch. There is ample free parking in the lots surrounding the Country Mart.

❋ 98% Angel

3835 Cross Creek Road
Malibu
310-456-0069
Return Policy: Store credit or exchange only within 7 days.
While 98% Angel is no longer the only children's store located in the Malibu Country Mart, it still has the best location on the popular sand-filled playground. Overall, it is a bit pricey, but it is a great place for unique gifts. There is a large selection of blankets, diaper bags, burp cloths, and bathing suits. It is a great place to stop before heading to the park. Brands carried: Petit Bateau, Superga, and Miniman.

❋ Planet Blue Kids*

3900 Cross Creek
Malibu
310-317-6157

Return Policy: Store credit or exchange only within 14 days.
The Planet Blue loyal customers finally have an offshoot for their kids in Malibu. The latest addition to the conglomerate carries clothes for babies and children, from newborns to size 14, including miniaturized versions of styles from the adult store and surf-inspired lines by local Malibu designers. Brands carried: Juicy, DaNang, Roxy, Billabong, Puma, and James Perse.

Manhattan Beach

Downtown Manhattan Beach (Highland and Manhattan avenues) is great for browsing and lunching. There are really only a few baby stores, but the scenery is great and the streets are wide with metered parking on both sides. There are a bunch of terrific restaurants and coffee shops that are kid friendly and your child will love taking a walk on the pier for a great ocean view.

❋ Baby A

1108 Manhattan Avenue
Manhattan Beach
310-798-8086
www.BabyA.com
Return Policy: Store credit or exchange only.
This baby boutique carries clothing, gifts, and furniture. The clothing is mainly infant layette, but they carry some toddler clothing as well. Brands carried: Baby Dior, Barefoot Dreams, Plum Pudding, Heartstrings Baby, and Kitestrings.

❋ Baby Wrights

1146 Highland Avenue
Manhattan Beach
310-546-3122
Return Policy: **Store credit or exchange only.**
We understand why this baby store is the most popular in Manhattan Beach: It carries just about every top-of-the-line brand you can imagine. This is one of the few places in Manhattan Beach where you can get Petit Bateau. Everything is displayed tastefully with shoes to match. There is also a fairly large toy and book selection, so it's a great place for gifts as well. Brands carried: Petit Bateau, Kenzo, Queen Bee, Juicy Couture Baby, Charabia, and Naturino.

❋ Girl Mania

916 Manhattan Avenue
Manhattan Beach
310-379-2250
Return Policy: **Store credit or exchange only.**
Girl Mania carries its own brand of clothing for girls sizes 4–14. It also does birthday parties, where girls can have their hair and makeup done, decorate clothes, and perform a dance number.

❋ Sprout*

904 Manhattan Avenue
Manhattan Beach
310-318-7870
www.sproutkids.com
Return Policy: **Full refund with receipt within 14 days.**
Sprout has fast become a favorite for moms in the South Bay. They carry an array of both classic and stylish clothing and accessories for boys and girls, newborn to size 10. They also have a large selection of books, toys, and gifts. Brands carried: Lilly Pulitzer, Zutano, Rubbies, and Mulberry Bush.

Pacific Palisades

Pacific Palisades village has many shops and restaurants, so it is a great place to spend an afternoon browsing. The main shopping streets are Swarthmore and Antioch, on either side of Sunset. There is metered parking all over the village. There's also a great farmers' market on Sunday mornings (see chapter thirteen).

❋ Ivy Greene For Kids

1020 Swarthmore Avenue
Pacific Palisades
310-230-0301
Return Policy: **Full refund with receipt.**
This neighborhood store located in the heart of the Palisades is divided—half for boys and half for girls. The infant and toddler section is small, but they carry some well-priced brands and have a great pajama selection. The owner, Ivy Greene, is friendly and helpful. There is a large LEGO table set up for kids to play with while their parents shop. Brands carried: Juicy, Charlie Rocket, At Home, and Flowers by Zoe.

❋ Petit Ami

15301 Antioch Street
Pacific Palisades
310-459-0011

Return Policy: Store credit or exchange only. Sale items are non-returnable.

Petit Ami, formerly Littlebits, is still a favorite among Palisades locals. While small, it is chock-full of clothing (from the well-priced to really expensive). They have an exceptionally large Petit Bateau selection, as well as hair accessories and books. Brands carried: At Home, Rosette Millington, and La Petite Ourse de Miniman.

Pasadena

Shopping in Pasadena is truly a delight. The streets are wide with plenty of room to push a stroller, and there are stores and restaurants dotting all the shopping areas, which consist of Old Pasadena, the Playhouse District, Paseo Colorado, South Pasadena, and the neighboring area of San Marino.

❋ Pumpkin*

956 Mission Street
South Pasadena
626-403-3366
Return Policy: Store credit or exchange only within 10 days.

Pumpkin is a welcome addition to the neighborhood. It is stocked with children's clothes and accessories, for newborns up to size 6. They also carry Bugaboo strollers and bedding from House Boutique. Brands carried: Oinkbaby, Charlie Rocket, Milk & Honey, Tea, and Icky Baby.

❋ Saturday's Child*

2529 Mission Street
San Marino
626-441-8888
Return Policy: Full refund within 14 days.

It is no surprise that this neighborhood store has been attracting customers from all over Los Angeles since 1972. They have a large selection of smocked clothing for boys and girls from Anavini and Mercatore, and it is a good place to find christening gowns and special occasion dresses. They also carry accessories and diaper bags and have a large shoe department. Brands carried: Heartstrings, Helena, Ralph Lauren, and Burberry.

Santa Monica

Montana Avenue is the heart of shopping in Santa Monica. It's a fun place to take your baby on a walk, grab a coffee at one of the many coffee houses, and enjoy the people watching. Stroll along this street and you'll find a baby store on almost every block. Salespeople tend to be friendly and recognize their regular customers. Prices run on the moderate to expensive side. There is metered parking on both sides of the street and a parking lot on the corner of Fifteenth and Montana.

Third Street Promenade is another excellent shopping alternative. Your child will love to watch the entertainers in the street. You can pick up some great bargains at babyGap or Old Navy, and then hit the mall at the end of the street. There is ample, free two-hour parking along the Promenade. There is also a large parking lot in the Santa Monica Place mall and the first three hours are free.

Cranky Pants*

1230 Montana Avenue
Santa Monica
310-917-1380
www.shopcranky.com
Return Policy: Store credit or exchange only within 14 days.
This is one of our favorite new stores. The owners are known for getting the latest styles of clothes, shoes, diaper bags, and toys from hot designers. They also have fun toys set up for your children to play with while you shop. Brands carried: C&C, Petit Bateau, James Perse, Paper Denim and Cloth, and Paulina Quintana.

Kids Bizz

908 Montana Avenue
Santa Monica
310-451-0237
This neighborhood store carries a good selection of clothes for both boys and girls. Don't be fooled by the store's size: Believe it or not, there is a lot of merchandise packed inside this small space. Brands carried: Miniman, Charlie Rocket, Flowers by Zoe, Baby Lulu, and Petit Bateau.

Little

1323 Abbot Kinney
Venice
310-396-2787
Return Policy: Store credit or exchange only within 10 days.
Little, located on Abbot Kinney in Venice, carries unique baby clothes for newborns to size 6x. It also has books, toys, and accessories.

Brands carried: Claude, Mothballs, Trunk, Robeez, and Coloso.

Papillon

2717 Main Street
Santa Monica
310-452-0969

21 North Fair Oaks Avenue
Pasadena
626-793-9912
www.papillonbaby.com
Return Policy: Full refund with receipt within 14 days.
This children's boutique carries unique clothing, toys, and books that are fair-trade certified and sweatshop-free. Brands carried: Tiki Baby, Under the Nile, Fleurville, Charlie Rocket, and Cake Walk.

Pookie Clothing

1740 Ocean Park Boulevard
Santa Monica
310-450-6593
Return Policy: Store credit or exchange only within 15 days.
This children's store located in the Sunset Park area of Santa Monica has clothes for boys up to size 8 and girls up to size 14. You can pick up something in just about any price range: from a $23 dress to a $180 diaper bag, Pookie has it all! Brands carried: Soup, Oinkbaby, Charlie Rocket, and At Home.

*Pump Station—Baby Boutique**

2415 Wilshire Boulevard

Santa Monica

310-826-5774

Return Policy: Full refund with receipt within 30 days.

No longer confined within the Pump Station's space, the Baby Boutique has expanded into a freestanding infant and toddler clothing boutique across the alleyway. The store's buyer really listens to what moms want for their babies. There's also a good selection of preemie clothing, diaper bags, and gadgets for babies. Brands carried: Petit Bateau, KissyKissy, Preemie Yums, Charlie Rocket, Robeez, and At Home.

*This Little Piggy Wears Cotton**

309 Wilshire Boulevard (across from Third Street Promenade)

Santa Monica

310-260-272

www.littlepiggy.com

Return Policy: Store credit or exchange only within 10 days.

This Little Piggy is located across from Third Street Promenade, and it's worth crossing Wilshire Boulevard for a visit. It is larger than most baby boutiques, beautifully decorated, and cleverly organized. In addition to clothing, it has a large toy section, books, shoes, hooded towels, diaper bags, and its own line of hair- and skin-care products. A great gift is their own line of "silkie" blankets in two sizes: large for the crib and small for trips around town. Brands carried: Petit Bateau, Juicy, Charlie Rocket, Baby Lulu, and Piggy Basics.

The Valley: Encino/Sherman Oaks/Woodland Hills

Van Nuys and Ventura Boulevard are dotted with all types of baby stores: some are located in strip malls and others inside malls. The chain stores that have locations in the Valley have been listed in the previous sections. Below we have listed a few of the popular boutiques.

Encino Kids

17157 Ventura Boulevard

Encino

818-990-4510

Return Policy: Store credit or exchange only.

This small store is well stocked with both European and American children's clothes for newborns through size 16. Don't let the size of the store fool you; there are tons of great brands offered here. Brands carried: Petit Bateau, JM Originals, Sara Sara, Cache Cache, and Miniman.

*Hopscotch**

16740 Ventura Boulevard

Encino

818-783-4080

Return Policy: Store credit or exchange only.

This welcome addition to Encino is located next door to Harry Harris shoes and carries newborn through size 14 clothes. It has equal amounts of boys' and girls' clothing and some furniture, with lovely fabrics to choose from. Brands carried: Hard Tail, Kissy Kissy, Juicy, and Petit Bateau.

❊ L.A. Babes

19837 Ventura Boulevard

Woodland Hills

818-704-4800

Return Policy: **Store credit or exchange only within 7 days.**

This small baby boutique is attached to the popular kids store A La Popcorn. They carry newborn to 6x clothes, and have a small play area in the front of the store. There are a bunch of well-priced lines and they also carry a large selection of tights, socks, and stuffed animals. Brands carried: Hard Tail, Flowers by Zoe, Quicksilver, and Perry Ellis.

❊ Oodles

13021 Ventura Boulevard

Studio City

818-783-2392

Return Policy: **Store credit or exchange only.**

Strategically located on the same stretch of Ventura Boulevard as the popular Stacey Todd women's boutique, Oodles is a small children's boutique stocked with all the latest designer clothing for kids, newborn to size 10. Brands carried: Charabia, Petit Bateau, and Queen Bee.

❊ Smooch

4774 Park Granada, Suite 2

Calabasas

818-222-4211

Return Policy: **Store credit or exchange only within 10 days.**

This new children's clothing boutique is a welcome addition for Calabasas moms. It's stocked full of kids' clothing and gifts, from newborn to size 14. Brands carried: Juicy, Paper Denim and Cloth, C&C, Nolita Pocket, and Puma.

West Hollywood/Hancock Park/Studio City

This area is so spread out that anything east of La Cienega seems to encompass "West Hollywood" and its surrounding areas. Studio City is just over the hill and many people travel back and forth, especially on Sundays for the great farmers' market (see chapter thirteen).

❊ Entertaining Elephants*

120531/2 Ventura Place

Studio City

818-766-9177

www.entertainingelephants.com

Return Policy: **Store credit or exchange only.**

This store, located on a nondescript side street in Studio City, is the find of a lifetime! Four years ago the owner, Ellen Massee, set out to bring sophisticated and unique children's clothing to L.A.—and she has accomplished it. Ellen has a great eye for color and textiles, and the store has become known for its line of custom-dyed, cotton-knit basics for babies and toddlers, with little embroidered elephants popping up on hip children from coast to coast. The store also features an eclectic mix of beautiful, soulful, and whimsical toys, furnishings, accessories, and decorative items for children. This store is a must for anyone looking for unique clothes and gifts.

Flicka

204 North Larchmont Boulevard
Los Angeles
323-466-5822
Return Policy: Store credit or exchange only.
This Hancock Park store is located on the popular strip of Larchmont between Third Street and Beverly. Larchmont is a great street for strolling and people watching. Brands carried: Petit Bateau, Tiki, Flowers by Zoe, and Cotton Caboodles.

For Kids Only

746 North Fairfax Avenue
Los Angeles
323-650-4885

18155 Ventura Boulevard
Tarzana
818-708-9543
Return Policy: Exchange only within 7 days.
This large discount children's store carries designer clothes and shoes at 25–60 percent off the retail price. The price tags are marked with both the retail price and the discounted price—in case you didn't already know you were getting a good deal. While you might have to spend some time searching, if you hit it on the right day you can walk away with some great bargains. It also has a large selection of dress blazers for boys.

Lost and Found*

6314 Yucca Street
Los Angeles
323-856-0921
Return Policy: Store credit or exchange only.

This brightly colored store located in the heart of Hollywood stocks trendy baby clothes. The owner, Jamie Rosenthal, designs her own label, which she carries exclusively. She really goes the extra mile to get a good selection of boys' clothes. Brands carried: Baby YaYa, Queen Bee, Marimekko, Bee and Dragons, Charlie Rocket, C&C, and Jeanbourget.

pip-squeak*

8213 West Third Street
Los Angeles
323-653-3250
www.pipsqueakinLA.com
Return Policy: Store credit or exchange only.
This adorable store is full of specialty-type clothes for newborns to size 10. It's located on a strip of Third Street that is great for lunching and shopping. The loft upstairs is available to mothers to rent out for Mommy and Me groups. Brands carried: Charabia, Nolita Pocket, James Perse, Quincy, Little Mass, Flora and Henri, and Chevignon.

Sunset Kids

8669 Sunset Boulevard
Los Angeles
310-659-4411
Return Policy: Store credit or exchange only.
This ultra-trendy kids' boutique, located in Sunset Plaza, carries the latest fashions and designer clothes for children. If you are looking for something unique, like a hand-painted pink leather jacket, this is the place! Brands carried: Petit Bateau, Miniman, Rocky T's, Riley, and Diesel.

Best Places to Find Preemie Clothes

❊ Gap
❊ Nordstrom
❊ Preemie.com
❊ The Pump Station

shoes

❊ **Brooks Shoes for Kids**
459 North Canon Drive
Beverly Hills
310-274-2278

Westside Pavilion
10800 West Pico Boulevard
Los Angeles
310-470-6040

1703 Wilshire Boulevard
Santa Monica
310-315-9898

Sherman Oaks Fashion Square
14006 Riverside Drive
Sherman Oaks
818-501-2982
Return Policy: Full refund within 15 days; thereafter exchange only.
This upscale chain of shoe stores has branches all over southern California and offers just about every kind of shoe your child will ever need. They carry moderately priced to expensive shoes, and while the prices are no better than anywhere else in town, they do have great end-of-season sales. Brands carried: Elefanten, Naturino, Stride Rite, and Skechers.

❊ **Harry Harris Shoes***
409 North Canon Drive
Beverly Hills
310-274-8481

16744 Ventura Boulevard
Encino
818-981-2641

2528 San Vicente Boulevard
Santa Monica
310-393-5718
Return Policy: Store credit or exchange only.
This is the place to buy kids shoes in L.A. It's not just that the store has a good selection (which it does), but also that the staff really know their stuff. If you want shoes that fit properly, this is the place to go. Bear in mind, service this good takes a while, so don't expect to be in and out in five minutes. Also, high style and service like this don't come cheap, but to compensate the store has a "Buy Twelve, Get One Free" card, so why not grab that extra pair while you're there? Brands carried: Stride Rite, Adidas, Skechers, and Naturino.

❊ **Ruby Slippers**
171 South Barrington Place
Los Angeles
310-476-0699
Return Policy: Store credit or exchange only.
Ruby Slippers carries shoes from size 4 and up.

They also have socks, tights, lunch boxes, and backpacks. Ruby Slippers doesn't have the same old-time neighborhood feel as Harry Harris, but they carry everything you'll need for your toddler's growing feet. Brands carried: Aster, Naturino, Stride Rite, New Balance, Adidas, Puma, and Skechers.

❋ Shoe Box
23673 Calabasas Road
Calabasas
818-222-8677
Return Policy: Full refund with receipt.
Located across the street from Calabasas Commons and carries a huge selection of shoes for growing girls and boys, from infants on up. Brands carried: Oilily, Nina, Primigi, Nike, Adidas, and Naturino.

❋ Skechers USA
8500 Beverly Boulevard (Beverly Center)
Los Angeles
310-652-5185

1343 Third Street Promenade
Santa Monica
310-899-0151
Return Policy: Full refund with receipt.
This popular shoe store has a children's section in the back where you can find a wide selection of trendy, quality shoes for your tots.

❋ Village Footwear Kids
115 North Larchmont Boulevard
Los Angeles
323-461-3535

Return Policy: Store credit or exchange only.
This Hancock Park store mostly carries shoes for bigger kids, but they have a small toddler section. Brands carried: Aster, Skechers, and Naturino.

resale

❋ Bearly Used
1136 North Hollywood Way
Burbank
818-954-9436
Return Policy: Store credit or exchange only.
This popular Burbank used-clothing store stocks clothes that are almost as good as new. They also carry strollers, high chairs, and other baby equipment in fairly good condition. They will give you store credit in exchange for your items for sale.

❋ Flap Jacks
10590 Pico Boulevard
Los Angeles
310-204-1896
Return Policy: Store credit and exchange only within 7 days.
This small resale shop carries clothes for newborns and up in reasonably good condition. We even found a three-piece Ralph Lauren outfit with the tags still on it! It also carries used toys and strollers. The owner will give you 40 percent of the price once it is purchased, and with shirts priced at $4.99 and lower, they go pretty quickly. Flap Jacks will only take one bag of clothes and one bag of toys at a time, because they have so much back stock.

❊ Noodles

4907 South Sepulveda Boulevard
Culver City
310-737-1766
Return Policy: Store credit or exchange only within 7 days.

This small resale shop is located in a Culver City strip mall. The store is stuffed with clothing, most of which is in pretty good condition. There is a smattering of toys, strollers, monitors, and books. On the day Linda was visiting, there even was a breast pump. You can sell your clothing here for store credit, or they'll give you 25 percent of the sale price. But the prices are pretty low. Given the $1 sale rack, we recommend opting for the store credit.

❊ Once Upon a Child

1032 West Alameda Avenue
Burbank
818-557-7400
Return Policy: Full refund within 7 days.

The motto at this children's resale shop is "kids' stuff with previous experience." It is part of a large national chain of stores that specialize in both new and used clothing, furniture, strollers, toys, and books. It will take your used items and give you between 20–40 percent of the resale price, in cash, at the time you drop it off.

❊ Once 'n' Again

3012 Santa Monica Boulevard
Santa Monica
310-315-1044
Return Policy: Store credit and exchange only.

This family-owned children's resale shop has everything from clothing to strollers. Bring in your old children's clothing, toys, or gear, and you get store credit for what's taken. If your items are not sold, you can opt to donate them to the Westside Children's Center.

❊ Twerps*

5060 Eagle Rock Boulevard
Los Angeles
323-256-7608
Return Policy: Store credit of exchange only on new items.

Twerps is a great find! This Eagle Rock store carries both used and new clothing. The back of the store houses the used clothing; they take consignments by appointment only, and pay 30 percent of the price in cash. In the front room, they have a large selection of new children's shoes, toys, and clothing.

Best Places to Find Bargains

- ❊ Gap
- ❊ Gymboree
- ❊ Old Navy
- ❊ Macy's
- ❊ Nordstrom
- ❊ Target

shopping malls

Beverly Center

8500 Beverly Boulevard
Los Angeles
310-854-0070
www.beverlycenter.com

This mall is located on the outskirts of Beverly Hills and is home to all the old standbys such as babyGap, Guess Kids, Gymboree, Skechers, Puzzle Zoo, and Sanrio. They also have a Bloomingdale's and Macy's. The food court is kid friendly and it has a freestanding California Pizza Kitchen and Hard Rock Cafe. The only downside to this mall is the parking lot; it is extremely confusing and has just one elevator, which can mean a long wait if you have a stroller in tow.

Glendale Galleria

2148 Glendale Galleria
Glendale
818-240-9481
www.glendalegalleria.com

This huge indoor mall in downtown Glendale attracts shoppers from Pasadena, Silver Lake, and even Burbank with just about every store you can imagine. There is a Nordstrom and Macy's, babyGap, Gymboree, Stride Rite, Disney Store, Janie and Jack, KB Toys, LEGO, Color Me Mine, and Build-a-Bear. Nordstrom has a large rest room if you need to take a break or feed your baby. There's a children's play area and a large food court.

The Grove

189 The Grove Drive (adjacent to Third and Fairfax)
Los Angeles
323-900-8000
www.TheGroveLA.com

This outdoor mall, located directly next to the farmers' market, is a great place to take the kids. There is a babyGap, Pottery Barn Kids, Janie and Jack, and Nordstrom. Your children will love the fountain that shoots water syncopated to music; and in the summer there are a multitude of kids' entertainers. There is plenty of parking, and a trolley that kids love, which runs between the farmers' market and Nordstrom. With all of the food stands at the farmers' market, plus a Cheesecake Factory, The Farm of Beverly Hills, and the Corner Bakery restaurant, you'll never run out of lunch options. This is yet another great way to spend an afternoon with your kids without having to go inside!

Santa Monica Place

395 Santa Monica Place
Santa Monica
310-394-1049
www.santamonicaplace.com

Located at the southern end of Third Street Promenade, Santa Monica Place has a bunch of kids' stores worth visiting. The three levels of shops are reached by walking through the food court, where you will find all the kid-friendly restaurants you want, including Hot Dog on a Stick. Although there are many kids' stores on Third Street Promenade, the mall has a babyGap,

Gymboree, and Three Cheeky Monkeys, along with Macy's and Robinson's-May.

✳ Westfield Century City

10250 Santa Monica Boulevard
Los Angeles
310-277-3898
www.westfield.com/centurycity

The beauty of this open-air mall is that it lets you shop at all your favorite stores, and still enjoy great weather. It is spacious, perfect for strolling and browsing the children's stores, which include babyGap, Puzzle Zoo, Riginals, Bloomingdale's, and Macy's. They have complimentary strollers shaped like cars! The food court is kid friendly, and there is a New York Deli, Houston's, Ben & Jerry's, and Johnny Rockets as well. The rest rooms are clean, large, and conveniently located close to the food court.

✳ Westfield Fashion Square

14006 Riverside Drive
Sherman Oaks
818-783-0550
www.westfield.com/fashionsquare

You'll find a great selection of kids' stores at this Sherman Oaks mall, including Brooks Shoes, Babystyle, babyGap, Gymboree, Kids Foot Locker, Janie and Jack, Pea in the Pod, and Bloomingdale's. The food court is large and there is a Coffee Bean and Tea Leaf, which you don't normally find in a mall. There is a Playtown for kids located near Bloomindale's and a Kids' Club, with activities scheduled the third Friday of every month. You can rent strollers on the first floor for $2.

✳ Westfield Topanga

6600 Topanga Canyon Boulevard
Woodland Hills
818-594-8740
www.westfield.com/topanga

This is one of the most family-friendly malls in the Valley. Kids' stores include babyGap, The Disney Store, Gymboree, and Sanrio, and are all located near one another on the ground level. The food court is nearby as well. The main attractions for kids are the train and coin-operated rides next to the food court. Complimentary strollers shaped like cars are available at the customer service desk. Kiosks around the mall include A Bear Is Born, where you can stuff and decorate your own teddy bear. There is also a Nordstrom, Robinson's-May, and Sears.

✳ Westside Pavilion

10800 West Pico Boulevard
Los Angeles
310-474-6255
www.westsidepavilion.com

This is one of our favorite malls to go to, with or without our children. Aside from the basic children's stores (babyGap, Gymboree, Kids Foot Locker, Right Start, Brooks Shoes for Kids, and The Disney Store) there are Gymboree classes, Music 'n' Me, Dance Studio No. 1, and a Build-a-Bear Workshop. The food court is kid friendly with plenty of options, and there is a small area with kids' rides. Strollers are available to rent at the guest services desk located on level two, and near Barnes & Noble on level one. The department stores, Nordstrom and Robinson's-

May, provide the best rest room options. We prefer Nordstrom; it has a large, fairly clean sitting area and changing table. On one of those rare rainy days, you can fill your day with a class at Gymboree or browsing through the many kid-friendly stores.

Our Top 5 Finds

* Cranky Pants
* La La Ling
* Planet Blue Kids
* Pumpkin
* Smooch

toys, toys, toys...

Having a baby is a great excuse to act like a kid again! Welcome back to the magical world of toys. From the dependable Toys "R" Us to a tiny neighborhood specialty shop, L.A. has wonderful toy stores for you to enjoy—with or without your child!

You will be surprised at how much toys have changed since you were young. But even though the new toys may have more glitz and glam, you will be pleased to hear that some of the old favorites are making a comeback. We have friends who have bid a pretty penny on eBay for the old Fisher-Price Animal Farm!

Magazines like *Parenting* and *Child* are good resources for finding out about the latest toys; check out consumer guides such as *Oppenheim Toy Portfolio*, as well. Each year it rates the best toys for every age group. The Consumer Products Safety Commission also recommends and rates toys on its website (www.cpsc.gov), as does Amazon.com and other toy store websites.

The Consumer Products Safety Commission requires manufacturers to recall any toy that it deems unsafe, and the manufacturer then notifies the retailers to pull any such toys from the shelves. You should always check to make sure that your toys have not been recalled. You can do so by calling the CPSC hotline at 800-638-2772 or checking their website (www.cpsc.gov). Most stores will post any recall information at the checkout counter. Some pediatricians do the same.

Toys have the power to rule your life. It is hard to keep up with the latest toy crazes and every parent wants to find the perfect toy that will educate, stimulate, and entertain her or his child forever. So be careful not to go overboard buying toys in the beginning; an infant really is just as happy with a set of plastic cups as he or she is with a V-Tech toy with all the bells and whistles. The best advice we received was to open up the Tupperware drawer; kids can play there for hours! Another tip: You may be tempted to duplicate every exciting toy your child plays with over at her friend's house. Don't give in! It is nice for children to have something new to play with at friends' houses; plus, if you buy them everything they see in playgroup, they will only grow tired of that toy more quickly.

Toy stores are like all other stores—there are chain stores and independent stores. The chains generally have better prices and more lenient return policies, but the independent stores often carry more unique (though often more expensive) toys and provide you with more personalized service. Many of these neighborhood toy stores are good for gifts and provide great gift wrapping. Don't forget to check the Internet, especially Amazon.com, which includes Toysrus.com and Imaginarium.com. It's a great place to shop for toys, especially when you know exactly what you are looking for. Just beware of buying bulky items online, because the shipping charges can become very pricey.

Here is our list of don't-miss toy stores in L.A.:

❋ *Acorn Store*
1220 Fifth Street
Santa Monica
310-451-5845
Return Policy: Store credit or exchange only.
Instead of the run-of-the mill plastic playthings, this gem of a toy store carries "natural toys." They have the best selection of wooden toys around, everything from kitchen stoves to

wooden animals. The store is associated with The Waldorf School in Santa Monica and all of the profits go to the school.

❄ Allied Model Trains

4411 Sepulveda Boulevard
Culver City
310-313-9353
Return Policy: Store credit or exchange within 30 days; collectors' items are final sale.

This large train store spans over thirteen thousand square feet and is a replica of L.A.'s Union Station. They carry an extensive selection of Thomas and Brio trains and have a large display and showroom that kids love. They also carry Playmobil toys and model airplanes.

❄ Dinosaur Farm

1510 Mission Street
South Pasadena
626-441-2767
Return Policy: Store credit or exchange only.

Dinosaur Farm is a great toy store in South Pasadena. Though the name says "dinosaur," they also carry dress-up clothes, Hello Kitty, Groovy Girls, science toys, and arts and crafts. There is a back room where they host story times, dance classes, and birthday parties.

❄ The Disney Store Westside Pavilion

10800 West Pico Boulevard
Los Angeles
310-441-1977
Sherman Oaks Fashion Square
14006 Riverside Drive
Sherman Oaks

818-907-5094
www.disneystore.com
Return Policy: Full refund with receipt. Item must be unopened with tags still on.

The Disney Store carries every kind of Disney paraphernalia imaginable, including toys, clothes, stuffed animals, and even toothbrushes. For a small child, visiting this store can be as much fun as a visit to Disneyland itself. This is a great place to find Halloween costumes as well. No gift wrapping available.

❄ Fire Fly's

27015 McBean Parkway
Santa Clarita
661-255-9144
www.fireflytoys.net
Return Policy: Store credit or exchange only.

Fire Fly's sells books and toys, including classic toys and European and educational toys. They have Corolle, Groovy Girls, Small World, Crocodile Creek, and Manhattan Baby and Toy. It is also one of the only dealers of Lilliput Play Homes.

❄ Gregory's Toys*

16101 Ventura Boulevard, #135
Encino
818-906-2212
Return Policy: Full refund with receipt.

Gregory's Toys is located in a large strip mall that has an old-fashioned carousel, making it a popular destination for kids in the Valley. Large and roomy enough to wheel your stroller up and down the aisles, you and your child could spend an entire afternoon here checking out the latest selections. They carry everything from dolls to tricycles, as well as popular toys like Thomas the Tank Engine, LEGOs, and Barbies. The prices are competitive and there are good sales. Gift wrapping is available.

❋ Jenny Bec's*

927 Montana Avenue
Santa Monica
310-395-9505
www.jennybecs.com
Return Policy: Store credit or exchange only.

Jenny Bec's carries a great selection of quality toys for newborns and up. You will find art supplies from Alex, as well as dolls, Thomas the Tank Engine train sets, a large truck selection, and much more. This store also does great gift wrapping.

❋ K•B Toys

10800 West Pico Boulevard
Westside Pavilion
Los Angeles
310-441-9034

13720 Riverside Drive
Sherman Oaks
818-907-6995
www.kbtoys.com
Return Policy: Full refund with receipt within 30 days; thereafter store credit only.

K•B Toys carries all the popular name-brand toys, including Fisher-Price, Little Tikes, LEGO, and Preschool. The stores also carry the hot toy of the moment, whatever that may be! Their prices are discounted and if you need an inex-

pensive gift, this is the place to find it. Gift wrapping is not available.

❋ Kip's Toyland

Farmers' Market
6333 West Third Street
Los Angeles
323-939-8334
Return Policy: Full refund with receipt within 30 days.

Located in the Original Farmers' Market behind The Grove, Kip's has been open for over sixty years. It carries old-fashioned and vintage toys, trains, and dolls, and tons of stuffed animals.

❋ Lakeshore Learning Materials Store*

8888 Venice Boulevard
Culver City
310-559-9630
www.lakeshorelearning.com
Return Policy: Full refund with receipt, otherwise store credit only.

Lakeshore specializes in educational toys and is one of Culver City's best-kept secrets. Just about every toy, climbing apparatus, art project, book, and doll that your child plays with in toddler classes and preschool is from Lakeshore. The store is nice to browse in, so it's worth the trip, and if you want something special from the catalog or website, call ahead. It can be ordered for you, and if you pick it up at the store, you won't have to pay shipping. Gift wrapping is available.

Puzzle Zoo

1413 Third Street Promenade
Santa Monica
310-393-9201

Century City Mall
10250 Santa Monica Boulevard
Los Angeles
310-284-8268

Palisades Playthings

1041 Swarthmore Avenue
Pacific Palisades
310-454-8648
www.puzzlezoo.com
Return Policy: Store credit or exchange only.
Puzzle Zoo is a small chain of toy stores (including Palisades Playthings) that carries a large selection of board games, stuffed animals, and arts and crafts toys. The Palisades and Century City stores carry more infant and children's toys, including LEGO, Playmobil, and Brio. Gift wrapping is available.

Right Start

Westside Pavilion
10800 West Pico Boulevard
Los Angeles
310-446-4770

2001 North Sepulveda Boulevard
Manhattan Beach
310-939-1147

2212 Wilshire Boulevard
Santa Monica
310-829-5135

13413 Ventura Boulevard
Sherman Oaks
818-817-6550
www.rightstart.com
Return Policy: Full refund with receipt.
Right Start is a great place to go for infant toys. The stores stock the latest developmental toys by Lamaze, Chicco, V-Tech, and Manhattan Toy. The stores are not large enough to keep all toys in stock at all times, so items are shifted seasonally. If there's something specific you want, and its "season" has passed, check the website. Along with toys, the stores carry a large selection of necessity items, which make them popular places to register for baby gifts. Gift wrapping is available.

San Marino Toy and Book Shoppe*

2424 Huntington Drive
San Marino
626-309-0222
www.toysandbooks.com
Return Policy: Full refund with receipt.
There is a good reason San Marino Toy and Book Shoppe has been in business for thirty years—the store has a great selection. You'll find every amusement you can imagine under one roof, including books for children of all ages, from newborns to teens, and a selection of toys that run the gamut from Madame Alexander dolls to board games.

Star Toys*
130 South Barrington Place
Brentwood
310-472-2422
Return Policy: Full refund with receipt.
Star Toys, a venerable Brentwood institution, is definitely worth visiting. The owner and staff always go the extra mile to help you find what you are looking for. There is an an array of toys, including Brio, Corolle, Melissa & Doug, and Chicco. Gift wrapping is available.

Three Cheeky Monkeys
10800 West Pico Boulevard (Westside Pavilion)
Los Angeles
310-470-7060

395 Santa Monica Place, Suite 273
Santa Monica
310-576-6226
Return Policy: Exchange or store credit only.
Three Cheeky Monkeys is not your average "toy store in a mall." This independent store carries an array of toys in every price range. The store itself is laid out perfectly: the aisles are wide enough so you can maneuver around the kids playing in the lane, and strollers can pass each other without creating traffic jams. They carry Brio, Corolle dolls, and Ryan's Room, and a good selection of books. Gift wrapping is available.

Tom's Toys
437 North Beverly Drive
Beverly Hills
310-247-9822
Return Policy: Full refund with receipt.

This popular toy store located in the heart of Beverly Hills carries toys for children of all ages. They have a large Brio selection, Madame Alexander dolls, and LEGOs. They also have stickers and electronic cars large enough for your child to drive. Gift wrapping is available.

Toy Crazy*
(formerly Country Mart Toys)
23140 Civic Center Way
Malibu
310-456-5969

225 Twenty-sixth Street
Santa Monica
310-394-6564
Return Policy: Store credit or exchange only.
This popular toy store has opened a second location in the Brentwood Country Mart, strategically located near the coin-operated rides. Both stores have a surprisingly large selection of toys, including trains, dolls, puzzles, books, and arts and crafts projects. Brands include Groovy Girls, Breyer, and Brio. Gift wrapping is available.

Toy Jungle
1104 Manhattan Avenue
Manhattan Beach
310-798-7744
Return Policy: Store credit or exchange only.
This quaint toy store located in the heart of Manhattan Beach's shopping district is full of wonderful toys. They only carry top-of-the-line toys, including Thomas the Tank Engine, Corolle dolls, Groovy Girls, and Lamaze. Gift wrapping is available.

Toys "R" Us

683 North Victory Boulevard
Burbank
818-841-5037

11136 Jefferson Boulevard
Culver City
310-398-5775

1833 South La Cienega
Los Angeles
310-558-1831

16040 Sherman Way
Van Nuys
818-780-5115
www.toysrus.com
Return Policy: Full refund with receipt, otherwise store credit only.
Toys "R" Us has just about every brand-name toy at the lowest prices around. The stores carry a ton of Fisher-Price, Safety 1st, Playskool, and Mattel items, as well as all of the hottest toys to date. The prices are just about the best you can find in L.A. If you are looking for something specific, you may be better off buying from the website; the stores always seem to be out of that hot toy that your child must have! No gift wrapping is available.

Costumes/Dance Clothes

As early as your child's first Halloween, you will feel the inescapable urge to dress her or him up and go out trick-or-treating. You can easily find costumes on the Internet, in specialty catalogs such as *Sensational Beginnings*, and in many clothing stores (including the Gap) around October.

The second your child shows an interest in dance classes you'll probably be out hunting for dance clothes. Most dance studios carry clothing, but we've found a couple of stores that carry them at really good prices. Your little ballerina will grow out of her slippers faster than you can say pirouette! The following are specialty stores that carry great costumes and dance clothes for children.

Aahs

1090 Westwood Boulevard
Los Angeles
310-824-1688

3223 Wilshire Boulevard
Santa Monica
310-829-1807

14612 Ventura Boulevard
Sherman Oaks
818-907-0300
www.aahs.com
Return Policy: Exchange or store credit only within 14 days of purchase.
Come the fall season, this huge novelty store carries just about every Halloween costume you can imagine.

Shelly's Discount Aerobic Wear

2089 Westwood Boulevard
Los Angeles
310-475-1400
www.shellysonline.com
Return Policy: Store credit or exchange only.

Don't let the name fool you. Shelly's carries a huge selection of costumes year-round. Shelly's is also the best place for well-priced ballet dancewear.

❊ *Ursula's Costumes*

2516 Wilshire Boulevard
Santa Monica
310-582-8230

Return Policy: No returns or exchanges.

This costume store stocks hundreds of children's costumes year-round. The costumes are mainly the generic polyester type and sold in small plastic bags, but there is a good selection, so you're sure to find whatever current character your child wants to dress as. There is an infant section as well. Prices are fairly reasonable, from $20 and up.

bookstores
and beyond

No doubt about it, L.A. babies and their moms love bookstores! The multimedia universe is one of the most exciting aspects of having a baby today. Talented writers, artists, and musicians are creating lasting treasures for you and your child. It seems like every celebrity today has lent her or his name to a children's book. Bookstores are the place for you and your child to listen to stories, pick out videos and CDs, and best of all, discover the joy of reading.

This section lists the best children's bookstores in L.A., including where you and your toddler can listen to a reading of his or her favorite book. We have listed all the major chain stores, as well as our favorite independent bookstores, each with its own unique charm and appeal. (We have omitted full descriptions of the chain stores because of their prevalence.) Don't forget to visit your local library: L.A.'s expansive public library system is a great way to introduce your child to the wonder of reading. The branches offer many services for children including book readings, puppet shows, and short films. Some branches even have a program called Grandparents and Books (GAB) where grandparents read stories to children. Best of all, library cards are free and are fairly easy to acquire. For a complete list of branches visit the website www.lapl.org, or call 213-228-7272.

best bookstores for children

+++ Denotes stores with story time for toddlers. Call for updated schedules.

❋ *B. Dalton Booksellers (owned by Barnes and Noble)*

6600 Topanga Canyon Boulevard
Canoga Park
818-883-8195

201 North Los Angeles Street
Los Angeles
213-687-3050

9301 Tampa Avenue
Northridge
818-886-5443

1815 Hawthorne Boulevard
(South Bay Galleria)
Redondo Beach
310-371-8737

12136 Ventura Boulevard
Studio City
818-505-9528
www.bn.com
Return Policy: Full refund with receipt within 14 days.

❋ *Barnes and Noble*
731 North San Fernando Boulevard
Burbank
818-558-1383

4735 Commons Way
Calabasas
818-222-0542

16461 Ventura Boulevard+++
Encino
818-380-1636

245 North Glendale Avenue
(Glendale Fashion Center)
Glendale
818-246-4677

189 The Grove Drive, Suite K30 (The Grove)+++
Los Angeles
323-525-0270

1800 Rosecrans Avenue
Manhattan Beach
310-725-7025

13400 Maxella Avenue
Marina del Rey
310-306-3213

111 West Colorado Boulevard
Pasadena
626-585-0362

1201 Third Street Promenade+++
Santa Monica
310-260-9110

160 South Westlake Boulevard
Thousand Oaks
805-446-2820

21500 Hawthorne Boulevard
(Del Amo Fashion Square)
Torrance
310-370-5552

10850 Pico Boulevard+++
West Los Angeles
310-475-4144

6100 Topanga Canyon Boulevard
Woodland Hills
818-704-3850
www.bn.com
Return Policy: Full refund with receipt within 14 days.

❖ *Borders*
6510 Canoga Avenue
Canoga Park
818-887-1999

100 South Brand Boulevard
Glendale
818-241-8099

1501 Vine Street
Hollywood
323-463-8519

9301 Tampa Avenue
Northridge
818-886-5443

475 South Lake Avenue
Pasadena
626-304-9773

1415 Third Street Promenade
Santa Monica
310-393-9290

14651 Ventura Boulevard
Sherman Oaks
818-728-6593

125 West Thousand Oaks Boulevard
Thousand Oaks
818-497-8159

3700 Torrance Boulevard
Torrance
310-540-7000

330 South La Cienega Boulevard
West Hollywood
310-659-4045

1360 Westwood Boulevard
West Los Angeles
310-475-3444

6081 Center Drive, Suite 118
Westchester
310-215-3720
www.borders.com
Return Policy: Full refund with receipt within
30 days.

❋ Brentano's (owned by Waldenbooks)

8500 Beverly Boulevard (Beverly Center)
Los Angeles
310-652-8024

10250 Santa Monica Boulevard
(Century City Mall)
Los Angeles
310-785-0204

14006 Riverside Drive (Fashion Square)
Sherman Oaks
818-788-8661
Return Policy: Full refund with receipt within
30 days.

❋ Chevaliers

126 North Larchmont Boulevard
Los Angeles
323-465-1334
Return Policy: Store credit or exchange only
with receipt.
Chevaliers is a favorite stop for book lovers in
Larchmont Village. This independent bookstore
has a room devoted strictly to children's books.
You will find a good selection of both hard- and
softcover books for newborn through grade-
school children. There is also a parenting section.

❋ Children's Book World +++

10580½ West Pico Boulevard
West Los Angeles
310-559-2665
Return Policy: Full refund within 2 weeks;
thereafter store credit only.
We love the selection at this store. They carry
books for children of all ages, from newborns to
teens. Books are classified by age and by con-
tent; there is a large area for pop-up books and
a special section of books for newborns. You
can also find a good selection of videos, CDs,
and cassette tapes. Parents will love the range
of the resource section; there are books dealing
with everything from attention deficit disorders
to sibling preparation. The store hosts a weekly
story hour for children ages three and up.

Diesel, a Bookstore

3890 Cross Creek Road
Malibu
310-456-9961
Return Policy: Store credit or exchange only within 5 days.

Malibu has been without a bookstore for years, so Diesel is a welcome addition. There is a small children's section in the back of the store and the owners are very knowledgeable and will help you find whatever it is you and your child are interested in reading.

Dutton's Books +++

447 North Canon Drive
Beverly Hills
310-281-0997
www.duttonsbeverlyhills.com

11975 San Vicente Boulevard
Brentwood
310-476-6263
www.duttonsbrentwood.com
Return Policy: Store credit only.

The Brentwood store is a true neighborhood bookstore, and has long been a favorite spot for locals. The eagerly anticipated Beverly Hills store is now open, with ample parking and an enviable Canon Drive location. This neighborhood bookstore continues its tradition as the best and most popular "independent" bookstore on the Westside. In Brentwood, the children's section is located in the "east wing" of the store; in Beverly Hills, the children's books are located in the rear of the store. Dutton's packs the books in, which makes for great browsing, but you may have to hunt if you are looking for something specific. Events include story times and author signings.

Every Picture Tells a Story +++

1311 Montana Avenue
Santa Monica
310-451-2700
www.everypicture.com
Return Policy: Store credit only for art; credit or refund for books.

This children's art gallery and bookstore has been around for over fifteen years and has become a "must stop" for parents and children browsing Montana Avenue. The store carries original and limited edition prints ranging from $100 to over $5,000. Besides artwork, you can find a good selection of classic and contemporary children's hardcover books. Any child who loves to read would enjoy one of the custom gift baskets. Events include story time and author signings.

Mrs. Nelson's Toy and Book Shop +++

1030 Bonita Avenue
La Verne
909-599-4558
www.mrsnelsons.com
Return Policy: Full refund with receipt.

Mrs. Nelson's is one of the last large independent children's bookstores still in existence. It carries every children's book you can imagine (over thirty-five thousand titles) and has some of the most knowledgeable staff around. They also have weekly story times with crafts.

❋ *Storyopolis* +++

12348 Ventura Boulevard
Studio City
818-509-5600
www.storyopolis.com
Return Policy: Store credit or exchange only within 30 days with receipt.

Though under new management and with a new location, Storyopolis remains one of the best bookstores for children. Aside from a large selection of books and gifts, Storyopolis is also an art gallery that represents over seventy artists. The store hosts many events such as a craft and story hour, book signings, and puppet shows. Free story readings are offered for children of different age groups: Tiny Tuesdays are for infants up to age two and Wee Wednesdays are for ages two to five. Other events, such as guest authors or activities revolving around a certain book or theme, cost a nominal fee (about $6) and you must reserve a spot in advance. The staff will work with you to create custom gift baskets, which make wonderful presents for any child. This store is great fun, so even if you don't attend a book reading or event, we encourage you to go to Storyopolis to browse the latest children's books and artwork.

❋ *Village Books* +++

1049 Swarthmore Avenue
Pacific Palisades
310-454-4063
Return Policy: Store credit or exchange only with receipt.

This small neighborhood bookstore has a section in the back devoted to children's books. You will find a good selection of unique and classic books for infants and up, along with a parenting resource section. Every Saturday morning is Story Time with Grandma Joan. She will read your toddler's favorite books, or let her or him read to her!

❋ *Vroman's Bookstore* +++

695 East Colorado Boulevard
Pasadena
626-449-5320
www.vromansbookstore.com
Return Policy: Full refund within 30 days with receipt.

Vroman's is as large as a chain bookstore, but still has the feel of an independent. Their huge children's section, located upstairs, has lots of space to read and play. Weekly story times and handwritten staff recommendations give it the personal touch. There is also a separate stationery and gift shop that carries announcements and invitations.

❋ *Waldenbooks*

124 Fox Hills Mall
Culver City
310-313-9352

700 West Seventh Street
Los Angeles
213-624-5137
www.waldenbooks.com
Return Policy: Full refund within 30 days with receipt.

birth announcements, stationery, and party invitations

It is time to let the world know that your baby has arrived! Those little cards announcing a child's birth can turn into quite a production these days. From hand-painted embossed papers to photo-cards, there are countless options for creating a birth announcement for your newborn. So here are a few tips to clear away the clutter.

First, decide what you're looking for. Most people we know still send out the traditional printed cards, but photo announcements and websites dedicated to your child's birth, ordered via the Internet, are also quite popular. You can buy ready-made cards that can be filled in by hand or, depending upon your level of computer literacy, fed through your home printer.

Second, keep your budget in mind. Announcements can get fairly costly depending upon how customized you want to get, and it is just as special to prepare handwritten or computerized announcements as it is to get an original letterpress design on handmade paper.

Third, if you want to include a photograph as well, this will take extra time and trying to get just the right shot of your newborn may add unnecessary stress.

We recommend choosing your announcements a month or so in advance, as it takes a few weeks to print and address your envelopes (or more depending on what you order). Once your baby is born, you can call the store and provide the pertinent information (name, weight, time, and date of birth) to print your final order. Consider ordering matching thank-you cards at this time. Be sure to order enough—you have no idea how many people will send you gifts and you can always use extra thank-you cards. Most stores charge less if you order a larger quanti-

ty at one time, so it actually saves money to order more than you think you need the first time around.

Photo-printing websites are popping up all over the Internet. Whether or not you use a digital camera (if you don't, your photo shop can put the images on a disc for you), you can design announcements with the ease of a mouse. Linda used www.shutterfly.com and both of us have received tons of baby announcements and holiday cards printed this way (the website address is printed on the back flap of the cards). It's a great alternative to traditional announcements. Many of the website cards are the same price as store-bought cards; but you don't have to leave your house to order them and you can see a mock-up of your announcement instantly on most websites.

We have compiled a list of the most popular L.A. stationery stores; each stocks books that the stationery companies provide with samples of their stationery for you to look through. Choose your source based upon how much personal service you are looking for and how customized you want your announcements to be. If you are not experienced in choosing stationery, you may want to find a store that will walk you through the maze of paper stock, fonts, and envelope-flap liners to make this process as easy as possible.

One last tip: Keep your address list handy. Before you know it, it will be time to print invitations to your one-year-old's birthday party! All of the stores listed below also stock birthday party invitations and we have noted some of our favorites. Remember, your child's first birthday will be just as memorable with a fill-in-the-blank card as with an expensive letterpress invitation, so don't get too carried away as they'll all get tossed after the party.

There are so many creative ways to express how excited you are about your baby's arrival that you should not feel limited by the stores and ideas we provide. If you have the time and inclination, nothing is more personal and special than something handmade. Have fun!

❊ Aahs

3223 Wilshire Boulevard
Santa Monica
310-829-1807
www.aahs.com

This novelty and gift shop carries an assortment of well-priced announcements that can be custom-printed, but the store also carries those that you can either fill out by hand or on your computer. An order of ten boxed baby announcements will cost you $4–$15, and if you want them printed you will be charged a $20 setup fee and 19 cents per card thereafter.

❊ Black Ink* (formerly Nest Egg)

873 Swathmore Avenue
Pacific Palisades
310-573-9905

Patty Black's Palisades shop caters to the kids' birthday party set. They carry custom-printed announcements from Prentiss Douthit, Blue Starr Design, Take Notice, and Pulp, and the walls are filled with boxed invitations from Meri-Meri, Itty Bitty, Cross-My-Heart, and Robin McGuire that you can print on your home computer or that can be printed for you for a $20 setup fee and 50 cents per card thereafter. An order of 100 baby announcements will cost $100–$500.

❊ Brenda Himmel Stationery*

1126 Montana Avenue
Santa Monica
310-395-2437

This great stationery store located on Montana Avenue carries its own card stock and letterpress stationery, and has books for several different companies, including Stacy Claire Boyd, Meri-Meri, Cross-My-Heart, Luscious Verde, Checkerboard, Peculiar Pair Press, and Inviting Company, and the old staples, William Arthur and Crane's. We can't say enough about the service; the staff is well versed in the business of stationery and will help you come up with the perfect announcement. The store also carries birthday and special occasion cards, which you can fill in yourself. An order of 100 baby announcements will cost $75–$400.

❊ Christie

1219 Highland Avenue
Manhattan Beach
310-545-1707

This popular stationery store in Manhattan Beach carries nearly every brand of birth announcements, and then some. This is just about the only place in the area to find all the popular brands under one roof including Cross-My-Heart, Sur Tout Pour Vous, Take Notice, Stacy Claire Boyd, William Arthur, and its own brand, Christie & Company, to name a few. An order of 100 baby announcements will cost $75–$350.

❋ Diana Dee's Stationery and Fine Gifts

2060 Huntington Drive
San Marino
626-289-1062

Diana Dee's carries all the traditional stationery brands like Crane's and William Arthur, as well as a good selection of blank card stock. It also carries the new stationery line from Disney. Announcements start at $85 for fifty.

❋ Embrey Papers*

11965 San Vicente Boulevard
Brentwood
310-440-2620
www.embreypapers.com

This popular Brentwood stationery store has a real neighborhood feel. They carry Luscious Verde, Meri-Meri, Cross-My-Heart, Stacy Claire Boyd, Crane's, and William Arthur, and the store will customize just about anything you can imagine. They have a letterpress in house, as well as a calligrapher for one-stop shopping. Depending upon how customized you want to get, you can purchase 100 baby announcements for as little as $100.

❋ Francis Orr

320 North Camden Drive
Beverly Hills
310-271-6106

Moms-to-be have been ordering from this Beverly Hills institution forever. Francis Orr stocks a variety of announcements from Crane's, William Arthur, Sweet Pea, and many others. An order of 100 baby announcements will cost approximately $160.

❋ La Partie

1628 Montana Avenue
Santa Monica
310-829-4021

We were pleasantly surprised by La Partie. The walls are covered with cute boxed cards that you can fill in yourself either by hand or on the computer, but the store will print for you as well. They have a great selection of individual sheets of Cross-My-Heart designs that start at $1.75 per sheet, including the envelope and an adorable sticker. In-house printing is $35 for setup and 75 cents per invite thereafter. An order of 100 baby announcements costs about $75 and up.

❋ Landis General Store

138-142 North Larchmont
Hancock Park
323-465-7998

Landis has that old-fashioned general store feeling, but carries a surprisingly large selection of baby announcements. This is just about the only place on this side of town that stocks such a large selection of baby announcements, from the traditional (William Arthur and Crane's) to the smaller lines (Sweet Pea and Bambino). They also carry boxed announcements; boxes of ten start at $14.50. An order of 100 baby announcements will cost approximately $150.

❋ Malibu Colony Company

3835 Cross Creek Road
Malibu
310-317-0177

This stationery store in Malibu carries unique gifts and announcements. Lines carried include William Arthur and Crane's. They also have an in-house calligrapher. An order of 100 baby announcements costs $120–$500.

Moss House*

1936 Hillhurst Avenue
Los Angeles
323-664-5801
www.themosshouse.net

The owner of the Moss House decided to turn her ten-year-old floral business in Los Feliz into a stationery and children's party store. This is a full-service event-planning center for kids, carrying everything from invitations to party favors and handmade banners. They offer an array of blank cards, invitations, and announcements, all of which can be printed for a $25 setup fee, plus $2 per card thereafter.

Paper Source

9460 Brighton Way
Beverly Hills
310-288-9700

163 West Colorado Boulevard
Pasadena
626-577-3825
www.paper-source.com

If you are looking for a place to find all the "fixings" to make really creative announcements yourself, look no further than Paper Source. Their motto is "do something creative every day." The stores are stocked with wall-to-wall dyed papers in every color imaginable, and they have entire sections of ink stamps and all the special knickknacks to personalize your stationery. The staff is creative and helpful, and there are even classes! Ten cards and envelopes start at $5 and depending on the amount of paper you buy, discounts of up to 30 percent are available.

Paper Whites

2491 Mission Street
San Marino
626-441-2196

Owned by two sisters, Paper Whites has been providing Pasadena locals with tasteful stationery for the past ten years. The store carries popular brands like Stacy Claire Boyd and Cross-My-Heart, and some from smaller companies like Prentiss Douthit. There is also a large selection of letterpress invitations and stationery. Announcements start at $200 for fifty.

Papyrus*

10800 West Pico Boulevard (Westside Pavilion)
Los Angeles
310-446-5314

8522 Beverly Boulevard (Beverly Center)
Los Angeles
310-360-0311

1412 Montana Avenue
Santa Monica
310-255-7909

14006 Riverside Drive (Fashion Square)
Sherman Oaks

818-981-5866

www.papyrusonline.com

Papyrus is an upscale chain of fine paper and cards, with lines like William Arthur, Stacy Claire Boyd, Cross-My-Heart, and others. The stores also carry boxes of ten cards that run between $10 and $20 each, which they will print for you in-house for a $10 setup fee and less than $1 per card. An order of 100 announcements will cost $100–$400. They work extremely fast, so if you need announcements in a hurry, Papyrus is your best bet.

❊ Salutations

900 Granite Drive

Pasadena

626-577-7460

Salutations stocks just about every brand of stationery you can imagine, including Crane's, William Arthur, Lallie, Prentiss Douthit, and Stacy Claire Boyd. The staff are knowledgeable and helpful. They offer calligraphy services as well. They can work in any price range and can fill an order of as few as twenty-five announcements, printed on-site for a $30 setup fee and $1 per card.

❊ Soolip Paperie

8646 Melrose Avenue

Los Angeles

310-360-0545

Soolip is a unique stationery, gift store, and gallery in West Hollywood. They offer both custom- and pre-made announcements and invitations, and will also work with you to create an original design, from the paper to the envelope

liner. Soolip is pricey: Custom announcements and invitations start at $6 each.

❊ Sugar Paper*

1749 Ensley

Los Angeles

310-277-7804

Brentwood Country Mart

253 Twenty-sixth Street

Los Angeles

310-452-7870

www.sugarpaper.com

Owners Chelsea and Jamie, both graphic artists, opened Sugar Paper armed with an antique letterpress and a love of paper. Tucked away in Century City, next door to the popular lunch spot Clementine and now their fabulous new store in the Brentwood Country Mart, Sugar Paper specializes in custom-designed letterpress stationery, baby announcements, and invitations. It offers a unique selection of cards and paper goods by terrific boutique designers. Prices start at $175 for fifty flat-printed announcements with a $25 setup fee.

❊ Tiffany & Co.

210 North Rodeo Drive

Beverly Hills

310-273-8880

www.tiffany.com

Tiffany & Co. has a large stationery department offering both its own brand and Crane's. The cards are timeless, but pricey. Still, if you're looking for something that is understated yet screams status, Tiffany is the answer. They have updated their books for those looking for something a bit more playful. Boxed cards start at $120 for 50 cards; custom cards will cost $280–$500 for fifty.

❋ Tina J
323-655-3005

www.tinaj.com

Tina designs custom-made stationery, birth announcements, and invitations by appointment out of her studio and through her website. Her designs are simple but unique; fifty announcements start at $150.

❋ William Ernest Brown
442 North Canon Drive

Beverly Hills

310-278-5620

This old-time Beverly Hills store, popular with the celebrity set, specializes in traditional stationery and announcements like Crane's and William Arthur, although it does carry some smaller, more specialized lines as well, such as Cross-My-Heart and Sweet Pea. An order of 100 baby announcements will cost you approximately $200.

❋ Wilshire West Fine Paper*
3023 Wilshire Boulevard

Santa Monica

310-828-6461

Tucked into an unassuming strip mall on Wilshire, this "bulk" stationery store stocks many of the most popular stationery, announcement, and invitation lines. Since the paper is stocked in bulk, you can buy exactly

how much you need and are not stuck paying for extra pieces as you often are with boxed cards. They offer discounts starting at 10 percent for twenty-five or more sheets and will do printing for a $20 setup fee and $1 per card thereafter; proofs are available within twenty-four hours. They also give a 15-percent discount on all of their traditional stationery books, including Crane's.

Independent Stationers

A trend we have noticed recently is small, independent stationery representatives who carry multiple stationery lines. You can either visit them at their homes, or they come to you. Most of these companies are able to provide discounts, because they don't have the overhead of a retail space. If you are strapped for time or unable to leave the house easily to run errands, this is a good option.

❋ Circle the Date
310-472-6830

www.circlethedate.com

By appointment

Circle the Date carries all of the most popular stationery lines, including Cross-My-Heart, Checkerboard, Inviting Company, and Real Card Studio. They also sell personalized baby gifts.

❋ JAM/Mindy Weiss
232 South Beverly Drive, #200

Beverly Hills

310-205-6000

www.mindyweiss.com

Mindy Weiss is the premier party planner in

L.A., and together with Janis Gurnick she owns JAM, a company that provides invitations, stationery, and baby announcements by appointment only. Lines include Lallie, Hello Lucky, Luscious Verde, Cross-My-Heart, and Stacy Claire Boyd. An order of 100 baby announcements starts at around $200.

❊ *Just for You*
310-470-3870
This private stationery company carries fine sta

tionery, baby announcements, invitations, and party accessories by appointment only. Lines include Robin Miller, Stacy Claire Boyd, Checkerboard, and Encore.

❊ *Linda Levie Paper Designs*
818-996-3306
Linda Levie carries the most popular lines of stationery, invitations, and birth announcements, and she will travel to your house with her books. She offers some discounts as well.

unique baby
and shower gifts

Any mother or mother-to-be who's been to a baby shower is familiar with the feeling of seeing a truly special and unique baby gift: You take a step back, and wonder in awe, Where did she find that? Finding an awesome gift basket, an exceptionally soft baby blanket, homemade sugar cookies, and other great gifts is no easy task. But have no fear. We have tracked down the secret treasures L.A. has available, so that you can pick out the perfect shower or baby gift that will elicit all the oohs and aahs you could hope for! A tip: You don't have to spend a lot of money to give a great gift. Presentation is often the key to creating unique gifts and there are hundreds of creative ways to wrap an outfit or toy. Also, keep in mind your time constraints. If you are pressed for time, which is a likely state to be in with a newborn at home, ordering a baby shower gift online is a great solution. There's no parking hassle, no schlepping your baby in and out of the car: just click and order! Leave yourself plenty of time to receive your order as many of the websites charge astronomical amounts for rush delivery. We have listed a few of our favorite baby gift websites at the end of the chapter.

❋ Anya Hindmarch
118 South Robertson
Los Angeles
310-271-9707
www.beabag.com
Return Policy: Store credit or exchange only within 14 days.
Anya Hindmarch, the fabulous bag designer, offers a great gift for someone who already has it all. Be a Bag allows you to have photographs transposed onto a bag of your choice. There are seven different styles available, from evening bags to beach bags. Prices start at $175.

❋ Auntie Barbara's Antiques
238 South Beverly Drive
Beverly Hills
310-285-0873
www.auntiebarbaraskids.com
Return Policy: Store credit or exchange only.
Barbara, of Auntie Barbara's fame, handpicks the best (and most expensive) clothing and accessories for newborns for her store. Staff will wrap the gift in a beautiful basket, or include a hand-painted rocking chair or step stool. And no matter how much you spend, Barbara will make your gift look fantastic.

❋ Blush
625A Montana Avenue
Santa Monica
310-899-3810
Return Policy: Store credit or exchange only.
Blush is a welcome addition to the less-traveled lower section of Montana Avenue. Look for baby gifts including toys, ponchos, booties, and backpacks.

❋ Further Kids
2901 Rowena Avenue
Los Angeles
323-661-2120
Return Policy: Store credit or exchange only.
If you're looking for children's gifts in Silver Lake, look no further! Further Kids carries a ton of books, specialty clothing, and toys.

House Boutique

1603 Montana Avenue

Santa Monica

310-451-1321

www.houseinc.com

Return Policy: Store credit or exchange only within 10 days.

House Boutique carries comfy newborn clothing, bibs, and booties along with some of the softest blankets and bedding around. The robes and booties make great gifts.

Intuition

10581 West Pico Boulevard

Los Angeles

310-234-8442

www.shopintuition.com

Return Policy: Store credit or exchange only.

Jaye Hirsch stocks both her small store in West L.A. and her website with the latest baby gifts. You can find everything from cashmere sweaters to receiving blankets, baby charm bracelets, and giant oil-cloth folders for storing children's artwork.

It's a Wrap*

12237 Wilshire Boulevard

Los Angeles

310-820-1322

www.itsawrap.com

This unique wrapping store not only wraps any gift you bring in, but it also has a great selection of baby gifts of its own. Whatever your gift is, it will be wrapped beautifully.

Jenny Bec's*

927 Montana Avenue

Santa Monica

310-395-9505

www.jennybecs.com

Return Policy: Store credit or exchange only.

Jenny, the owner of this Montana Avenue store, listens to her customers, and has stocked her store with the gifts they want. You can choose from the large selections of toys, books, and furniture, and then have the gift wrapped in the store's adorable signature wrapping.

Just Had a Baby

310-476-0470

www.justhadababy.com

The "Just Had a Baby" T-shirts and "baby" onesies make great gifts for new moms. Visit the website to see styles and to buy online.

Kitson Kids

108 South Robertson Boulevard

Los Angeles

310-246-3829

www.shopkitson.com

Return Policy: Store credit or exchange only.

If you are looking for something that screams Hollywood Baby, Kitson's newest store is your place. You will find the latest trends in everything from clothing, stuffed animals, nightlights, and toys, to hair accessories for babies and children.

Monogram Market*

Brentwood Country Mart

253 Twenty-sixth Street, Suite D

Santa Monica

310-395-7373

Return Policy: Personalized items are final; everything else is exchangeable within 14 days of purchase.

Monogram Market will personalize almost anything for both moms and babies. The small store has a bunch of baby items, including beautiful quilts, sweaters, sheets, small suitcases, diaper bags, and silver spoons.

❋ Nana's Garden

426 North Robertson

Beverly Hills

310-288-3024

Return Policy: Store credit or exchange only.

Nana's Garden has a small selection of children's clothes, toys, and books for you to choose from while your child plays in the "indoor garden."

❋ Pink Pineapple

827 Via de la Paz

Pacific Palisades

310-230-6822

Return Policy: Store credit or exchange only.

This women's clothing shop in the Palisades is a hidden gem, known mostly to locals. They also carry baby gifts, including books, pajamas, robes, and shoes.

❋ Pump Station—Baby Boutique

2415 Wilshire Boulevard

Santa Monica

310-826-5774

www.pumpstation.com

Return Policy: Store credit or exchange for gifts without receipt; full refund with receipt.

Pump Station's Baby Boutique is stocked with everything a baby (and mommy) could ever need. A gift certificate from here is a great present.

❋ Room with a View

1600 Montana Avenue

Santa Monica

310-998-5858

www.roomview.com

Return Policy: Store credit or exchange only.

Room with a View carries only the most high-end baby clothes, furniture, and accessories. Items include exquisite handmade European clothes, the softest down blankets with silk duvets, diaper bags, and beautiful hand-knit sweaters. For a perfect shower gift, have the staff wrap your items in a beautiful bassinet. A gift registry is available.

❋ Saks Fifth Avenue

9600 Wilshire Boulevard

Beverly Hills

310-275-4211

www.saks.com

Return Policy: Full refund within 60 days.

The Saks baby department's renowned layette selection has everything a new mom needs. The staff will help you pick out your gift, and wrap it in a Moses basket that the baby can actually sleep in!

Salutations

900 Granite Drive
Pasadena
626-577-7460
Return Policy: Store credit or exchange only.
This home store is known for its excellent gift selection. They carry an array of clothing, books, blankets, frames, and photo albums. The staff can wrap all of your purchases in a beautiful package.

Simply Fresh

2628 Mission Street
San Marino
626-441-7250
Return Policy: Store credit or exchange only.
Simply Fresh is simply great for finding a unique and special gift for a new parent or baby. Custom gift baskets are also available.

This Little Piggy Wears Cotton

309 Wilshire Boulevard
Santa Monica
310-260-2727
www.littlepiggy.com
Return Policy: Store credit or exchange only within 10 days.
This Little Piggy has expanded its toy selection into a small department in the back of the store. It carries an array of toys that make the perfect gifts, including Woodkins dolls, Groovy Girls, great books, cars, and cleaning and gardening tools. Giftwrapping is available.

Tiny Treasures for Tots

310-471-6066
www.tinytreasuresfortots.com
By appointment only
Return Policy: Store credit or exchange only.
Tiny Treasures for Tots specializes in newborn gift baskets that are filled with cute clothing and blankets from its own line, Tiny Tots, along with towels, books, toys, and much more. We especially loved the bath basin filled with bathing supplies.

Udderly Perfect

1203 Highland Avenue
Manhattan Beach
310-546-5322
Return Policy: Store credit or exchange only within 7 days.
This boutique is easy to find—just look for the cow-print doorway! It specializes in gift items such as blankets, bibs, and soft books, and has a selection of delightful ducks, both rubber and stuffed.

Uncle Jer's

4459 Sunset Boulevard
Los Angeles
323-662-6710
Return Policy: Store credit or exchange only.
This boutique located at Sunset Junction carries toys and gifts with a "vintage" feel.

*Yolk**

1626 Silver Lake Boulevard
Los Angeles
323-660-4315
Return Policy: Store credit or exchange only within 10 days.

At Yolk, owner, furniture designer, and mom Melanie Miller carries her own furniture designs, along with others, all with a decidedly modern bent. Look for sleek rocking horses, high chairs, chalk tables, and bedding unlike any others.

❊ Zipper

8316 West Third Street
Los Angeles
323-951-0620
www.zippergifts.com
Return Policy: Store credit or exchange only within 30 days.
The inventory at this great gift store is constantly changing to keep ahead of the trends. If you are looking for something different, they always have interesting and unique baby gifts.

Baskets, Cookies, and Party Favors

❊ Captain Wayne's First Class Cookies

310-451-2601
www.firstclasscookies.com
Captain Wayne, an airline pilot, turned his love of baking chocolate chip cookies into a business. His cookies are delivered in metallic lunch box pails with custom covers, such as a baby announcement or birthday wish.

❊ Cookies by Design

Several locations throughout Los Angeles
800-945-2665
www.cookiesbydesign.com
Cookies by Design is best known for its "cook-

ie bouquets," featuring the new baby's name, weight, and other personal information on delicious sugar cookies. They also do an adorable "pregnancy bouquet" that is perfect for a baby shower centerpiece.

❊ Cyn's Cookies

323-384-3155
Cyn's Cookies make great baby gifts and party favors. They will design sugar cookies with just about any theme you can imagine. We especially loved the baby booties and duckies.

❊ Deluscious Cookies & Milk

323-460-2370
www.delusciouscookies.com
If you're looking for something to send to the hospital room or home of a new parent, Deluscious Cookies & Milk is the answer. These handmade cookies, delivered with milk, are so big they come in a pizza box!

❊ Mrs. Beasley's*

Several locations throughout Los Angeles
800-710-7742
www.mrsbeasleys.com
Everyone loves Mrs. Beasley's cakes, muffins, and cookies, so what better way to celebrate a new baby than with a miniature wire baby carriage brimming with the bakery's best treats? It offers an array of choices, including the option to scan a photo of your baby onto a cookie! You can either visit the stores or log on to the website to see all of the offerings.

✳ *Star Treatment*
818-781-9016
www.startreatment.com

Star Treatment started out catering to studios, preparing "wrap gifts" for the cast and crew of television or film productions. They have since expanded, offering amazing baby baskets at just about every price point.

Websites

There is an overwhelming number of baby resources on the Internet these days, with new websites popping up daily and old ones closing down. To help you navigate this ever-changing landscape, we have hand-picked a few of our favorites for great baby and shower gifts:

www.babystyle.com
www.deborahsharpelinens.com
www.hottoddieonline.com

www.planetjill.com
www.plumparty.com
www.pokkadots.com

www.poshtots.com
www.silverlakekids.com
www.totshop.com
www.tuttibella.com

Top Five Baby Gifts:

1. home-cooked meal delivered to the family
2. scrapbook
3. photography session
4. massage
5. magazine subscriptions (*Child*, *Parent*)

Chapter Twelve

classes, play spaces, and other indoor activities

So you've survived the first couple of months and you finally feel like you're getting a handle on this motherhood business—you could probably pack a diaper bag with your eyes closed. Now you're ready to venture out with your little one and start having some fun!

In this chapter, we list the most popular classes and activities for kids all around the city. In addition to classes for infants and toddlers, we've included activities for older kids as well, because as your child gets older, naps go by the wayside and those half days at preschool will not be enough for her or him—or you. We will guide you through the endless array of activities for your child, from discussion-based Mommy and Me classes to gymnastics, music, sports, theater, and even etiquette classes for older kids. If you still do not find what you are looking for here, check out your nearby hospital or medical center, the local church or synagogue, or your health club for other classes and activities.

Before you start signing up for activities, we have one warning about monitoring your child's schedule. Many first-time moms "overbook" their children, signing them up for music, dance, art, and tumbling—you name it. When our first children were just months old, we had them all over the city trying out different classes. In hindsight, we realize it was more for us than for them. We see now that time with mom in the park can be just as valuable as a Gymboree class.

Here are some other things to keep in mind when checking out a class (some of these are more applicable to infants than school-age children):

Sick policy: Check the sick policy. The number one complaint we hear from other moms is about parents bringing their children to class when they are sick. Our Mommy and Me class had a "two wipe" policy—if you had to wipe your baby's nose more than once during the class, you were asked to leave. While this policy might seem overly conservative, it was very effective in keeping sick babies at home.

Time and location of class: When your child is young, consider the class as the "event of the day." When your baby is under age one, he or she is probably taking two naps a day. By the time you pack the diaper bag, load up the car and get on your way, there is not a whole lot of time left over for activities. So pick classes that meet at times that work with your baby's schedule. If the class is held at noon and you know that your baby usually naps around this time, don't sign up for it. It won't be enjoyable for you, your baby, or the other children in the class. Also, keep in mind how close a class is to your home. We all know that traffic in L.A. is unpredictable, and you don't want to spend the better part of your baby's awake time sitting in bumper to bumper traffic.

Trial classes: Many programs offer a free trial class. This is an excellent way to check out the instructor and the classroom, as well as meet some of the other mothers in the class. You may find that some programs are heavily attended by caregivers, rather than parents, which may or may not be what you're looking for. Look around and see if the place feels clean. When the children are really little, it is a good idea to ask how often they clean the toys and equipment. Don't be afraid to try three or four different classes until you find one that you like. This way you won't waste your money.

Teachers: The teacher makes all the difference, and some are better than others. If you really like a place, but aren't thrilled with the teacher, try another class.

Below is a list of classes for newborns and older children, organized by activity.

Infant Massage

Infant massage is a practice that has become popular as a great way to soothe and bond with your baby. We've had friends who swear massage helped calm the most colicky baby. Below are some certified infant massage instructors:

❋ **Heather Archer**
310-503-1439
Heather is trained in prenatal massage as well as infant massage.

❋ **Karen Blackmore**
310-456-7499
Karen is a certified pregnancy massage therapist and a certified infant massage instructor with over twenty-three years of experience. Her private classes cost $125 and include a book on infant massage.

❋ **Octavia Lindlahr**
818-645-4692
www.sacredmotherdoula.com
Octavia is a certified infant massage instructor who teaches private classes ($125 for four classes) and group classes ($115 for four classes) at several locations in Los Angeles. She specializes in helping parents of premature babies. Check her website or call for a current list of classes.

❋ **Lynn Oyama, RN**
310-395-7220
Lynn has been teaching infant massage, as well as CPR and safety, for over ten years. Her massage technique is wonderful, and many mothers swear it got them through colic.

❋ **Cathy Vorse**
310-458-0680
Cathy is a certified infant massage instructor who teaches in Santa Monica. She holds group classes ($150 for a four-week session) and private sessions ($150 for a three-week session).

Mommy and Me Classes

Remember the line the Beatles sang, "Help! I need somebody!"? Well, all moms feel this way every once in a while when they have a new baby at home, and there's no better place to turn than a group of women going through the exact same thing. Lucky for us, L.A. is filled with a wide variety of different educational and support groups for new parents, including Mommy and Me, Daddy and Me, Working Mom, Single Parent, and Grandparents and Me classes. A good Mommy and Me class is like group therapy for parents, combining playtime for babies with discussion for parents. Discussions generally address parenting, and developmental issues, and are usually led by professionals with backgrounds in child development, child behavior, or early childhood education. Most classes require parent attendance, rather than a caregiver. During the discussion, the children play together, supervised by the parents, the "coaches," and the teacher. Many of our friends found classes such as these to be essential in helping them transition during the first year of motherhood. Some classes continue until children are two or even three years old, which can be a great benefit since the members of these groups often grow quite close and develop friendships outside of class. Other classes have more of a drop-in policy, which is great if you just need some extra support every now and then. We met in a Mommy and Me class when Jack and Sarah were just ten weeks old, and our group continued to meet until they were two. We both made some of our closest friends in this class, as did our children.

❊ Babies First Class/Jackie Rosenberg*

14368 Ventura Boulevard
Sherman Oaks
818-501-BABY
Ages: newborn to 18 months
Jackie Rosenberg has been running Mommy and Me groups for over twenty years, and many mothers think Jackie's word is gospel. There are approximately fifteen parent/baby participants in each class, and it is recommended that you get on the waiting list soon after you conceive. Jackie is a mother of two and has a background in child occupational therapy. She teaches every class herself (sixteen a week total). The cost per ten-week session is $300. Classes generally start when your baby is three months old and continue until babies are between sixteen and eighteen months old. Classes begin with

Jackie leading a discussion on a specific topic, followed by a sing-along, exercises, dance, and other activities to stimulate your child. Dads are always welcome. Babies First also offers a class for mothers of twins run by Sue Darrison. Jackie teaches evening lectures for second- or third-time parents on topics such as discipline and bringing home the new baby.

❊ Babygroup, Inc./Donna Holloran*

Santa Monica
310-397-3975
Ages: newborn to 2 years
Donna Holloran, a child development specialist and a certified infant mental health specialist with a master's degree in social work, has been leading "baby groups" for over seven years. She has become a household name on the Westside, so much so that "Donna says . . ." is frequently how many of our friends start conversations. Her classes have such a following that many women sign up during their first or second trimester, and go back to her after their second and third pregnancies. In addition to her advice, Donna's groups have the reputation of gathering great women who develop friendships outside of class. Classes, taught by either Donna or one of the other two professionals that work for Babygroup, are intended to increase parents' awareness of their child's natural abilities while supporting them. Each class addresses a different parenting topic, and is followed by "singing circle" with parents and babies. During the discussion, children are free to move and explore in the play area supervised by at least two assistants. There is a designated "dad's day" each

session, but they are welcome to attend any class. Classes meet once a week for seventy-five minutes, and cost between $375 and $425 for ten weeks. She offers specific classes for second-time moms, third-time moms, and single moms.

✳ Shelley Breger
Community Methodist Church
801 Via de La Paz
Pacific Palisades
310-459-1217
Ages: newborn to 2½ years

Shelley is a licensed marriage, family, and child counselor who has been leading Mommy and Me classes for over fifteen years. Her groups are smaller than many other Mommy and Me classes, and have a wider variety of participants, often including both first- and second-time moms and babies of different ages. While the discussion portion of the class revolves around parenting issues, ensuing conversations can lead to other family or personal issues. During discussions, children are supervised by two assistants who lead them in various activities such as free play, arts and crafts, and snack time. Older children can bring lunches and are allowed in the outdoor area to play. Classes are limited to ten moms, and some have a waitlist. Many of Shelley's groups aren't ready to graduate when the toddlers reach preschool-age, so Shelley has some groups that still meet without their children. She even has one group that still meets and the children are now fourteen!

✳ Childsleep
Santa Monica
310-230-1823
www.childsleep.com
Ages: 2 months to 18 months

Childsleep is run by Jill Spivak, Tracy Smolin, and Jennifer Waldburger, all of whom hold master's degrees in social work and have experience running support-education groups for mothers and families. They hold mother-infant and mother-toddler groups for children ages two to eighteen months, and offer private parent education sessions on issues such as toilet training, siblings, and behavioral problems, and, of course, sleep. While sleep training is not the sole focus of this class, we can speak highly of Jill's expertise in this area. After attending their seminar on this topic, we were able to get our babies on regular sleeping, napping, and eating schedules. Additionally, they regularly speak in the community on a variety of child development topics.

✳ Early Childhood Parenting Center
Various locations throughout L.A.
310-281-9770
www.parentingtots.org
Ages: newborn and up

The Early Childhood Parenting Center is a nonprofit organization that was established over thirty years ago as part of Cedars-Sinai. They offer several parenting groups including Parent and Toddler, Working Mom, Daddy and Me, and Single Parent. Groups are led by professionals with a background in either education or child development and generally have eight to ten people in a class. The groups offer parent support and education, and include discussions of topics raised by either the parents or the group leaders. Infant groups cost $125 for a six-week session; toddler groups cost $125 for a month-long session. Classes meet weekly for an hour and a half. The center also offers a "warm line" for parents who have general questions about child-related issues, such as sleeping, feeding, and tantrums. You can leave a message and a professional will return your call.

Kidspace Children's Museum

480 North Arroyo Boulevard
Pasadena
626-449-9144
www.kidspacemuseum.org

Kidspace Children's Museum holds popular Baby and Me classes in the Museum's Early Childhood Center taught by a child develop-ment expert. Classes are one and a half hours long and cost $150 for an eight-week session. Registration is done via email at ccoleman@kidspacemuseum.org.

La Canada Presbyterian Church Parent Education Class

626 Foothill Boulevard
La Canada
818-790-6758
www.lacanadapc.org

This Mommy and Me is a favorite among Pasadena-area moms. Teachers who are trained in child development lead the group in age-appropriate topics, allowing moms to ask ques-tions, get support, and make friends. Classes

meet once a week for two (or two and a half) hours, and cost $380 for a thirty-four-week session.

South Bay Adult School

Various locations in the South Bay
310-937-3340 (main number)
310-376-3514 (hotline)
www.southbayadult.org
Ages: newborn and up

The South Bay Adult School is a fantastic resource for families. Programs include parent-child participation classes, lectures, support groups, and parent information and discussion groups. Our friends rave about its Mommy and Me program. Classes address topics such as discipline, sleep issues, and power struggles. Classes are offered in English and Spanish and are open to both residents and non-residents of the South Bay. Costs are based on income level.

Terry Stansfield

818-342-3725

Terry has degrees in child development and music and has been teaching children for over twenty years. She holds Mommy and Me class-es through LAUSD (Los Angeles Unified School District) in Woodland Hills and West Hollywood. The three-hour classes are free (with a $20 registration fee) and run for twenty-week sessions with eighteen to twenty moms in a class. The classes consist of music, art, parent discussion, and playtime. This has to be one of the best bargains in L.A.!

Play Activities

Once your child starts to "wake up" from his or her first few months of sleep, it's time to go out and have some fun! In a city the size of L.A., it can be overwhelming trying to decide what places are right for you and your child. No matter how many toys and activity centers you have at home, you will always find yourself searching for new ideas and activities to do with your child. Fortunately, we are blessed to live in a city rich in parks and beaches. If you are looking for something a little more structured, a place you can go week after week, we have some ideas for you, but keep in mind that although some classes start at three or four months of age, you and your child will find an organized class much more enjoyable once she is able to sit up and, depending on the activity, crawl and/or walk.

The classes listed below are all activity-based. Generally, classes for children three years old and younger require an adult presence in the room or gym alongside each child (most allow grandparents or caregivers in lieu of parents). Some places offer transition classes (sometimes called Preschool Alternative) for children approximately two and a half years old and up. These classes are generally two or three hours long and allow you to leave for a few minutes or even the whole time once your child is comfortable. These classes are good for kids who may have just missed the cut-off date to start preschool, those whose parents choose not to send them to preschool, or for children who are ready for something a little more stimulating than a one-hour class. Once your child starts preschool (or in some cases turns four years old), the classes tend to be "drop-off," where you either watch from an "obser- vation deck" or leave altogether, to enable your child to have some independence and allow the classes to run without parent interference. Some of the places below also offer camp sessions that are usually held during winter, spring, and summer breaks from school and are generally half- or whole-day sessions.

When your child reaches three or four years of age, we recommend trying out a variety of classes. By then, your child will have preferences of his own, and teachers and activities vary from place to place. Your child may not like karate at one place and absolutely love it at another. Most of these classes offer free trial sessions, so take advantage of this. You don't want to listen to your child cry his way through eight weeks of soccer classes!

Art Classes

❈ *Armory Center for the Arts*
145 North Raymond Avenue
Pasadena
626-792-5101
www.armoryarts.org
Ages: 3 years and up
The Armory offers art classes that introduce children to materials, concepts, and techniques starting at age three (children must be toilet trained). They also offer adult classes at the same time, so you can enjoy a class while your child has his or her own.

❈ *Art for Tots*
291 South La Cienega, Suite 102
Beverly Hills
310-855-1291
www.artfortots.com

Ages: 1 year and up

This art studio and enrichment center offers a variety of art and music classes, such as art, knitting, scrapbooking, jewelry making, and cooking for children ages five and up. Infant and toddler classes are forty-five minutes long and cost $200 for an eight-week session. Afterschool classes are one and a half hours and cost $225 for a four-week session.

Brentwood Art Studio

13031 Montana Avenue
Santa Monica
310-451-5657
www.brentwoodart.com

Ages: 4 years and up

This art studio offers mixed-media classes for children ages four to twelve. The classes include painting, sculpture, collage, and many other art techniques. Weekly classes start at $165 per month, which includes supplies.

Children's Art Studio*

12401 Wilshire Boulevard, Suite 105
Los Angeles
310-207-0076

Ages: 2½ years and up

This is creativity for kids at its best! Children sculpt with clay, make buildings out of Styrofoam and cork and paint, all while listening to Mozart in the background. Classes cost $400 for a ten-week session.

Crayon Box

818-983-7757
www.crayonboxart.com

Ages: 1 year and up

Crayon Box was created by an educator and art instructor with over thirty years of experience. They teach children ages one to four about all mediums of art, and classes foster both cognitive and physical development. Sessions are held in Studio City and Santa Monica.

KidsArt

2400 Foothill Boulevard
La Canada
818-248-2483

18399 Ventura Boulevard, #16
Tarzana
818-996-1822

600 East Colorado Boulevard
Pasadena
626-577-7802

1804-B South PCH
Redondo Beach
310-316-9331

13401 Ventura Boulevard, #104
Sherman Oaks
818-783-1161
www.kidsartclasses.com

Ages: infant and up

KidsArt has been teaching kids for over seventeen years. They take a traditional approach to drawing and painting and offer classes for all levels, including Mommy and Me.

Shakuntala Creative Art

310-497-3802

www.shakuntala.net

Ages: 2½ years and up

Shakuntala and her mother, Jennifer, teach private art classes in parents' homes for small groups of children (maximum ten kids) starting at two and a half years old. You provide the workspace, and they will bring all the supplies for a fun hour of art. Prices are $40 per child.

Music, Dance, and Theater Classes

The Adderley School

522 Palisades Drive

Pacific Palisades

310-230-1185

Ages: 3 years and up

This popular theater school offers a variety of music and dance programs. Classes meet for fourteen-week sessions and end with a performance at a local theater. Recent performances have included *The Little Mermaid* and *Annie*.

American National Academy

10944 Ventura Boulevard

Studio City

818-763-4431

Ages: 3½ years and up

Children's classes combine ballet, jazz, tap, acting, and singing and meet once a week for 1½ hours.

Dance for Kids Malibu

3898 Cross Creek Road

Malibu

310-456-8821

Ages: 3 years and up

Dance for Kids has recently taken over this popular Malibu dance studio. Classes include tap, ballet, and Mommy and Me.

The Classical Ballet School

22817 Ventura Boulevard

Woodland Hills

818-610-1091

www.classicalballet.com

Ages: 3 years and up

At this ballet school, started in 1947 in London, classical ballet based on the Cecchetti method is taught; it is a balanced and analyzed system of dance theory. The school has recently started a new Tiny Tots class for three- to five-year-olds.

Creation Station

8520 Pico Boulevard

Beverly Hills

310-659-3267

21616 Sherman Way

Canoga Park

818-598-0135

3601 Ocean View Boulevard

Glendale

818-248-7655

11239 Ventura Boulevard
Studio City
818-509-8888
www.creationstations.com
Ages: 15 months and up

Creation Station offers a variety of music, dance, and theater classes for children, including ballet, tap, jazz, hip hop, and karate. It also offers a three-hour drop-off "preschool alternative," where children learn through music, art, literature, and peer interaction. Weekly classes cost $150 for a ten-week session.

❄ Creative Kids

11301 West Olympic Boulevard, Suite 110
Los Angeles
310-473-6090
www.mycreativekids.com
Ages: newborn and up

Classes at Creative Kids include arts and crafts, Mommy and Me, cooking, chess, music, and dance for children ages three and older. Each class includes a snack, story time, music, and free play in the play area, which has mats, slides, tunnels, and toys. It also has a transition program where you can leave your child for part of the class. Twelve-week sessions cost between $200 and $650, depending on the class. Additionally, it offers camp sessions year-round. A free trial class is offered.

❄ Creative Space*

6325 Santa Monica Boulevard
Los Angeles
323-462-4600

11916 West Pico Boulevard
West Los Angeles
310-231-7600
www.creativespaceusa.com
Ages: 4 months to 12 years

Creative Space was founded by a group of moms who felt that traditional classes for kids lacked imagination. The classes here focus on inspiring children and promoting self-esteem, and are among the most creative we have seen. Classes include Be an Architect, where children build their own fantasy building from the ground up; Little Heroes, a fantasy play and art class; Magical Fairy Garden, where children create their own fairy wings and pretend to fly away; and Skateboard Art, where the kids decorate and design their own skateboards. Be sure to check the website, as new classes are always being introduced. It also offers transition classes and summer camp.

❄ Dance and Jingle

Various locations throughout L.A.
818-845-3925
Ages: 18 months and up

This music program introduces children to music starting at eighteen months old. It is designed to help children reach musical, social, emotional, physical, and academic goals. Classes are $15 each and run for forty-five minutes, with thirteen to fifteen children.

Dance for Kids/Brentwood Academy of Dance

Brentwood Gardens
11677 San Vicente Boulevard, Suite 312
Los Angeles
310-820-5437
Ages: 1 year and up

This popular dance school in Brentwood starts with kids as young as age one, with drop-in classes (accompanied by an adult) where you only pay by the class ($10 each). More structured classes start at age three and include ballet, tap, jazz, and hip hop; these culminate with an end-of-year recital. They also have a dance team for girls ages seven and older.

Debbie Allen Dance Academy

3623 Hayden Avenue
Culver City
310-280-9145
www.debbieallendanceacademy.com
Ages: 4 years and up

Debbie Allen's Early Bird program consists of a ballet/jazz/tap class, plus two electives of your choice (including flamenco, hip hop, and African dance). Classes meet three times per week (twelve hours per month), or for one long day on Saturdays.

Dramagination

323-856-8177
Ages: 3 to 5 years

These popular fairy-tale theater classes are held at various locations in Pasadena and La Canada. Each location has its own registration, policies, and prices. Contact "Queen Laura" for more information.

Fancy Feet Dance Studio

881 Alma Real Drive, Suite T-27
Pacific Palisades
310-459-7203
Ages: 2 years and up

This dance studio is located in the basement of an office building in downtown Pacific Palisades, and offers ballet, tap, and jazz classes. If you sign up for the session, classes are $13.50 each. If there is room, you can drop in at $15 per class.

Focus Fish

6121 Santa Monica Boulevard
Hollywood
323-957-0901
www.focusfish.com
Ages: 2 years and up

Focus Fish is a new, warehouse-size fitness and dance center in Hollywood; their philosophy is based upon community fitness and wellness. Dance classes start as young as two years old; adult classes are scheduled at the same time. They have baby-sitting and a salon, and a juice bar is opening.

For Kids Only*

The Sports Club/L.A.
1835 Sepulveda Boulevard
Los Angeles
310-445-6640
Ages: 3 months and older

For Kids Only at The Sports Club/L.A. calls itself "a club within the Club." It is a bright and colorful room outfitted with all sorts of toys and play equipment, and offers a variety of classes for children of members and non-members. One of the most popular classes is Half Music Half Mush, and is offered for children ages ten months to four years. The class is an hour long, and is divided between music and playing the "mush room," which is filled with buckets of edible "sand" (oatmeal and bran), that the kids can play in (they even rotate the flavors weekly)! Eight-week sessions are $120 for members of Sports Club/L.A. and $160 for nonmembers. Makeup classes are allowed within the session, and a free trial class is offered.

❋ Kids on Stage

Various locations throughout L.A.
310-314-0035
www.kidsonstage.com
Ages: 3 months and up

Kids on Stage was founded to help kids develop self-expression and creativity through acting, singing, dancing, and filmmaking. Classes include Parent and Me, ballet, tap, creative dance, comedy improvisation, and imagination theaters.

❋ Kindermusik International

Various locations throughout L.A.
800-628-5687
www.kindermusik.com
Ages: 3 months to 7 years

Kindermusik is an international music program that has several licensed teachers in the L.A. area. Classes incorporate singing, dancing, and playing instruments. Children are grouped according to age, and classes are forty-five minutes long. Check the website or call to find a class near you.

❋ Le Studio

100 West Villa Street
Pasadena
626-792-4616
www.lestudiodance.com
Ages: 3 years and up

Le Studio is a professional dance school that has been around for over twenty-five years. Creative movement classes start at three years old. Each season ends with a spring gala performance.

❋ Miss Claire

626-403-3828 (South Pasadena)
626-0308-2875 (San Gabriel)
Ages: 2 years and up

Miss Claire teaches tap, ballet, and hip hop at various locations around Pasadena. Classes include Musical Fun for Tots, Tiny Tots Dance, Parent and Me, and Dance Combo (ballet, tap, and jazz) classes.

❋ MNR Dance Factory

11606 San Vincente Boulevard
Los Angeles
310-826-4554
www.mnrdancefactory.com
Ages: 3 years and up

Formerly Molly & Roni's Dance Factory, this studio recently relocated to this new space. Dance classes start at three years old and combine ballet and tap. Also offered are pretoddler and toddler classes for children under three years old.

Music and Movement

Janet Hopper

Classes held at Westside and Valley locations

310-396-6333

Ages: 3 months to 3 years

Janet Hopper has been running music classes in people's homes since 1980. She brings music, toys, blankets, and an electric keyboard to entertain between six and ten children. You can either join an ongoing class or form your own with your friends.

Music 'n' Me

Westside Pavilion

10850 West Pico Boulevard, Suite 607

Los Angeles

310-441-1800

Ages: newborn to 5 years

Music 'n' Me is a music education class founded by Daniel Rosa, who wanted to share his love of music with children. The teaching staff includes college graduate music majors who aim to make the class fun and not forced. Classes are forty minutes long and include singing and playing musical instruments. Fees are $70 for a four-week session and $120 for an eight-week session (a free trial class is offered). Private lessons with different instruments are available for older children.

Music 'n' Motion

Rancho Palos Verdes

Torrance

310-373-0280

Ages: newborn to 7 years

Music 'n' Motion offers music classes at several different locations in Torrance and Rancho Palos Verdes. Classes are formed with a minimum of six students and a maximum of twelve students, and cost $10 each. Private home classes are also available.

Music Rhapsody

310-376-8646

Various locations throughout L.A.

www.musicrhapsody.com

Ages: 3 months to 12 years

The classes here incorporate singing, dancing, and playing musical instruments. When you sign up for the class, you must purchase the "music backpack" ($40) filled with all types of instruments and a video. There is a registration fee of $20 each year, and tuition is about $96 for a six-week session (there is a discounted annual fee). Teachers and locations vary, so take advantage of the free trial class. Music Rhapsody also offers summer camp programs.

Music Together

Various locations in L.A.

www.musictogether.com

Ages: newborn and up

Music Together is a nationwide program designed to introduce children to music. The program focuses on teaching children musical notes and sounds, rather than singing nursery rhymes. One session consists of ten weekly forty-five-minute classes and costs $165. The fee includes a CD, cassette tape, songbook, and parent guide to music development. Two makeup classes are permitted during each session. Call to take a free trial class.

Pacific Academy of Dance

1100 South Beverly Drive
Los Angeles
310-277-9779
Ages: 2 years and up
Dance classes here combine ballet and tap to help children develop coordination by learning basic positions. The school is very flexible about class time, and if you have a group of at least four children, it will work to form a class at a time that is best for you. The dance year culminates with an end-of-the-year recital.

Pasadena Civic Ballet

25 South Sierra Madre Boulevard
Pasadena
626-792-0873
www.pcballet.com
Ages: 3½ years and up
Introduction to dance and tap classes at PCB start at three-and-a-half years old and continue into pre-ballet, and pre-tap and hip-hop classes for five- to seven-year-olds. Ballet classes begin at age six and students can audition for the company when they are ten years old, members of which have the opportunity to perform in major productions before large audiences.

Piano Play*

14237 Ventura Boulevard
Sherman Oaks
818-789-6110
www.pianoplaymusicsystems.com
Ages: 19 months and up
Piano Play classes include Tiny Fingers (nineteen months to two years) and Little Hands (two to three years), which introduce young children to early fundamental music skills; Music for Fun (ages five and up) teaches beginner keyboard and fundamental music concepts. Advanced classes for ages six and older are also offered. The fee is $303 for a five-month period, but they will prorate the fee for partial sessions. Materials are $20 for Tiny Fingers and $50 for Little Hands. There are five to eight kids in a class and private instruction is also available.

Rana's Art Club

Various locations on the Westside
310-786-5925
www.ranasartsclub.com
Ages: 3 years and up
In addition to teaching yoga and dance at various area schools, Rana also offers classes and camps through the City of Santa Monica Parks and Recreation Department. Classes include Parent and Me yoga, Crafty Creativity, Fairytale Drama, and hip hop. She also created a kids' yoga video called "I Can Do Yoga" which is available on her website.

Rhythm Child

3025 West Olympic Boulevard
Santa Monica
310-204-5466
www.rhythmchild.net
Ages: 6 months and up
Rhythm Child introduces the ancient concept of drumming circles to young children. The Parent and Me Rhythms classes are for children ages six months to four years old.

Santa Monica Academy of Music

2414 Wilshire Boulevard
Santa Monica
310-828-8025
www.bestmusiclessons.org

Classes at the Santa Monica Academy of Music start at eighteen months with a musical instrument class. Their new transition classes for three-and-a-half- to five-year-olds introduce children to basic music concepts, recognizing notes and sounds, and beginning piano skills. Piano classes are for four-and-a-half- to six-year-olds, and singing groups are open to first graders and up.

Lou Stratten*

310-280-3378
Ages: 3 months to 6 years

Children in L.A. are bound to meet Lou Stratten at some point during their toddler years, whether it is in a music class, at a puppet show, or at a birthday party. Lou is an excellent entertainer and great with children. While she teaches music classes at various locations around Los Angeles, she is also available to teach small groups of children at your home for $20 per child, with a minimum of six children.

Studio A Dance

2306 Hyperion Avenue
Silver Lake
323-661-8311
www.studioadance.com
Ages: 2 years and up

Studio A offers a variety of classes including ballet and tap, creative ballet, move and groove, and karate.

Totally Kids

8291/2 Via de la Paz
Pacific Palisades
310-573-7073
www.totallykidscenter.com
Ages: infant and up

Totally Kids offers music and dance classes, a mixed-media art class, nature and hiking in the Temescal Canyon, and gymnastics with the popular teacher Dan the Man (see page 180). Classes cost between $160 and $200 for an eight-week session, depending on the class. They also have a three-hour drop-off program for preschoolers available every day of the week.

Village Arts and Enrichment Center*

15200 Sunset Boulevard, Suite 111
Pacific Palisades
310-454-4245
Ages: 6 weeks and up

Founded by local parents, this enrichment center is designed to be a place where children can express themselves creatively. Classes offered include Mush and Gush, which is a combination of art and music; Little Princesses, which includes dress-up, art, cooking, and dancing; Swashbucklers, Knights, and Pirates, which includes fantasy play and treasure hunts; and A World of Science, where children explore and discover through science. There is also a Daddy and Me class on Saturday mornings. Classes cost between $175 and $225 for an eight-week session.

❄ *Wondernation*

3625 North Sepulveda Boulevard

Manhattan Beach

310-545-4550

www.wondernation.com

Ages: infants and up

Wondernation is a discovery and enrichment studio that offers a variety of classes such as yoga, music, martial arts, hula, and book buddies, a class designed to help early reading and language skills.

Cooking

❄ *Chefmakers Cooking Academy**

872 Via de la Paz

Pacific Palisades

310-459-9444

www.chefmakers.com

Ages: 3 years and up

Chefmakers's Junior Chef program for young children includes Mommy and/or Daddy and Me for three- to five-year-olds (ten-week session is $325); Preschool Prodigy for four- to six-year-olds (ten-week session is $350); and Kids for seven- to eleven-year-olds (ten-week session is $400). All the children's classes are held in the same high-tech kitchen the adult classes are, and children cook everything from the usual kiddie fare (mac and cheese and cookies) to more sophisticated cuisine (lasagna and egg cups). Depending upon their age kids learn about ingredients, measurements, and following instructions.

Language Classes

❄ *La La Ling*

1810 North Vermont Avenue

Los Angeles

323-664-4400

www.lalaling.com

Ages: 6 months and up

La La Ling, a baby lifestyle boutique, holds classes in its back room for toddlers. They currently offer baby sign language, Kindermusik, toddler Spanish, and art.

❄ *Language Door*

11870 Santa Monica Boulevard, Suite 202

Los Angeles

310-826-4140

17200 Ventura Boulevard, Suite 305

Encino

818-995-3667

www.languagedoor.com

Ages: 1 year and up

The Language Door offers classes in Chinese, French, Spanish, Arabic, German, Italian, Farsi, and several other languages, which are taught through music, games, and other interactive activities. They use the immersion approach, which means that no English is spoken in class from the start. There is a Mommy and Me program for ages one to three. A free trial class is offered. There is a one-time registration fee of $30 and classes range from $69–$89 a month for weekly classes.

World Speak (formerly Baby Genius)

Westside Pavilion
10850 West Pico Boulevard, Suite 607
Los Angeles
310-441-5222
Ages: 10 months and up

World Speak offers classes for children in ten different languages, including French, Spanish, German, Italian, Hebrew, Russian, Chinese, and Japanese. They also offer Mommy and Me classes, preschool transition classes, and preschool alternative classes. Classes are $160 (seven to eight children per class) for an eight-week session with two makeup classes, or $128 for an eight-week session with no makeup classes.

Gym Classes

Bright Child

1415 Fourth Street
Santa Monica
310-393-4844
www.brightchild.com
Ages: 7 months to 6 years

This indoor play space (see entry on page 191) offers parent-participation classes for different age groups that include activities such as singing, exercise, and obstacle courses. They also have an arts and crafts room for children two years and older. Classes are $80 a month for one hourly class a week, plus a one-time enrollment fee of $125. All children must be supervised by an adult in both the classes and in the play space.

Broadway Gymnastics*

5433 Beethoven Street
Los Angeles
310-450-0012
www.broadwaygym.com
Ages: 18 months to adults

Broadway Gymnastics has been around for years, but recently moved to this large (over 25,000 square feet) state-of-the-art location. Children as young as eighteen months old can start classes at Broadway Gymnastics in the Tumbling Toddlers class. The facility is large enough that there are often multiple classes taking place at the same time. This makes for a somewhat loud and chaotic environment, but it doesn't seem to distract the kids! Once your child is old enough to take a class on his own, you can watch him from the observation deck. There is an annual registration fee of $50 per student. Eight-week sessions cost between $172 and $268, depending on the time of the class (forty-five minutes, sixty minutes, or ninety minutes).

Child's Play

2299 Westwood Boulevard
Los Angeles
310-470-4997
Ages: 9 months to 12 years

The classes offered at this indoor play space include Mommy and Me, ballet, tap, and jazz. Ten classes are $149. There is a separate eating area and a small shopping section that sells popular clothing and toys (see entry on page 191).

❊ Dan the Man

310-887-0042

www.dtmsupergym.com

Ages: infant and up

Dan the Man teaches sports and gymnastics classes at various locations around town and will also teach private classes in your home. For one to five kids, the cost per class is $20; $15 for six to ten kids; and $10 for eleven to twenty kids.

❊ Fit for Kids, Inc.

1106 North La Cienega Boulevard, Suite 105

Los Angeles

310-360-6282

Ages: 6 months to 6 years

Fit for Kids, Inc. offers gym classes involving music and play equipment. Classes are $60 for an eight-week session plus a one-time family membership fee of $30. They also offer a summer camp for children ages three to five and a half that is unique in its flexibility: You can choose the number of days and when you wish to attend and pay accordingly. A free trial class is offered.

❊ Fun and Fit Gymnastics

1919 West Burbank Boulevard

Burbank

818-845-0700

www.funandfit.com

Ages: 2 years and up

Fun and Fit offers gymnastics classes for all ages as well as day-camp sessions year-round. They also offer a parents' night out, free play, and other family events. The school is so confi-dent that your child will love gymnastics at Fun and Fit that they will give you your money back after thirty days if you are not happy.

❊ Gymboree

443 East Irving Drive, Suite F

Burbank

818-955-8964

4719 Commons Way

Calabasas

818-224-4695

4469 Chevy Chase Drive

La Canada

818-955-8964

10850 West Pico Boulevard

Los Angeles

310-470-7780

220 Aviation Boulevard

Manhattan Beach

310-798-8996

9301 Tampa Avenue

Northridge

818-905-6225

435 South Fair Oaks

Pasadena

626-445-1122

14801 Ventura Boulevard

Sherman Oaks

818-905-6225

2825 Pacific Coast Highway
Torrance
310-257-8059

3825 East Thousand Oaks Boulevard, Suite D
Westlake Village
805-529-8499
www.gymboree.com
Ages: newborn to 4 years

With locations all over L.A., Gymboree has been one of the most popular places for kids' gym classes for over twenty years. Their classes engage kids in fun activities in an encouraging setting. Classes are divided by age group, and involve music, parachutes, slides, and other play equipment meant to foster a child's physical and social development. They also have music and art classes. Prices vary with location, but generally there is a $25 one-time family membership fee. A session of twelve weekly classes costs approximately $175 and a $30 music materials fee is required for music classes. Discounts are available for siblings and multiple classes. Free trial classes are available.

Joey's Gym for Children
275 South Robertson Boulevard
Beverly Hills
310-855-0146
Ages: 4 months to 11 years

Joey's Gym is open seven days a week, and offers over twenty gym classes at a time. Parent/caregiver involvement is required for children three years old and younger. An eight-week session is $120 for forty-five-minute classes and $140 for sixty-minute classes. A one-

time membership fee of $25 is required. They also have transition classes, and summer, spring, and holiday camps.

Josephson Academy of Gymnastics*
8640 Hayden Place
Culver City
310-287-9886
www.jaggym.com
Ages: 1 year and up

This new gymnastics school has quickly become a favorite among parents for its brand-new, state-of-the-art facility (over twenty-four thousand square feet) and excellent teachers. Kids love it too, and will beg to come back after their trial class is over! Classes start as soon as your child is walking, and there is even a sibling area where small children can play while they wait.

Kidnasium*
808 Wilshire Boulevard
Santa Monica
310-395-6700
www.kidnasium.com
Ages: 6 months to 8 years

Kidnasium's mission is to promote fitness, balance, and coordination with classes that are part exercise, part music, and all fun! One-hour classes cost $154 for an eight-week session, with a $26 one-time membership fee.

Kids Gym, USA
5520 Crebs Avenue
Tarzana
818-343-1120
Ages: 6 months to 8 years

Kids Gym has been in its current location for almost thirty years. The classes teach coordination, balance, and strengthening skills through exercises with equipment. The apparatus is changed weekly to keep the environment fun and challenging. Parent-participation classes are offered for children ages six to nineteen months. Ten-week sessions cost $140 for forty-five-minute classes and $165 for sixty-minute classes. A free trial class is offered.

❋ *Los Angeles School of Gymnastics*

8450 Higuera Street
Culver City
310-204-1980

3639 Eastham Boulevard
Culver City
www.lagymnastics.com
Ages: 18 months and up
Los Angeles Gymnastics has been around since 1975 and prides itself on its high-quality (Olympic) coaches and its top-notch training facility. Classes start at $150 for an eight-week session.

❋ *Malibu Gymnastics**

29769 Heathercliff, #79 (Point Dume Plaza)
Malibu
310-589-5538

1145 Lindero Canyon, #c1
Westlake Village
818-889-4647
www.malibugymnastics.com
Ages: 2 years and up

This gymnasium offers a wide array of gymnastics classes for children of all ages, starting with Mommy and Me. They also offer popular indoor rock climbing classes for all levels, as well as a summer camp and "free play" time when the kids have the run of the place. Prices vary according to the age and level; private lessons are also offered.

❋ *My Gym*

1837 South La Cienega
Beverly Hills
310-287-1496

17175 Ventura Boulevard
Encino
818-385-0888

9420 Reseda
Northridge
818-998-7496

839 South Arroyo Parkway
Pasadena
626-441-7800

1216 Beryl Street
Redondo Beach
310-318-2288

12422 Santa Monica Boulevard
Santa Monica
310-820-0155

2701 Thousand Oaks Boulevard
Thousand Oaks
805-494-4154

4821 Lankershim Boulevard
Toluca Lake
818-509-1077

22027-B Vanowen Street
Woodland Hills
818-702-6946
www.my-gym.com
Ages: 3 months to 13 years
My Gym is a nationwide franchise, with over nine locations in Los Angeles alone. Classes are designed for specific age groups and include Tiny Tykes for children ages three to eleven months, and karate and hip-hop classes for older kids. Classes and prices vary at each location. Discounts apply for multiple classes or children.

Karate

❋ Champion Martial Arts

137 South Barrington Place
Los Angeles
310-440-1947
www.championsbrentwood.com
Ages: 4 years and up
Led by world champion martial artist Keith Cook, Champion Martial Arts focuses on character development. An introductory special for $19.95 includes a half-hour private class and one free group class.

❋ Dawn Barnes Karate Kids

17205 Ventura Boulevard
Encino
818-789-4400

23681 Calabasas Road
Calabasas
818-591-2424

3015 Wilshire Boulevard
Santa Monica
310-449-1700

13409 Ventura Boulevard
Sherman Oaks
818-906-2100
Ages: 4 to 14 years
www.karatekids.net
Dawn Barnes is one of the most popular karate studios in Los Angeles. Their martial arts classes aim to build students' confidence, discipline, and respect, and incorporate yoga, Shotokan karate from Japan, animal card games, and cardiovascular exercise. A free trial class is offered.

❋ United Studios of Self Defense

Various locations throughout Los Angeles
www.ussd.com
Ages: 4 years and up
This martial arts studio has twelve locations in the Los Angeles area. The children's program emphasizes building self-discipline and a positive self-image. A free trial class is offered. Check the website for a studio near you.

Sports Classes

Below are some of the most popular sports programs, but also be sure to check with your local parks and recreation center. Many offer some type of sports program.

❊ *Adventure Plex**

1701 Marine Avenue
Manhattan Beach
310-546-7708
www.adventureplex.org
Ages: infants and up

This fitness facility run by the Beach Cities Health District offers a variety of classes including sports classes and gym classes for toddlers, hip hop and ballet classes, and rock climbing. The facility is really clean and is a great place to introduce the family to fitness. There is an upstairs gym area, and a courtside café with healthy fare—no sodas here!

❊ *American Youth Soccer Organization (AYSO)*

www.soccer.org

AYSO is a nationwide youth soccer program that follows these principles: 1. Everyone plays; 2. Teams are fair and balanced in regard to ability; 3. Registration is open to everyone; 4. Coaching is positive; and 5. Good sportsmanship is mandatory. Check the website to find a location near you.

❊ *Coast Sports/Coach Steve Morris**

310-451-4220
www.coastsports.com
Ages: 3 years and up

Soccer is the core of this sports program; however, Coach Steve also offers baseball, golf, and a Super All-Stars class, which is a mix of sports, races, and games. Classes are offered at Barrington Park. Summer and spring break camps are also offered.

❊ *Culver Ice Arena*

4545 Sepulveda Boulevard
Culver City
310-398-5718
www.culvericearena.com
Ages: 3 years and up

Ice-skating classes start as early as three years old in the Mommy and Me program at Culver Ice Arena. These classes are forty-five minutes long and meet once a week for ten weeks ($135). Solo ice-skating classes begin at age four, and are forty-five minutes long. They meet once a week for ten weeks ($100), and also include one free practice day. Public skating sessions are also available.

❊ *Fun and Sports/Coach Samir Sakar*

323-934-1979
www.funandsportscamp.com
Ages: 2½ years and up

Coach Samir has been teaching sports classes all over Los Angeles for over ten years, from Santa Clarita to Malibu. His philosophy is that learning proper sports techniques will help kids develop self-esteem and build positive character traits, such as respect and good manners. Group classes are held at over twenty locations throughout the city, or you can put together your own group.

Ice & Roller Blade Hockey/private instruction with Ethan Rill

818-469-8837

Ages: 3 years and up

Ethan teaches private roller hockey classes to children all over Los Angeles. "If they can walk, they can skate" is his motto. Private classes are $40 per hour; he also holds semiprivate lessons with small groups.

Pasadena Ice Skating Center

310 East Green Street

Pasadena

626-578-0801

www.skatepasadena.com

Ages: 3 years and up

Skating lessons at Pasadena Ice Skating Center start at three years old. Classes are thirty minutes long and meet once a week for ten weeks ($125).

SoccerKids USA

310-737-0174

www.soccerkidsUSA.com

Ages: 2½ years and up

SoccerKids USA was created by husband-and-wife coaching team, Julie and Justin. In their classes, they try to maintain a nurturing environment, emphasizing playfulness rather than competition. They teach group and private lessons as well as clinics, classes, and camps at parks around Los Angeles.

YMCA

www.ymca.com

The YMCA brings sports programs to almost every community in Los Angeles. They offer programs in almost any sport, including basketball, soccer, baseball (and T-ball), and volleyball. Teams are usually coached by parent volunteers. Each community center offers a different program, so check with the YMCA in your neighborhood to find out which programs are offered.

Etiquette Classes

Perfect Angels

310-230-6877

Ages: 3 years and up

Perfect Angels, run by Chase Holiday, teaches social graces and character education for children ages four and up. Classes teach kids about virtues such as kindness, honesty, and charity in a fun and entertaining setting. Private and group classes, parties, and workshops are offered.

Petit Protocol

Hotel Bel-Air

701 Stone Canyon

Bel Air

310-472-1211

Ages: 6 years and up

This unique etiquette program at the Hotel Bel Air offers one-session classes four Saturdays a year, from 9 A.M.–1 P.M. ($250). The classes teach children everything from telephone etiquette to how to set a table, and include lunch, as well as baking a dessert in the hotel kitchen.

Swim Classes

❋ *Family Life Aquatics*
310-264-SWIM
www.familylifeaquatics.com
Ages: infant and up
Family Life Aquatics offers private and group swimming lessons either at Westside or Thousand Oaks locations, or at your home (for an additional fee). The schools offer lifeguards-for-hire for parties, as well as surfing instruction and synchronized swimming classes.

❋ *Head Above Water Swim School*
310-738-SWIM
www.headabovewater.net
Ages: infant and up
Head Above Water offers swim lessons for all ages, including a Mommy and Me program either at your home or at locations in Beverly Hills, Culver City, Woodland Hills, and Pasadena. They also offer a water safety class for parents and caregivers, lifeguard services, and pool parties.

❋ *Rosebowl Aquatics*
360 North Arroyo Boulevard
Pasadena
626-564-0330
www.rosebowlaquatics.org
Ages: 6 months and up
Rosebowl Aquatics offers year-round swimming lessons in its large facility, including Mommy and Me classes and instruction for swimmers of all ages and levels. Private lessons are also available. Classes are $72 for a four-week session.

Yoga

Almost every yoga studio in the city offers some type of class for children, starting with infants! One of the most popular programs is called Itsy Bitsy Yoga, which was started by Helen Garabedian, an infant developmental movement educator and registered yoga teacher. This program teaches more than seventy-five yoga poses and techniques for babies from three weeks to twenty-four months. There are several trained instructors in the L.A. area. Children's yoga classes are generally for ages four and up, and teaches them mental and physical flexibility and coordination.

The following is a list of yoga studios and yoga instructors that offer yoga for children.

❋ *Angel City Yoga*
12408 Ventura Boulevard
Studio City
818-762-8211
www.angelcityyoga.com
Mommy and Me yoga

❋ *Golden Bridge Yoga*
6322 DeLongpre Avenue
Hollywood
323-936-4172
www.goldenbridgeyoga.com
Mommy and Me yoga, children's yoga

❋ *Karuna Yoga*
19391/2 Hillhurst Avenue
Los Feliz
323-665-6242
www.karunayoga.net
Itsy Bitsy yoga, children's yoga

Khefri/Urban Goddess
323-549-5383
www.khefri.net
Itsy Bitsy yoga, Yoga for Tots, and family yoga

Jenny Jamrog
310-387-5902
Mommy and Me yoga, and Itsy Bitsy yoga

Jiva Yoga
15327 Sunset Boulevard
Pacific Palisades
310-454-7000
www.jivayoga.com
Mommy and Me yoga, children's yoga

Shana Meyerson
310-478-2266
www.miniyogis.com
Available for private instruction or group classes

Mission Street Yoga
1017 Mission Street
South Pasadena
626-441-1144
www.missionstreetyoga.com
Children's yoga, family yoga

Silver Lake Yoga
2810 Glendale Boulevard
Silver Lake
323-953-0496
www.silverlakeyoga.com
Children's yoga

Yoga House
11 West State Street
Pasadena
626-403-3961
www.yogahouse.com
Mommy and Me, children's yoga

Yoga West
1535 South Robertson
Beverly Hills
310-552-4647
www.yogawestla.com
Children's yoga

Yoga Works
1426 Montana Avenue, Second Floor
Santa Monica
310-393-5150

2215 Main Street
Santa Monica
310-393-5150

1256 Westwood Boulevard
Los Angeles
310-324-1200
www.yogaworks.com
Mommy and Me yoga, children's yoga

Transition/Enrichment

A Kid's Place
12306 Venice Boulevard
310-390-0401
A Kid's Place was founded by Susie Leonard, who has over twenty years of experience as a

preschool director and administrator. This large developmental center has several different rooms in which children engage in physical, creative, social, and imaginative play. There is a toddler class (Mommy and Me), a transition class, and preschool playgroups. They are currently in the process of getting preschool accreditation. A Kid's Place has open play several times during the week and is also available for birthday parties.

❋ IDEAS Studio
16550 Marquez
Pacific Palisades
www.theideasstudio.com
This new enrichment center offers science- and technology-related programs, and includes a computer lab designed to resemble NASA's Mission Control, a robot center, an art/media lab, and a play area for toddlers.

The following places are listed in the above activity section, but also offer transition classes:

❋ Creation Station
8520 Pico Boulevard
Beverly Hills
310-659-3267

21616 Sherman Way
Canoga Park
818-598-0135

3601 Ocean View Boulevard
Glendale
818-248-7655

11239 Ventura Boulevard
Studio City
818-509-8888
www.creationstations.com

❋ Creative Kids
11301 West Olympic Boulevard, Suite 110
Los Angeles
310-473-6090
www.mycreativekids.com

❋ Creative Space*
6325 Santa Monica Boulevard (Eastside)
Los Angeles
323-462-4600

11916 West Pico Boulevard (Westside)
Los Angeles
310-231-7600
www.creativespaceusa.com

❋ Joey's Gym for Children
275 South Robertson Boulevard
Beverly Hills
310-855-0146

❋ Totally Kids
8291/2 Via de la Paz
Pacific Palisades
310-573-7073
www.totallykidscenter.com

※ *World Speak (formerly Baby Genius)*

Westside Pavilion
10850 West Pico Boulevard, Suite 607
Los Angeles
310-441-5222

Indoor Play Spaces

Indoor play spaces are great on rainy days or when you just can't think of anything else to do with your child! These places have either built-in or freestanding equipment such as climbing structures, slides, and trampolines. There is generally no supervision, so a parent or caretaker is required at all times. These are also great spots for birthday parties, since they can accommodate a large number of children and usually offer something for everyone.

Before you head on over, here are a couple of tips. Indoor play spaces can get crowded in bad weather and school holidays, so go early and be prepared. Also, make sure to wash your little one's hands when you leave; germs spread quickly indoors, especially in ball pits and anywhere children can put things in their mouths.

※ *Adventure Plex**

1701 Marine Avenue
Manhattan Beach
310-546-7708
www.adventureplex.org
Ages: infants and up
This fitness facility has lots for kids and their families beyond the classes offered (see entry in Sports Classes section), including a play structure (the largest we've ever seen!), basketball

court, and rock-climbing wall. There are also fitness memberships available, after-school programs, camps year-round, and family activities such as movie nights. Admission is $5 for children under three; $10 for children three and older, and includes one adult. They are open Monday through Friday from 9 A.M.–9 P.M.; Saturdays from 10 A.M.–7 P.M.; and Sundays from 10 A.M.–6 P.M.

※ *Bright Child**

1415 Fourth Street
Santa Monica
310-393-4844
www.brightchild.com
Ages: 7 months to 6 years
The indoor play space at Bright Child has a mini putting green, a basketball court, rope climbing, and a huge climbing and slide maze. We love that it has an area exclusively for toddlers to play in. (Diaper-wearers only!) This place can get crowded, so come early on rainy days and school holidays. They are open seven days a week, and it has a snack bar. Regular admission is $9.75 per child for up to two hours of play and $4 for an additional two hours. All children must be supervised by an adult.

※ *Child's Play*

2299 Westwood Boulevard
Los Angeles
310-470-4997
Ages: 9 months to 12 years
The indoor play space at Child's Play has a bouncer, crawling equipment with slides and balls, lots of cars for kids to ride around in, a

stage, and a full trunk of clothes for dress up. Child's Play is great for toddlers because it is big enough for them to run around but small enough that you can still keep your eye on them at all times. They also have a separate eating area and a shopping section where toys and clothes are sold. Child's Play is open for free play during the week from 10 A.M.–6 P.M. (it stays open until 8 P.M. on Thursdays), and costs $8 per child. They are closed on the weekends for private birthday parties.

Funshineland

17200 Ventura Boulevard
(Encino Town Center)
Encino
818-386-9600
www.funshineland.com

This indoor playground is good for children up to age five. There is a small bouncer, air hockey table, and roller coaster, as well as cars. They are open during the week from 10 A.M.–6 P.M. and there is family night every Wednesday, which features characters such as Sponge Bob. They are closed on the weekends for private birthday parties. Admission for free play is $7 per child with a discount for siblings. Look for music and Mommy and Me classes coming soon.

Kid Concepts, USA

22844 Hawthorne Boulevard
Torrance
310-465-0075
www.kidconceptsusa.com

This indoor playground has a large play structure, pretend kitchen, dress-up area and stage, rock climbing wall, block area, arts and crafts room, toddler area, and a new lightspace interactive system, which is a special floor that lights up and plays music where the children move. There is also a café and small toy store. Admission for children under two is $5; over two is $8. One adult per child is free; additional adults are $4.

My Playroom

4954 Van Nuys Boulevard
Sherman Oaks
818-784-PLAY

This indoor playground is open weekdays for free play for ages ten months to five years. They are closed on the weekends for private parties.

Nana's Garden

426 South Robertson
Los Angeles
310-288-3042
www.nanasgarden.net

This unique indoor play space is a great place for moms to relax without leaving their kids at home. For kids, there is a small play area, a teacher who leads art projects, and music classes with Lou Stratten (see entry under Music Classes). For moms, it offers facials, massages, manicures, and pedicures; or you can just have a nice lunch while your child plays. They also have a Mommy and Me mani/pedi, and a great kids' menu at the cafe.

Playland

18555 Ventura Boulevard
Tarzana
818-343-6444

The equipment and toys at this indoor playground are most appropriate for children under six. Its facilities include a bouncer, putting green, play structure, and infant center, with toys geared for those under eighteen months. Playland is open weekdays from 9:30 A.M.– 6 P.M. Weekend hours depend on scheduled birthday parties.

✽ *Under the Sea**

2424 West Victory Boulevard
Burbank
818-567-9945

12211 West Washington Boulevard, #120
Culver City
310-915-1133

19620 Nordhoff Street
Northridge
818-772-7003

20929 Ventura Boulevard
Woodland Hills
818-999-1533
www.choicemall.com/underthesea
Ages: 6 months to 14 years
This indoor gym has a bouncer, ball pit, sea castle, fun house, and tons of other activities that toddlers will love. They are open for free play Monday to Friday from 10 A.M.–6 P.M. (though they host birthday parties, so call ahead). The cost for free play is $7 per child; adults are free (maximum two adults per child). A discounted monthly rate gives you and your child unlimited access.

out and about

Let's face it, if you love the outdoors L.A. is the best place to live! Before we had kids we may have taken it for granted, but L.A. has some of the most beautiful beaches, parks, and hiking trails in the world. Now that you have a baby it's time to get out of the house and enjoy all the city has to offer!

In this section, we discuss parks and playgrounds, beaches, and other places to picnic and hike. We also list museums, amusement parks, and zoos that are of interest to L.A. families. You are sure to find some educational and entertaining family activities.

parks/playgrounds

A visit to the park is an easy way to get out of the house without making a big production of it. Every kid loves swings, slides, and sand, and many women we know have met their best mommy friends at the park.

There are more parks in L.A. and the surrounding cities than we could ever list here, so we have limited ourselves to only those that have playgrounds, sandboxes, and at least one climbing structure. Many parks have recreation centers that offer fabulous classes for older children. (Some even offer Mommy and Me types of classes as well.)

The City of Los Angeles Department of Recreation and Parks has a directory of services and locations on its website www.laparks.com. For outlying cities, call your local Department of Recreation and Parks for information. If you have a dog, please note that most playgrounds don't allow them, or at least require them to be leashed. We have divided this section by geographic area so that you can easily locate the best playgrounds near your home.

Hollywood

❋ *Griffith Park*
4730 Crystal Springs Drive
Los Angeles
323-913-4688
Griffith Park is L.A.'s answer to New York's Central Park. At a sprawling 4,107 acres, Griffith Park is the largest park in L.A. and offers everything you can imagine for children, including seven playgrounds. Wherever you live in the city, it is worth the effort to make a visit, even if it is a day trip. Please be aware that since the park is so large, the activities listed below can be spread out. You can either park and take a stroller, or drive between sites. Some of the best spots in Griffith Park for children are:

Griffith Park Merry-Go-Round (in the center of the park). This antique carousel, built in 1926, is complete with wonderful organ music. Your child will love riding with you on a horse that moves up and down, or, once they are older, riding alone.

Griffith Park Observatory and Planetarium (2800 Observatory Road). Currently under construction, the remodeled Observatory is due to reopen in 2005. It has a temporary home, the Observatory Satellite located near the Los Angeles Zoo, which houses a telescope and exhibits. If your child is a budding astronomer, visit the website, www.griffithobs.org, for more information.

Travel Town Museum & Southern Railroad (Riverside entrance). The Travel Town Museum and the Southern Railroad will keep a train-loving toddler enthralled for years to come. There is a miniature train that looks like a steam engine, which kids can ride on (it costs $1.50 for a seven-minute ride). It is a bargain and a great hit with the kids! Further down the main road, you'll find Travel Town Museum. It has an amazing collection of trains that your child can play on and explore. The gift shop sells just about every train-related toy (including Thomas the Tank Engine products) imaginable.

Pony Rides (Riverside entrance). What better way to follow up a train ride than with a pony ride? The ponies are located just next door to the Southern Railroad. A concession stand and rest rooms are nearby.

Shane's Inspiration (Griffith Park Drive near the Park Center). Shane's Inspiration has the first "boundless playground" built in California. This unique park is a place where children of all abilities can play together. Seventy percent of the equipment is accessible to a child in a wheelchair, a walker, or other support apparatus. Children with and without disabilities play side by side and it is a great way to inspire compassion and understanding. The equipment is truly amazing—the floors and ramps are cushioned, as is the climbing apparatus—and there are big bucket swings.

Beverly Hills/Bel Air

✷ *Coldwater Canyon Park*
1100 North Beverly Drive
Beverly Hills
This great park located north of Sunset Boulevard has just recently been renovated and is a favorite for toddlers. The playground is just the right size for the little ones. There is also a running stream, which the kids love to play in on hot days.

✷ *Roxbury Park*
471 South Roxbury Drive
Beverly Hills
310-550-4761
Roxbury Park is the best park for toddlers in Beverly Hills. If you live in the area, this venue is sure to become part of your life for years to come. This great playground has a separate toddler area, with a dinosaur-shaped climbing apparatus that sprays cool mist in the summertime. This is also where most local soccer and baseball teams hold their games, which are fascinating for babies and toddlers to watch.

You might also check out:

✷ *La Cienega Park*
8400 Gregory Way
Beverly Hills
310-550-4625

Westwood/West L.A.

❊ *Aidan's Place**

Westwood Recreation Complex
1350 Sepulveda Boulevard
Los Angeles
310-473-3610

Since its opening in December 2001, Aidan's Place has become a popular destination for families on the Westside. Aidan's Place is the second "boundless playground" in the western United States, and like Shane's Inspiration in Griffith Park (see page 195), it is designed to allow children with and without disabilities to play alongside each other. The equipment is very imaginative, including stand-alone trucks with push-button spritzers to cool your child off on the hottest of days. The climbing structures have all sorts of hidden surprises: big puzzle letters, mirrors, maps, and steering wheels. There is a covered sandbox with built-in shovels that is also quite popular, especially since it is shaded.

❊ *Holmby Park*

601 Clubview Drive
Los Angeles
310-276-1604

This park, nestled in between the trees just north of Wilshire Boulevard in Westwood, is the perfect place to meet neighborhood moms. The playground is ideal for toddlers. The most popular attraction has to be the stream; running the full length of the park, it is shallow enough for a toddler to stomp around in for hours when the weather is hot.

You might also check out:

❊ *Cheviot Hills Park*

2551 Motor Avenue
Los Angeles
310-837-5186

❊ *Irving Schachter Park*

2599 Beverwil Drive
Los Angeles

❊ *Stoner Park*

1835 Stoner Avenue
Los Angeles
310-479-7200

Santa Monica/Venice

❊ *Douglas Park**

2439 Wilshire Boulevard
Santa Monica

This is one of our children's favorite parks. There is something for kids of all ages, and enough to do that you can spend an afternoon here. There is a separate playground for babies and toddlers, with clear signs to keep those "big kids" away. There are two great rubber bucket swings for babies and a couple of teeter-totters as well. With another swing set, three other climbing structures, and a great fort with a picnic table inside, it is sure to be a hit. There is also a large concrete area designed for children to ride their bikes, tricycles, and skateboards. During the summer, water shoots up from the middle of the concrete ground, drenching all who want to play! The recently renovated duck pond on the Wilshire side is also a favorite. These ducks are always hungry and glad to be fed. There are numerous picnic benches, walkways, and bridges for exploring.

❊ Ocean Park

2500 Barnard Way
Santa Monica

This small park located on Santa Monica Beach is really popular with toddlers. They have bucket swings and great climbing equipment with all sorts of hidden surprises, including steering wheels and a small spaceship made for two. With the backdrop of the bike path and the Pacific Ocean, it is an ideal location.

❊ Rustic Canyon Park*

601 Latimer Road
Santa Monica
310-454-5734

This great park is one of L.A.'s best-kept secrets. (In fact, we almost hate to include it here for fear it will become too crowded!) Rustic Canyon is nestled in the trees between Santa Monica and Pacific Palisades. Its hard-to-find location makes it popular with locals who want to get away from the crowds at spots like Douglas Park. There is a shaded playground with swings and a climbing apparatus small enough for toddlers. The bigger kids tend to go for the trees, which have lots of low branches for climbing. Because of its shady location, it never gets too hot, making it a popular destination in the summer months.

You might also check out:

❊ Christine Emerson Reed Park

1133 Seventh Street
Santa Monica
310-458-8540

Pacific Palisades

❊ Palisades Park

851 Alma Real Drive
Pacific Palisades
310-454-1412

Not to be confused with Palisades Park in Santa Monica, this park has a great playground for toddlers and is the best place to meet Palisades moms. Located just south of Palisades Village, the playground has a cool climbing apparatus, swings, and a fabulous fire truck that always fascinates the kids. Note that there is not much shade so it can get very hot in the summer.

Valley

❊ Lake Balboa Park*

6300 Balboa Boulevard
Van Nuys
818-756-9743

This popular park has a great playground with swings, sand, and a climbing apparatus, all just for toddlers. The most popular feature is Lake Balboa, where you can rent paddleboats and feed the ducks. There are always lots of moms around. The ducks are a perennial hit with the toddlers. The park is so large you can take a long walk with a stroller and actually get some exercise while enjoying the view.

Manhattan Beach

❄ *Live Oak Park**

1901 Valley Drive
Manhattan Beach
310-802-5421

Live Oak Park is the most popular spot for toddlers in Manhattan Beach. The "tot lot" is filled
with structures for climbing and playing. There is
a great train that gets a lot of attention, as well as
swings and a playhouse. Everyone in town con-
gregates around this great playground, so it is the
perfect place to meet other moms and their kids.

❄ *Polliwog Park*

1601 Manhattan Beach Boulevard
Manhattan Beach

This popular spot is known for its summer concert series, but it also has playgrounds with
climbing equipment and swings that are very
popular with toddlers. The main draw is the
large pond, where there is always something
going on (weddings, concerts, etc.). There are
tons of ducks to feed and great places to
explore around the pond.

Malibu

❄ *Malibu Country Mart Park**

3835 Cross Creek Road
Malibu

This popular park located in the center of the
Malibu Country Mart has certainly become the
"center" of Malibu. Everyone from celebrities
and their children to families from Calabasas
escaping the summer heat converges at this
park. The park has a large sandbox, two swing

sets, and a new climbing apparatus, and it is
surrounded by quaint stores, restaurants, and a
Coffee Bean and Tea Leaf. The scenery, along
with the shops and people watching, make this
a popular spot year-round.

Pasadena

❄ *Victory Park*

2575 Paloma Street
Pasadena
626-744-7500

This is everyone's favorite park in Pasadena.
There is a baseball diamond, children's playground, and a picnic area.

You might also want to check out:

❄ *Garfield Park*

Mission Street and Park Avenue
South Pasadena
626-403-7385

❄ *Lacy Park*

1485 Virginia Drive
San Marino

Hikes/Walks/Picnics

The following parks offer some of the best hikes,
walks, picnic areas, and relaxation spots set in the
most unbelievable surroundings we have ever seen.
If you want to visit a great park without pushing a
swing or spotting a slide even once, these are the
locations you should know about.

Also, check out the Family Nature Walks organized by the Children's Nature Institute. Go to the organization's website www.childrensnatureinstitute.org, for a schedule of family walks held at various trails around Los Angeles. Led by Children's Nature Institute docents, walks are two hours with many fun and educational activities. Be sure to call ahead for reservations.

❊ Franklin Canyon
2600 Franklin Canyon Drive
Beverly Hills

Franklin Canyon is not too strenuous to hike, which makes it a popular spot for parents with strollers and backpacks. Despite being located above the heart of the city, there is plenty of wildlife to be seen along the trails. The Franklin Canyon Reservoir has been the site of many film and television shoots over the years, and it is really as picturesque as it is in the movies.

❊ Huntington Park Children's Garden
1151 Oxford Road
San Marino
626-405-2100

The new Children's Garden in the Huntington Botanical Garden is a great way to introduce your children to everything the garden has to offer. They will enjoy exploring the series of sculptures set in the whimsically landscaped one-acre garden.

❊ Palisades Park
Ocean Avenue
Santa Monica

Overlooking Santa Monica beach and the Pier,

Palisades Park is a great place for a stroller. There are always tons of moms, nannies, babies, and toddlers out and about, and bikes are strictly forbidden on the path, so you can mosey along without any trepidation. There are benches on the way, so make sure to stop, relax, and take in the scenery. Even though there is no playground, children are fascinated by the surrounding nature, so be sure to let them out of their stroller to explore!

❊ Runyon Canyon Park
2001 North Fuller Avenue
Los Angeles

This Hollywood park is really popular with dog lovers, as there is an entire area for dogs to roam leash-free. If you and your children like dogs, this is a great place to come for a hike; but be sure your child is in a backpack or jogging stroller, as it can get pretty steep. The park also has a playground for children.

❊ Temescal Canyon (Gateway) Park
15601 Sunset Boulevard
Pacific Palisades
310-454-1395

If you're looking for a "rustic" family experience, Temescal Canyon is the answer. The park spans 141 acres and has waterfalls, streams, and access to all sorts of different hikes. This is a great place to put your child in a backpack and go for a great hike.

❊ Will Rogers State Park
1501 Will Rogers State Park Road
Pacific Palisades

310-454-8212

This fabulous park has a pretty steep hike up to "inspiration point." At the entrance you will find the infamous polo fields (they do actually play polo here), along with a bunch of other sports fields, and picnicking areas for relaxing.

Playground Equipment

You will be pleasantly surprised about how much backyard swing sets have changed since you were a kid! Depending on how much room you have, you can virtually build a playground that will grow with your children. Two popular companies that make great playground equipment are Swings 'n' Things (818-222-4967) and Play-Well Equipment (626-793-0603). You can check out the offerings on their websites, at www.swingsnthingsca.com and at www.playwell.com.

Beaches

No matter how far you live from the coastline, it would be a shame not to introduce your child to the beach at a young age—this is L.A. after all! When choosing a beach, look for one with easy access and parking as close to the beach as possible. The parking charges are most expensive in the summer. It also helps to find a beach with public rest rooms and food nearby. The following are some of the best beaches for families in L.A.:

Leo Carillo State Beach (Pacific Coast Highway and Mulholland Highway) has great tide pools for exploring sea creatures.

Manhattan and Redondo beaches both have tons of parking and kids everywhere.

Marina or "Mother's Beach" (Admiralty Way and Via Marina, Marina del Rey) is located just behind the Cheesecake Factory. Locals call this "Mother's Beach" because of the many moms and kids it attracts. There are no waves, so it's the perfect cove for your little one to wade into the water. There is a small playground adjacent to the beach. It also has a protected lagoon, lifeguard, and picnic tables, and you can rent bikes and skates at the shop next to the parking lot.

Paradise Cove (28128 West Pacific Coast Highway, Malibu) is a very popular beach for children. The beach itself is private and sits directly in front of the Paradise Cove Beach Café restaurant. If you order food and drinks at the restaurant, your parking will be validated. It has great Adirondack chairs that you can sit in as well. The beach is small but great for little children.

Santa Monica Beach (445 Pacific Coast Highway, Santa Monica, see chapter fourteen) has plenty of parking near Back on the Beach restaurant, as well as rest rooms and a small swing set.

Venice Beach (Ocean Front Walk at Washington, Venice) is known for people-watching, live music, and roller skaters. There is also a great park with three jungle gyms and plenty of snack shops nearby. You can rent bikes and skates as well. Parking is close to the beach and plentiful.

Zuma Beach (30050 Pacific Coast Highway, Malibu) has tons of convenient parking (2,082 spaces), a food stand in the summer, swings, and plenty of rest rooms.

Amusement Parks, Zoos, and Other Activities

Los Angeles offers so many options for weekend excursions with your children. There are great activities for children of every age at many city museums and attractions, like the Saturday children's series at Disney Hall and the Sunday programs at the Los Angeles County Museum of Art and at the Museum of Contemporary Art. A good resource to check for happenings around town is the "With the Kids" column in the Weekend Calendar section of Thursday's *L.A. Times*.

❋ Disneyland
1313 Harbor Boulevard
Anaheim
714-781-4565 (recorded)
714-781-7290 (operator)
www.disneyland.com
Disneyland has many attractions geared toward toddlers including Mickey's Toon Town, where kids can visit Mickey's and Minnie's houses, and Goofy's Bounce House, where kids can meet their favorite Disney characters. The rides that are great for young children include It's a Small World, the spinning teacups, and A Bug's Land. Be sure to check out whether Fast Pass is available; it is a great alternative to waiting in long lines with your children. It allows you to show up for a particular ride at a designated "return time," so you can bypass the long lines. Also check out the vacation-planning website www.mouseplanet.com. It even has reviews of the rest rooms at Disneyland!

❋ Family Room at the Getty Center
1200 Getty Center Drive
Los Angeles
310-440-7330
www.getty.edu
The Family Room at the Getty Center is an interactive space that introduces kids to the artworks in the Getty collection. Offering a place for children to discover a world of wonders, delights, and hands-on activities, it's the perfect place for families to learn about art together.

❋ Kidspace Children's Museum*
480 North Arroyo Boulevard
Pasadena
626-449-9144
www.kidspacemuseum.org
This fabulous children's museum recently re-located to a brand-new state-of-the-art facility featuring interactive exhibits, gardens, waterways, digging stations, and climbing towers, with much more coming in 2006. The water play at the entrance of the museum is really popular with kids, but be sure to bring a change of clothes—they get soaked!

❋ Legoland California*
One Legoland Drive
Carlsbad
760-918-5346
www.legoland.com

Legoland is the park of choice for children between two and six years of age. Unlike Disneyland, almost everything at Legoland is suited for toddlers. On a recent visit we didn't see many children over the age of ten. The park itself is built out of LEGOs and Miniland is at the center; over twenty million LEGOs re-create landmarks from all over the world. This is definitely a "don't miss" for toddlers.

Long Beach Aquarium of the Pacific

100 Aquarium Way
Long Beach
562-590-3100
www.aquariumofpacific.org

This amazing aquarium is definitely worth the drive down to Long Beach. Children as young as eighteen months will enjoy looking at the fish in the huge tanks housed on each floor, which are stroller friendly throughout. There is an outdoor tank too, and your child can actually touch the fish as they swim by. Check the website to find out about new exhibits.

❊ Los Angeles Children's Museum

213-687-8800
www.childrensmuseumla.org

The Los Angeles Children's Museum has plans to reopen in a new home in Hansen Dam in the Northeast San Fernando Valley in 2007. Check the website for exciting programs such as Children's Museum2Go, which is a mobile program that brings the museum to your site.

❊ Los Angeles County Museum of Art (LACMA)

5905 Wilshire Boulevard
Los Angeles
323-857-6000
www.lacma.org

Visit LACMA on Sundays from 12:30–3:15 P.M. for free programs designed for families. Activities include artist-led workshops and family gallery tours for children ages twelve and under. During the week, the Boone Children's Gallery is a place where kids can do projects such as painting, drawing, and building that are inspired by the museum's permanent collection. (Closed Wednesdays.)

❊ Los Angeles Zoo

Griffith Park
5333 Zoo Drive
Los Angeles
323-644-4200
www.lazoo.org

The L.A. Zoo is a great place for kids of all ages, but the Winnick Family Children's Zoo and the Riordan Kids' Korner feature tons of activities perfect for toddlers. There are many hands-on activities, including an area where your child can pet and feed the animals. There is a mazelike entrance with a wonderful mosaic hand-washing device that allows kids to clean their hands before entering or leaving the area. There is also a story-time area and a theater. The baby-animal nursery is always a big hit with children.

Magicopolis

1418 Fourth Street
Santa Monica
310-451-2241
www.magicopolis.com

Magic shows play here on Fridays, Saturdays, and Sundays. The shows are kid friendly, with much audience participation. Available for birthday parties (see page 229).

Mountasia Family Fun Center

21516 Golden Triangle Road
Santa Clarita
661-253-4386
www.mountasiafuncenter.com

Mountasia is an entertainment complex located in Santa Clarita that has great activities for older kids, including LazerDome lazer tag, a twenty-foot rock-climbing wall, a huge video and redemption arcade, two eighteen-hole miniature golf courses, go-kart rides, bumper boat rides, batting cages, and everyone's favorite, the old-fashioned Farrell's Ice Cream Parlour.

The Museum of Contemporary Art (MOCA)

250 South Grand Avenue
Los Angeles
213-626-6222
www.moca-la.org

One of the best-kept secrets in town is the drop-in art program at the MOCA, held the first Sunday of every month. Families with children ages seven and older are invited to create art together in an artist-led workshop; no reservation required.

Pacific Park at Santa Monica Pier

Ocean Avenue
Santa Monica
310-260-8744
www.pacpark.com

Located on the Santa Monica Pier, Pacific Park is a great amusement park for toddlers. For children starting at twenty-four inches in height, there are some nice rides. It also has games and food, making this a popular spot for birthday parties (see page 231). There is a carousel and arcade located on the pier as well.

Roundhouse Aquarium

Manhattan Beach Pier
310-379-8117

This marine science education center is free and is located at the end of the Manhattan Beach Pier. They host classes and birthday parties among other programs.

Santa Barbara Zoo

500 Ninos Drive
Santa Barbara
805-962-6310 (recorded)
805-962-5339 (zoo offices)
www.santabarbarazoo.com

If you are up for a drive, we have many friends who swear that the Santa Barbara Zoo is the best for toddlers. You can stroll the entire zoo in less than one hour. There also is a small area where children can feed the animals.

SEA Lab

1021 North Harbor Drive
Redondo Beach

310-318-7438

The SEA Lab is a hands-on coastal science education center in Redondo Beach offering activities and programs such as fish feeding, beach exploration, and birthday parties. Fishtivities (arts and crafts, story time, and puppet shows) are held the first Saturday of every month.

Skirball Cultural Center

2701 North Sepulveda Boulevard
Los Angeles
310-440-4500
www.skirball.org

The Skirball Cultural Center is a Jewish cultural institution where children (and adults) of all cultures and ethnicities learn about one another's backgrounds. Skirball has diverse activities for children, including Stories on Sundays by Book PALS and Toddler Time on Thursdays.

Troutdale

2468 Troutdale Drive
Agoura
818-889-9993

This fishing pond is packed with trout, and it makes a great outing for kids. Admission is $5 for adults, $3 for kids, plus an extra charge per fish you catch (depending upon the size of the fish). They have all the equipment you need, including ice packs to take home the fish you catch. We recommend bringing your own fishing pole if you have one; the pole you get here consists of stick and string. We found our luck was better using a real pole.

UCLA Ocean Discovery Center

Santa Monica Pier
1600 Ocean Front Walk
Santa Monica
310-393-6149
www.odc.ucla.edu

Located beneath the Santa Monica Pier, this aquarium is fun for toddlers. The greatest attractions are the touch tanks where children can feel all different types of sea creatures. They also have arts and crafts tables set up with art supplies, puzzles, and books.

Underwood Family Farms

3370 Sunset Valley Road
Moorpark
805-529-3690

Underwood is a great day trip for kids, because they get out of the city and see a real working farm. Kids can pick their own fruits and vegetables to take home, ride ponies, and visit pigs, goats, and emus in the petting zoo.

Walt Disney Concert Hall

111 South Grand Avenue
Los Angeles
323-850-2000
www.musiccenter.org

Walt Disney Concert Hall offers two series for children, Pillow Theatre and Toyota Symphony for Youth, on Saturday mornings. Reservations are required, and season ticket holders have priority. Before the Toyota concerts, the Walt Disney Concert Hall becomes a cultural playground with hands-on arts and crafts projects, musical activities, dance, theater, and storytelling.

❋ The Will Geer Theatricum Botanicum

1419 North Topanga Canyon Boulevard

Topanga

310-455-3723

www.theatricum.com

This amazing outdoor theater located in the heart of Topanga Canyon hosts a children's concert series, Family Fundays, on weekends from June through October. The intimate outdoor theater (ninety-nine seats) is a great place for kids to experience music and nature together. Call ahead for tickets and bring along a picnic lunch for after the show.

❋ Zimmer Children's Museum

6505 Wilshire Boulevard

Los Angeles

323-761-8989

www.zimmermuseum.org

The Zimmer Museum is located on the lobby level of the Jewish Federation building. The museum is a wonderful experience for both Jewish and non-Jewish visitors. Even very young children will enjoy the interactive exhibits and Sunday family programs, which change regularly and are appropriate for children of all ages. In addition, it has recently introduced art classes for toddlers and open art studio time for ages four to eight. The permanent exhibit, Main Street, has stores, a playhouse, and restaurants (where children can pretend to be customers or waiters), along with a rocket ship and a library.

farmers' markets

Farmers' markets are located all over L.A. and the neighboring cities. Each location has its own days and hours. The basic farmers' markets sell fresh fruits, vegetables, and flowers. On the weekends some of the locations expand into full-blown street fairs, with pony rides, live music, and food stands. They attract families from all over and are a great place to meet up with your other friends with children or even meet new families. You can visit www.farmernet.com to find out the days and locations of all farmers' markets in Southern California. Below, we have listed the most popular locations with fun activities for kids.

Beverly Hills

200 block of North Canon Drive

Sundays 9 A.M.–1 P.M.

Brentwood

South Gretna Green Way and San Vincente Boulevard

Sundays 9 A.M.–1 P.M.

Calabasas:

23504 Calabasas Road

Saturdays 8 A.M.–12 P.M.

Hollywood

Ivar Avenue between Sunset and Hollywood boulevards

Sundays 8:30 A.M.–1 P.M.

Pacific Palisades

1000 block of Swarthmore Avenue

Sundays 8 A.M.–12 P.M.

Santa Monica
2000 block of Main Street
Sundays 8 A.M.–1 P.M.

Silver Lake
3700 Sunset Boulevard
Saturdays 8 A.M.–12 P.M.

Studio City
12000 block of Ventura Place, near Ventura and Laurel Canyon boulevards
Sundays 8 A.M.–1 P.M.

West Los Angeles
11338 Santa Monica Boulevard at Corinth Avenue
Sundays 9 A.M.–2 P.M.

kid-friendly restaurants

Angelenos love to dine out, and believe it or not, doing so with your new baby or toddler can be an enjoyable experience. That said, keep in mind that your child will likely go through various stages of eating, so sometimes the dining experiences will be more enjoyable than others. The good news is that more and more restaurants today welcome children and are even catering to children's needs—although you still can't waltz into Spago with a screaming infant and expect to be welcomed with open arms! In this section we list some of the most popular family-friendly restaurants in town, along with some tips on how to make the most of dining with your toddler. First, the choice of restaurant is critical. Certainly, if you have a favorite neighborhood spot with food you love, you can always look around to see if children are dining there. But what do you do when you are in an unfamiliar neighborhood or restaurant? Look for kid-friendly clues such as paper rather than cloth table coverings, children's menus, booster seats and high chairs, and interesting features such as gardens and playgrounds. Second, fast service is crucial to making a restaurant kid-friendly. We all know how quickly a child can go from "merry" to "meltdown," especially when she is hungry! You need a place that understands the true meaning of fast food! Third, diversions are key. It may be the basket of bread on the table, a box of crayons, or a fish tank. These things will keep your child entertained while you wait for your food. Fourth, ethnic restaurants, such as Mexican, Chinese, and Japanese, are especially popular with kids. Mexican restaurants in particular tend to be on the noisy side and offer quick service. And the baskets of chips with salsa come in handy: Jack and Will are always on their best behavior if allowed to partake! Chinese restaurants that serve dim sum are great because the portions are perfect for little hands. Pizza parlors are also favorites for families. We couldn't possibly list every kid-friendly restaurant in town, but here are some tried-and-true places where you don't have to worry if your child is not on his or her best behavior. All of the following restaurants have high chairs or booster seats. Most have children's menus, but if they don't, the kitchen will adapt items from the regular menu for you.

Chain Restaurants

Most chain restaurants today cater to kids. These chains can be found in almost every L.A. neighborhood, so check the websites for locations in specific areas.

❋ *Baja Fresh*
www.bajafresh.com

❋ *Benihana*
www.benihana.com
The chefs at this restaurant cook the food right at your table, which makes for an entertaining experience.

❋ *Buca di Beppo*
www.bucadibeppo.com
Kids love that they can tour the kitchen with a member of the waitstaff.

❋ *California Pizza Kitchen*
www.cpk.com

* **The Cheesecake Factory**
www.thecheesecakefactory.com

* **Chuck E. Cheese**
www.chuckecheese.com
The games and shows here provide entertainment both before and after dining.

* **Corner Bakery**
www.cornerbakery.com

* **Daily Grill**
www.dailygrill.com

* **Du-Par's**
www.dupars.com
Kids get free ice cream with their meal.

* **Islands**
www.islandsrestaurants.com

* **Jerry's Famous Deli**
www.jerrysfamousdeli.com

* **Johnny Rockets**
www.johnnyrockets.com
There are jukeboxes at each table, which kids love.

* **Koo Koo Roo**
www.kookooroo.com
Chicken fingers here are baked, not fried.

* **Louise's Trattoria**
www.louises.com

* **Rosti**
www.rostituscankitchen.com

* **Ruby's Diner**
www.rubys.com

* **Souplantation**
www.souplantation.com

Santa Monica

* **Back on the Beach**
445 Pacific Coast Highway
Santa Monica
310-393-8282

* **Blueplate**
1415 Montana Avenue
Santa Monica
310-260-8877

* **Border Grill**
1445 Fourth Street
Santa Monica
310-451-1655
www.bordergrill.com

* **Broadway Deli**
1457 Third Street Promenade
Santa Monica
310-451-0616

* **Coogies Café Santa Monica**
2906 Santa Monica Boulevard
Santa Monica
310-829-7871

❋ *El Cholo*
1025 Wilshire Boulevard
Santa Monica
310-899-1106
www.elcholo.com

❋ *Jinky's Café*
1447 Second Street
Santa Monica
310-917-3311

❋ *Kay and Dave's*
262 Twenty-sixth Street
Santa Monica
310-260-1355

❋ *Newsroom Café*
530 Wilshire Boulevard
Santa Monica
310-319-9100

❋ *Reel Inn*
1220 Third Street Promenade
Santa Monica
310-358-0312

❋ *Royal Star Seafood*
3001 Wilshire Boulevard
Santa Monica
310-828-8812

Beverly Hills

❋ *El Torito Grill*
9595 Wilshire Boulevard
Beverly Hills
310-550-1599
www.eltorito.com
One night a week, each adult entrée comes
with a free meal for children twelve and under.

❋ *Kate Mantilini*
9101 Wilshire Boulevard
Beverly Hills
310-278-3699

❋ *Nate 'n' Al's Deli*
414 North Beverly Drive
Beverly Hills
310-274-0101
Children are presented with a bagel on a string
as soon as they are seated.

❋ *Solar Harvest*
242 South Beverly Drive
Beverly Hills
310-777-6527
www.solarharvestfood.com
Healthy children's menu.

Brentwood/West Los Angeles/Rancho Park

❋ *Apple Pan*
10801 West Pico Boulevard
Los Angeles
310-475-3585

❋ *Good Stuff*
11903 West Olympic Boulevard
Los Angeles
310-477-9011

❋ *Jack Sprat's Grille*
10668 West Pico Boulevard
Los Angeles
310-837-6662
www.jackspratsgrille.com

❋ *John O'Groats*
10516 Pico Boulevard
Los Angeles
310-204-0692

❋ *Junior's Deli*
2379 Westwood Boulevard
Los Angeles
310-475-5771
www.jrsdeli.com
Kids eat free Monday through Friday from
4–7 P.M.

❋ *Reddi Chick*
225 Twenty-sixth Street
Los Angeles
310-393-5238

❋ *Taiko*
11677 San Vicente (Brentwood Gardens)
Los Angeles
310-207-7782

Pacific Palisades

❋ *Cafe Vida*
15317 Antioch Street
Pacific Palisades
310-573-1335

❋ *Gladstone's*
17300 Pacific Coast Highway
Pacific Palisades
310-573-0212
www.gladstones.com

❋ *Kay and Dave's*
15246 Sunset Boulevard
Pacific Palisades
310-459-8118

❋ *Mort's Deli*
1035 Swarthmore
Pacific Palisades
310-454-5511
On Wednesday nights the restaurant has video
night, where families can dine and watch a
movie at the same time.

❋ *Terri's*
1028 Swarthmore
Pacific Palisades
310-454-6467

Malibu

❋ *Bob Morris' Paradise Cove*
28128 Pacific Coast Highway
Malibu
310-457-2503
The beach provides the perfect backdrop for dining.

❋ *Coogie's Beach Café*
23750 Pacific Coast Highway
Malibu
310-317-1444

❋ *Howdy's Taqueria*
3835 Cross Creek Road
Malibu
310-456-6299
Kids can play in the adjacent park while waiting for their food.

❋ *Reel Inn*
18661 Pacific Coast Highway
Malibu
310-456-8221

Marina del Rey

❋ *C&O Trattoria*
31 Washington Boulevard
Marina del Rey
310-823-9491

Valley

❋ *Hugo's*
12851 Riverside Drive
Studio City
818-761-8985

❋ *Jinky's*
14120 Ventura Boulevard
Sherman Oaks
818-981-2250

❋ *More than Waffles*
17200 Ventura Boulevard
Encino
818-789-5937
www.morethanwaffles.com

❋ *The Stand*
17000 Ventura Boulevard
Encino
818-788-2700
www.thestandlink.com

L.A. Central (Beverly/Fairfax/La Brea)

❋ *Eat Well*
8262 Santa Monica Boulevard
West Hollywood
323-656-1383

❋ *Newsroom Café*
120 North Robertson Boulevard
West Hollywood
310-652-4444

The Original Farmers' Market

6333 West Third Street
Los Angeles
323-933-9211
www.farmersmarketla.com

Toast Bakery Café

8221 West Third Street
Los Angeles
323-655-5018

Los Feliz

Mexico City Restaurant

2121 Hillhurst Avenue
Los Feliz
323-661-7227

West Hollywood/Hollywood

101 Coffee Shop

6145 Franklin Avenue
Hollywood
323-467-1175

Carney's

8351 Sunset Boulevard
West Hollywood
323-654-8300
www.carneytrain.com
Kids love the novelty of eating in an old train car.

Hugo's

8401 Santa Monica Boulevard
West Hollywood
323-654-3993

Pink's

709 North La Brea
West Hollywood
323-931-4223

Silver Lake/Glendale/Pasadena/ Eagle Rock

Alegria

3510 West Sunset Boulevard
Silver Lake
323-913-1422

Avanti Cafe

111 North Lake Avenue
Pasadena
626-577-4688
www.avanticafe.com

Brite Spot

1918 West Sunset Boulevard
Echo Park
213-484-9800

Busters

1006 Mission Street
Pasadena
626-441-0744

Casa Bianca

1650 Colorado Boulevard
Eagle Rock
323-256-9617

❋ Coffee Table
1958 Colorado Boulevard
323-255-2200
Eagle Rock

❋ Eat Well
1013 South Brand Boulevard
Glendale
818-243-5928

3916 West Sunset Boulevard
Silver Lake
323-664-1624

❋ Malo
4326 West Sunset Boulevard
Silver Lake
323-664-1011

❋ Swork Coffee
2160 Colorado Boulevard
Eagle Rock
323-258-5600

South Bay

❋ Good Stuff
1286 The Strand
Hermosa Beach
310-374-2334
1300 Highland Avenue
Manhattan Beach
310-545-4775

1617 South Pacific Coast Highway
Redondo Beach
310-316-0262
www.eatgoodstuff.com

❋ Sharkeez
3801 Highland Avenue
Manhattan Beach
310-545-6563

❋ Taiko
2041 Rosecrans Avenue
El Segundo
310-647-3100

❋ Uncle Bill's Pancake House
1305 Highland Avenue
Manhattan Beach
310-545-5177

traveling

Traveling with your children for the first time (or anytime!) can be a nerve-racking experience. Before motherhood, you probably prayed that your seat on the airplane wasn't next to a bawling baby. (We did!) And remember that age-old question, typically asked a mere ten minutes into the drive, "Are we there yet?" Hotels are a new experience with children too. If you are a first-time mom, you've probably never checked to see if there was a separate children's pool or if the hotel offered babysitting services.

Whether you are traveling by plane, train, or automobile, it is best to be prepared. While we don't have any advice that can guarantee you a pleasant airplane ride or vacation stay, we do have some tips that may increase your chances of getting there without going crazy!

airplanes

* Children under two years of age are not required to have a separate paid ticket and are permitted to sit in an adult's lap. But if possible, buy your child a ticket, as it's always helpful to have an extra seat. Most airlines offer tickets at fifty percent off for a child under two years old when traveling with a paying adult.

* The U.S. Federal Aviation Administration recommends that all children be protected by an approved child restraint system (CRS), i.e. car seat, appropriate to the child's size and weight. Children under twenty pounds should be in an approved rear-facing CRS; children between twenty and forty pounds should be in an approved forward-facing CRS; and children over forty pounds should use the standard lap belt in the airline seat. For more information on federal regulations, you can call 1-800-FAA-SURE, or check out its website www.faa.gov.

* A few airlines offer built-in bassinets in some rows, but make sure to ask when choosing your seat.

* Always consider bringing a stroller and/or a car seat with you when you fly. You will likely need a stroller to navigate the airport, and you may need the car seat in the airplane (you will probably need at least one of these at your destination, too). Car rental agencies rent seats, but the quality, cleanliness, and availability are unpredictable, and vary greatly. If you won't be using the car seat on the plane, you can buy a travel bag for it, and check it with the rest of your luggage. Invest in a cheap umbrella stroller; these are lightweight, easy to use, and small enough to store in an overhead bin. (You also can usually check strollers at the gate.) An alternative to carrying both a car seat and stroller is the Sit 'n' Stroll 5-in-1. Doubling as a car seat and a stroller, the Sit 'n' Stroll is FAA approved, and will fit through most airplane aisles and into the seat, although you may need a seatbelt extension. While you would never want to use this as your primary stroller, we found it a huge help when traveling with our kids.

* Allow a lot of time to get through security. All child-related equipment must pass through the X-ray screening. This means that even if your child is asleep, you must take him or her out of the car seat or stroller so it can be inspected. Also, remember all travelers are subject to search. Lisa was randomly pulled out of line for

a security search and was shocked that Jack had to be as thoroughly searched as she was.

- Be nice to the flight attendants. They can make or break your flight. Tell them ahead of time of any needs you might have during the flight, i.e. a bottle to be warmed, medical conditions, and so on. Order any special meals several days in advance.
- Forget your "no video" rule for the time being, and bring a DVD player for children. These were lifesavers when we were traveling on long plane rides—our children watched the same film over and over. If you don't have one and can't find one to borrow, check the airports. Many large airports now rent the DVD players and have a large selection of movies to choose from.
- Bring your own food and snacks.
- Pack a bag of new toys or surprises. Some small toys and games that we have found to be entertaining are Silly Putty, Play Doh, crayons, Magna Doodle or Etch-a-Sketch, and small books and puzzles.
- Check out the rest room situation ahead of time. Changing a diaper in an airplane lavatory takes a bit of creative gymnastics. Some newer planes have a built-in diaper table but many planes don't.
- Pack all essential items in carry-on luggage. It is a good idea to pack an entire day's worth of clothing, diapers, and supplies such as food and medicine, in case your luggage is misplaced.
- Give your baby something to suck on during takeoff and landings, such as a bottle or pacifier. The change in air pressure can be painful for them and this helps them "pop" their ears.
- Take advantage of pre-boarding. If you are traveling with your spouse, one of you can board the plane and get situated, while the other one lets the little ones tire themselves out in the waiting area.
- You need a passport for your child if you are traveling out of the country. One of our friends discovered this the hard way!

For a map of LAX, as well as a listing of all its restaurants and stores, check out the website, at www.los-angeles-lax.com.

cars

- If possible, leave during nap time.
- Use car shades to keep the sun out of your child's eyes.
- If going on a long ride, stop every couple of hours. A good rule is to take a fifteen-minute break every two hours at a rest stop or restaurant and let your kids run around. Fast food restaurants often have play areas for kids.
- Audiotapes are great.
- Pack your own snacks.
- Pack your own bag of toys or surprises.

hotels

- Pick a hotel that is kid friendly. If you don't know anyone who has stayed at a particular hotel, ask about the child-related amenities offered. If there aren't many (for example, no children's menu at the restaurant), you can assume it is not the most kid-friendly place.
- Some hotels offer cribs, bathtubs, high chairs, and changing tables. But keep in mind that a hotel's definition of a crib may be a pack 'n' play.

* Bring your bedding from home, if possible. We take the sheet right from our kids' cribs (unwashed so it still smells like home). Or bring a favorite blanket or toy to give your child a sense of comfort.

* Ask if the hotel will safety-proof the room. If not, bring your own supply of outlet and knob covers.

* Ask if the hotel has a baby-sitting service. Most hotels contract out with baby-sitting agencies. We prefer to speak to the agency directly and tell them exactly what we are looking for. Don't be afraid to ask about the agency's screening process and their employees' qualifications.

* Find out where the nearest store is, for when you need those necessary supplies, such as diapers.

Travel Resources

* Baby's Away

www.babysaway.com

This baby/child equipment rental company has over fifty locations in the US and will deliver whatever you need to your destination, including cribs, strollers, and beach equipment.

* Babies Travel Lite

www.babiestravellite.com

Babies Travel Lite will send anything you need for your baby to your travel destination so that you don't have to pack it. They have everything from Huggies diapers to baby food.

* Jetsetbabies

www.jetsetbabies.com

Jetsetbabies will deliver diapers, formula, food, and other baby necessities to your travel destination. They offer live personal service twenty-four hours a day. It's recommended that orders be placed at least two weeks prior to arrival.

* Seatguru

www.seatguru.com

This ingenious website gives you the scoop on the best seats to request in an airplane. You pick the airline and type of plane and it gives you the details.

part four

Keeping Up With Your L.A. Baby: Everything You Need to Grow!

Chapter Sixteen

let's celebrate

Your child's first birthday can either be a small family affair or an affair to remember! Some parents go all out for their child's first birthday, and we've all heard stories about the extravagant parties people throw, while their one-year-old is either napping obliviously or hysterically crying because it is all too overwhelming. If you have a party at your house, your child will at least be in familiar surroundings. But if you decide that you want to celebrate away from home (which is always easier on the parents), try to keep the party as low-key as possible. Remember, most of your little guests will not be used to being around so many people.

We have split this chapter into two sections: house parties and location parties. Whatever you want for the first birthday, we've got it covered. Our list of party places and activities will be good for many birthdays to come, so keep it in mind for the future.

House Parties

If you are thinking about hosting your child's party at your home, you will probably be interested in hiring outside entertainment. Lucky for you, there are a lot of options. There are probably more struggling actors and actresses in L.A. working the party circuit than any other city in the world. However, for your child's first birthday, remember that kids this young might be just as happy with a bunch of toys they have never seen before. If you decide to hire outside entertainment for your child's first birthday party, another thing to keep in mind is that one-year-olds spook easily. You may want to stay away from costume characters, as these tend to really freak out the little ones.

If you plan to have a swimming party, we can't recommend enough that you hire a lifeguard. Two companies that provide lifeguards are Head Above Water (310-738-SWIM) and Family Life Aquatics (310-264-SWIM).

Below is a list of some of the best children's entertainment for hire in L.A.:

❋ *Amazing Parties**
818-981-4321
www.amazingparties.net
Owners Matt and Eric do a great job of taking care of birthday boys and girls, and make sure they have fun on their special day. They have hundreds of party games and age-appropriate toys. They do parties for two- to twelve-year-olds, and the kids love them! For $280, they will come to your home for two hours of serious fun.

❋ *Animal Guys*
310-392-5909
The Animal Guys will give your guests an up-close-and-personal look at exotic mammals, reptiles, amphibians, and bugs for one hour at a cost of $395 (plus a $20 driving charge). This is the perfect party for an animal lover.

❋ *The Bear Builders*
310-325-1575
The Bear Builders will bring the Bear Factory machine and canopy to your home. Each child chooses an animal from over twenty-two choices, which he or she will stuff and dress. The company can design the party around your theme, and the children take home their new

stuffed animals in a box. The basic party is ninety minutes and is $175, plus $16.50 per animal, for a minimum of eight children.

❖ Celebrations Entertainment*
818-508-5777

Maura and Adam, owners of Celebrations, are birthday party experts who can make your child's birthday dream come true. Whether you need help organizing the entire event—including food, balloons, and entertainment—or if you just need the perfect cupcakes for that special day, Celebrations can take care of it. The entertainment provided ranges from characters to jugglers and live animals. Prices start at $200.

❖ Michael Cladis
310-396-3366

Michael sings and plays guitar, and he knows all of the kids' favorite songs. His show, "Fun with Music" is interactive and includes sing-alongs, music and movement, and play-alongs, with small guitars, drums, and other instruments, which he brings for all of the kids to play together. Bubbles and parachutes are also included. The cost is approximately $100 per hour.

❖ Cookie Construction Company
818-681-1141

This creative party idea includes everything you need for a cookie-decorating party—cookies, frosting, and decorations. Cost is $225 for thirty children.

❖ Creative Faces
323-662-8713
www.creativefaces.net

For $125 an hour, Creative Faces will come to your child's birthday party and do face painting.

❖ Dan the Man
310-827-0042
www.dtmsupergym.com

Kids love Dan the Man's parties, which involve him leading children in activities tailored to your child's age. These parties are good for kids ages one through eleven, and party games include sports races, parachutes, bubbles, and scavenger hunts. The cost is $250 for a one-and-a-half-hour party for up to thirty kids.

❖ Event Solutions
310-815-2440
800-850-9979
www.EventSolutions.com

Event Solutions can take care of all of your party needs, including planning, catering, party rentals, and entertainment. Moon bounces and other inflatable toys are also available. The company helps you develop a theme for your party, whether it is a puppet or magic show, pony rides, or a sports party.

❖ Jim Gamble Puppet Productions
310-541-1921
www.jimgamble.com

Jim Gamble has been performing puppet shows nationally for over twenty years, and he offers a variety of shows to choose from that are customized for parties. For a toddler's party, he recommends either the "Wonderful World of Puppets" or the "Enchanted Toy Shop." The cost is $225 for a half-hour show, which includes a puppet video for the birthday boy or girl.

Giggles and Glamour

310-679-8610

www.gigglesandglamour.com

Giggles and Glamour is a great party for kids ages three and up who like to dress up. The company brings everything needed for the ultimate dress-up party. Prices start at $225 for six children; additional children are an extra charge. They will also provide goody bags and invitations for an extra charge.

Kids on Stage

310-314-0035

www.kidsonstage.com

Kids on Stage plans one-of-a-kind theater parties for your child's birthday, which are tailored to his or her wishes. Starting at $200 for ten kids, it brings costumes, props, and music to your party. Older kids will put on a live stage show for their audience, while the younger ones can just play dress-up and party games.

Mad Science

888-885-9777

www.madscience.org/losangeles

The Mad Science entertainers will come to your party with an entire science lab. During their one-hour show, kids can get in on the fun by making putty and bouncy balls to take home. Parties start at $160, and they will add on laser

lights, party favors, cotton candy, and other fun for your party upon request.

Merrymaking*

818-846-9811

www.merrymaking.biz

Merrymaking will provide just about everything you need for a great theme party in honor of your child's birthday, from one year and up. Once you have decided on the theme (such as *Blues Clues*, *Sesame Street*, fireman/trucks, or a fairy party), Merrymaking provides decorations, centerpieces, paper goods, a cake, two hours of games appropriate to the age group, various characters, and party favors. Parties start at $750 for fifteen kids and include a staff member for every ten kids.

Claire Mills Entertainment

310-358-7324

www.clairemills.com

Claire Mills will entertain your little ones at your home for one hour; the cost is $175. Claire's cute pigtails and her cheery demeanor work wonders with even the crankiest partygoer! Claire brings all of her own equipment, including instruments, puppets, and a parachute. For older children, Claire leads dress-up and dance parties.

North Hollywood Ice Company

818-984-3774

Did you know that it snows in L.A.? Yes, for those parents from the East Coast or those that are just crazy enough to love snow, this is the party for you. North Hollywood Ice Company will bring man-made snow to your house and create a winter wonderland, complete with a hill for sledding. This is one of the most original parties we have ever seen. For $130 per ton (there is a five-ton minimum) your child can really have a party to remember.

❋ Joe Ortiz Fire Trucks
818-768-1678

For a really unique party, Joe Ortiz will bring his shiny new fire truck to your house, and take the birthday kid, friends, and their parents on rides all around the neighborhood—heads will turn! The cost is $400 for Joe, the truck, and firefighters to come to your house for three hours. This gives the birthday partygoers plenty of time to explore the truck and to take as many rides as they like!

❋ Playparty
866-544-9591

www.playparty.net

Playparty brings race car and LEGO parties to your home. For $225 they will set up a huge track or LEGOs around your home for one hour of "hands-on" entertainment (additional playtime is $25 per fifteen minutes). This is a great party for a child who loves cars or LEGOs.

❋ Ponderosa Pony Parties*
818-353-2222

Ponderosa keeps the cleanest ponies and petting zoos in town. They charge $260 per hour for one pony and a petting zoo with twenty to twenty-five animals.

❋ Prancing Ponies
800-54-PONYS

Prancing Ponies brings the petting zoo to you, complete with a pony and wagon rides. For $225 you can have two ponies or a petting zoo; for $350 you can have both.

❋ Rhythm Child
310-204-5466

www.rhythmchild.net

Rhythm Child arranges drum circle sing-along parties using every percussion instrument imaginable. The parties are geared for one- to three-year-olds. For $200, the musicians will entertain for forty-five minutes with drumming, songs, games, and more.

❋ Send in the Clowns
310-399-3733

818-563-2409

Don't let the name fool you, this company offers much more then just clowns. Owner and fellow mom Leesa Zelken will help you plan a unique party—either big or small. Possibilities include carnival parties with a kiddie train, dress-up tea parties with a one-of-a-kind princess carriage, toddler parties with a create-your-own bubble station, and so much more! Prices start at $160 for a one-hour clown; $185 for a one-hour character. For the ultimate party experience, creative full-service party planning is available.

❋ Side Street Projects
626-577-7774

Side Streets Projects, a non-profit organization

supporting artists, will bring a bus outfitted with a wood-working project for partygoers to complete. For $275 per every ten children, they will provide two teachers and a bus (for ages five to eleven).

✳ Lou Stratten*
310-280-3378

Lou Stratten comes to your home and entertains the birthday child and friends with her guitar, puppet, musical instruments, and toys. She charges $255 for one hour (plus extra for travel outside of the L.A. area) and has an amazing rapport with children, especially those three years and under.

✳ Twinkles the Clown
1-800-4CLOWNS

Twinkles the Clown has been entertaining little ones for over twenty years and it shows. She comes to your house and performs an engaging puppet show that your child and her friends will love. Twinkles charges $135 per hour and $40 for an additional half hour.

✳ Wild about Balloons*
562-809-6980

Shellyann is the best balloon entertainer in L.A. She will come to your party for $150 per hour.

✳ Zanzibar
310-322-4409

Zanzibar parties are great for children between the ages of three and six who have lively imaginations. The party begins inside a safari tent erected in your backyard, where the children listen to a story about a different culture. This is followed by an arts-and-crafts project based on the story. Parties are $25 per child with a minimum of twelve and maximum of twenty-five children.

Rentals/Caterers

✳ Advanced Backyard Carnivals
818-767-1255

This is a great place to find carnival rides to rent for a party. Prices range from $34 for a balloon pump to $169 for a three-horse carousel.

✳ Awesome Bounce
800-226-8623
www.awesomebounce.com

Awesome Bounce rents bouncers starting at $69. They also rent cotton candy, sno-cone, popcorn, and hot dog machines.

✳ Classic Party Rentals*
310-202-0011
www.classicpartyrentals.com

Although a bit pricier than other rental companies, Classic is reliable and offers good-quality products for all of your party needs.

✳ Jump for Fun
800-281-6792
www.jumpforfun.com

Jump for Fun has themed inflatable jumpers, from the elegant castle to the licensed Disney character jumpers and the extreme water-slide option. Some of these jumpers will take up an entire tennis court! They also rent popcorn and cotton candy machines. The jumpers are a great deal; an eight-hour rental (including delivery and setup) starts at $64.

❊ Let's Have a Cart Party*
310-839-6749

Let's Have a Cart Party rents antique food carts that include everything from hot dogs to frozen drinks. The food is always a big hit, especially the hot dogs (beef, chicken, or turkey) and french fries. The carts are $85 per day and charges for food are per serving. You will also pay $70 per attendant for four hours.

❊ Party On Rentals (formerly Ninja Jumps)
800-200-0744

www.partyonrental.com

No matter what your child's party theme, from Disney princesses to Dora the Explorer, Party On Rentals carries every character inflatable jumper you can imagine. If you're planning a party on the beach, the company has the only jumpers that can be used in the sand. Prices start at $69. They also rent sno-cone, popcorn, and cotton candy machines.

❊ Pico Party Rents
2537 South Fairfax Avenue
Culver City
310-275-9431
818-789-6559
323-936-8268

www.picopartyrents.com

Pico Party rents and sells anything and everything you might need for a child's party including linens, serving pieces, Astroturf, paper goods,

helium tanks, carousel horses, cribs, strollers, car seats, and kiddie-size tables and chairs. Items can be picked up or delivered. There is a $50 minimum for delivery, and the delivery fee starts at $40 and varies depending on location.

The following is a list of party-supply stores that stock the standard party paraphernalia—plates, hats, cups, tablecloths, balloons, and party favors:

❊ Aahs
3223 Wilshire Boulevard
Los Angeles
310-829-1807

1090 Westwood Boulevard
Los Angeles
310-824-1688

14612 Ventura Boulevard
Sherman Oaks
818-907-0300
www.aahs.com

❊ Moss House
1936 Hillhurst Avenue
Los Feliz
323-664-5801

❊ Party America
Numerous locations throughout L.A.
www.partyamerica.com

❊ Party City
Numerous locations throughout L.A.
www.partycity.com

❋ *Party On*
358 La Cienega
Los Angeles
310-360-1786

❋ *Party Pizzazz*
15121 Sunset Boulevard
Pacific Palisades
310-454-2307

❋ *Standard Brands Party Supplies*
3020 Wilshire Boulevard
Santa Monica
310-453-1094

Location Parties

If you choose to have a party at a location other than your home, there are plenty of options. If you want something outdoors, one alternative is to reserve a space at your local park. Call the recreation division in your city for rules and regulations. If you want something indoors, though, there are party places that will provide everything from the food to the favors—although many moms we know still bring in birthday cakes and favors to match the theme. Most of the places on our list are equally great for children who are older; we've been to second, third, and even fifth birthday parties at many of the places listed below. Another good idea is to call the people who run your child's favorite class, activity, or sport; many also do parties.

Beware of the expanding guest list at location parties. Parents may ask to bring siblings, so know that most places charge extra per child over the base amount, and some have a maximum amount of children allowed. Also, tip is not included in the prices listed below. Many of the places listed have exceptional party entertainers on staff, and you may want to tip them separately from the party fee.

❋ *Bright Child**
1415 Fourth Street
Santa Monica
310-393-4844
www.brightchild.com
Bright Child birthday parties are much like their classes—fun, loud, and exciting! The parties are for children ages one and up and are two hours long. Partygoers can use the "free play" area, which includes a maze, slides, tubes, pulleys, swings, a basketball court, and a putting green. The party includes a host, pizza, juice, cake, paper plates, napkins, and balloons for fifteen children for $345 during the week and $395 on the weekend (each additional child is $15). If you want the exclusive use of the place, you can do so after hours (6:30–8:30 P.M.) for $1,400 for fifty children.

❋ *Broadway Gymnastics*
5433 Beethoven Street
Los Angeles
310-450-0012
www.broadwaygym.com
Broadway Gymnastics will entertain your child and his friends (for children ages two and older) with a two-hour gymnastics party. The party includes gymnastics, an obstacle course, parachute play, and other great activities in a huge gym space. After all the fun, you can serve refreshments (which you supply) in the party

room. Prices start at $549 for a two-hour party on weekend days for up to twenty-one children (additional children are an extra charge).

Chefmakers Cooking Academy*
872 Via de la Paz
Pacific Palisades
310-459-9444

A party at Chefmakers, a new cooking school in the Palisades, is a great way to entertain kids with something new and different. The standard parties include an Iron Chef party, where the children compete to make the best-tasting pizza from scratch; the school also does customized parties, depending on the age and tastes of the child. Prices start at $45 per child for a maximum of thirty-two children (depending upon the age of the attendees and complexity of the menu).

Child's Play
2299 Westwood Boulevard
Los Angeles
310-470-4997

You can rent out Child's Play exclusively for your child's party (starting at $395). They supply everything from pizza to cake and party favors. There is an entire playroom with toys, jumper, ball pit, dress-up clothes, cars, and trains. In the back there is plenty of seating to enjoy food and cake. Theme and character parties are also available. On the weekends you get the entire space to yourself; during the week you get a room in back, but other children will be in the play area.

Claudia's Teacup and Dress Up
13630 Ventura Boulevard
Sherman Oaks
818-783-6654

Parties for little girls at Claudia's Teacup and Dress Up start at $325 for eight children and include food, party favors, and paper goods (you bring your own cake). Additional children are $25 each with a maximum of eighteen.

Creation Station
11239 Ventura Boulevard
Studio City
818-509-8888

At Creation Station, your child can choose from a variety of themes, such as fairy princess and pirate parties, and then the party hosts will entertain your child and his or her friends with activities and party games. The cost is $325 (up to twenty kids); and for an additional $15 per child you're supplied with invitations, party favors, paper goods, pizza, and drinks. Parties take place on weekends only.

Creative Kids
11301 West Olympic Boulevard, Suite 110
Los Angeles
310-473-6090
www.mycreativekids.com

During the weekends, twenty partygoers can play exclusively in the huge Creative Kids space for two hours ($9 per additional child). Starting at $395, your child's party will have open access to the gym, art room, dance room, and party room with three party hosts to supervise. There are a variety of "signature" theme parties for children as young as one; our favorites are the fairytale princess party, where your party is visited by a costumed princess, and the conductor's special, a great train party where the children take a train ride and have their faces painted. A party at your home costs $150 per hour.

❊ Creative Space*

6325 Santa Monica Boulevard (Eastside)
Los Angeles
323-462-4600

11916 West Pico Boulevard (Westside)
Los Angeles
310-231-7600
www.creativespaceusa.com

Kids three and up can have their parties here on Friday nights and during the day on Saturdays and Sundays. Starting at $550, your party gets use of the entire space. Creative Space is known for their original party themes, including an art party, a royal tea party, a cooking party (our favorite), and a wacky science party. You bring the food, cake, and paper goods.

❊ Dance for Kids

Brentwood Gardens
11677 San Vicente Boulevard, Suite 312
Los Angeles
310-820-5437

You can rent out Dance for Kids on Sundays for your child's birthday (for children ages two and older). You choose the theme (ballet, hip hop, fifties), and for $525 you get a studio, including balloons. You supply your own food, drinks, cake, and party favors.

❊ Fit for Kids

1106 North La Cienega Boulevard, Suite 105
Los Angeles
310-360-6282

This popular gym is available for rent for two-hour birthday parties on the weekends, for children as young as age one. For $400 (thirty-two children maximum), they coordinate the activities; you bring the food, drink, and cake.

❊ Focus Fish

6121 Santa Monica Boulevard, Studio B
Hollywood
323-957-0901
www.focusfish.com

This warehouse-size fitness and dance center holds birthday parties for young children that combine dance, music, and obstacle courses. The older children's parties incorporate aerial equipment including the trapeze, hoop, and fabric. The cost is $10 per child (minimum of twenty children) plus a $50 cleanup fee.

❊ Funshine

17200 Ventura Boulevard
Encino
818-386-9600

Encino's newest indoor playground will host your toddler party and take care of everything except for the cake, for $360 for twenty children.

❊ Joey's Gym

275 South Robertson
Beverly Hills
310-855-0146

Joey's Gym will host your child's birthday party,

for children as young as age one. For $375, your child and twenty-five friends (additional children are an extra charge) will have the run of the gym, and the party coordinator will lead them through a series of activities until they are too tired to do anything but eat (food is not provided). Decorations and balloons are provided.

Kid Concepts USA

22844 Hawthorne Boulevard
Torrance
310-465-0075
www.kidconceptsusa.com

A party at Kid Concepts USA includes pretty much everything you need for your child's birthday party. Starting at $300 for up to ten children, Kid Concepts will provide the invitations, food, entertainment, and goody bags. Add-ons include make-your-own ice cream sundaes and food for the adults.

Kidnasium*

808 Wilshire Boulevard
Santa Monica
310-395-6700
www.kidnasium.com

This gym in Santa Monica is a great place to have a birthday party. For $385, you get the exclusive use of the gym for two hours, including entertainment, party hosts, and a cleanup crew, with a maximum of thirty children. You bring your own food, drinks, cake, and decorations. Parties can be held on Saturdays and Sundays during the day.

Kids Gym, USA

5520 Crebs Avenue
Tarzana
818-343-1120

Kids Gym, USA will take care of everything for your child's party (for children ages one to eight). Starting at $350 for twenty children (additional attendees are an extra charge), the party coordinators will run the party from start to finish, and even provide food, cake, and party favors for an additional charge.

Magicopolis

1418 Fourth Street
Santa Monica
310-451-2241
www.magicopolis.com

Parties at Magicopolis are for children ages four and up. The party is two-and-a-half hours long, and includes a magic class, party favors, pizza, cake, drinks, and a ninety-minute magic show with the party child featured on stage. The cost is $500 for fifteen children.

Music Rhapsody

1603 Aviation Boulevard
Redondo Beach
310-376-8646
www.musicrhapsody.com

Music Rhapsody provides entertainment for your child's party that includes music, instruments, and puppets (for children ages one and older). If you live in the South Bay you can have your party at the "birthday center," otherwise Music Rhapsody will come to your house and entertain your child and his friends. Forty-five minutes costs $225.

❋ My Gym

1837 La Cienega
Beverly Hills
310-659-8453

17175-B Ventura Boulevard
Encino
818-385-0888

9420 Reseda Boulevard
Northridge
818-998-7946

839 South Arroyo Parkway
Pasadena
626-441-7800

1216 Beryl Street
Redondo Beach
310-318-2288

12422 Santa Monica Boulevard
Santa Monica
310-820-0155

2701 Thousand Oaks Boulevard
Thousand Oaks
805-494-4154

4821 Lankershim Boulevard
Toluca Lake
818-509-1077

22027-B Vanowen Street
Woodland Hills
818-702-6946
www.my-gym.com

My Gym parties are some of the most popular with the two- to four-year-old set. A My Gym party includes the exclusive use of a play area complete with swings, ball pits, mazes, slides, and climbing apparatuses; also, the party hosts will lead the group through "free play," with a series of obstacle courses and toys. The party breaks for pizza and cake in the back room. Parties are available only on the weekends and prices start at $350 (prices vary depending upon location).

❋ My Playroom

4954 Van Nuys Boulevard
Sherman Oaks
818-784-PLAY

Parties at the My Playroom indoor gym start at $345 for twenty children ($10 per additional child) and include free play in the open play space, face painting, games, and other activities. Decorations and invitations are included.

❋ Nana's Garden

426 South Robertson
Beverly Hills
310-288-3024
www.nanasgarden.net

The indoor play space and restaurant at Nana's Garden can be exclusively yours for your child's party. Everything you need including food, decorations, party hosts, arts and crafts projects, and goody bags—is provided for $875.

❋ Olivia's Doll House Tea Room

8804 Rosewood Avenue
West Hollywood
310-273-6631

1321 Thousand Oaks Boulevard, #110
Thousand Oaks
805-381-1553
www.oliviasdollhousetearoom.com
Olivia's Doll House hosts dress-up parties that, in addition to clothes, makeup, and hair styling, include a fashion show and a tea party with cake. Parties start at $275 for a minimum of six guests (or seven depending upon location); $25 for each additional guest.

Pacific Park
Santa Monica Pier
310-260-8744, ext. 283
A party at the Santa Monica Pier features unlimited access to the rides, a private cabana for your party, decorations, and food. A party coordinator will organize, set up, and clean up after your party. Prices start at $21 per child, with a ten-child minimum. They have a kiddie ride area for the young children (they must be twenty-four inches or taller to ride) along with the famous Pacific Wheel that overlooks the ocean.

Pagoda Artworks
17161/2 Ocean Park Boulevard
Santa Monica
310-452-8820
www.pagodaartworks.com
You can take over this art studio for your child's birthday party for two hours of arts and crafts. The party includes a craft project for ten party-goers. It costs $250; each additional guest is $10. You bring your own decorations, food, and cake.

Santa Monica Pier Carousel
310-395-4248
The carousel at the Santa Monica Pier is owned separately from Pacific Park, but it is also available to rent for semiprivate and private parties. A semiprivate party is limited to thirty people and will cost $200 for three hours ($5 per additional child). You will be provided with two tables on which to serve your refreshments (which you must bring). Semiprivate parties are available every day between 11 A.M.–2 P.M. and 3–6 P.M. For private parties, call for information and date and time availability.

Santa Monica Playhouse
1211 Fourth Street
Santa Monica
310-394-9779, ext. 2
Parties at the Santa Monica Playhouse are hosted by storybook characters and are $15 per child and $12 per adult (minimum is $150).

Star Eco Station
10101 Jefferson Boulevard
Culver City
310-842-8060
www.ecostation.org
This two-hour party takes place at the Eco Station, an environmental science and exotic wildlife rescue center. The parties start at $300 and include a guided tour of the Eco Station and a party favor from the gift shop; for an additional charge, food will be provided.

Sweetpeas and Snapshots

11726 West Pico Boulevard
Los Angeles
310-479-2444

Dress-up tea parties are really fun at this scrapbooking parlor in West L.A. Each guest makes a page for the birthday child's scrapbook, which she takes home as a keepsake. The cost is $20 per child, with a maximum of twenty children.

Travel Town Railroad

5200 West Zoo Drive
Griffith Park
323-662-5874

Travel Town is the ultimate place to have a party for a child with a train fascination. For $140, your child and friends can celebrate in the "party car" train; there are special Thomas the Tank Engine parties as well. Afterward, they can ride the Southern Railroad train down the street (an additional $1.25 per child) and explore the exhibit halls, gift shop, and the antique trains.

Under the Sea

12211 West Washington Boulevard
Culver City
310-915-1133

19620 Nordhoff Street
Northridge
818-772-7003

1182 East Thousand Oaks Boulevard
Thousand Oaks
805-373-5580

20929 Ventura Boulevard
Woodland Hills
818-999-1533

Starting at $289 (prices vary depending on location), you can have a private party in this indoor playground for two hours. A large number of kids can be accommodated at these venues. They will provide the decorations, balloons, and face painting; cake, party favors, pizza, juice, characters, and a treasure hunt are available for an extra charge.

If you don't plan ahead, you may find that many of the entertainment companies are already booked. We once had to call four different pony companies until we found one available! Just in case, here is a list of some additional party resources:

Entertainment

Fay Face Painter
323-309-0109

Kathy's Critters
310-318-1389

Life of the Party
800-527-4310
www.lifeoftheparty.com

Once Upon a Party
310-441-2400

Ponies for Parties
626-350-3049

* *Reptile Family*
  310-822-5585

* *Smokey's Fire Department*
  888-347-3878

* *Wondergirl Balloons*
  310-370-4065
  www.wondergirlballoons.com

Food

* *Artie's Parties*
  818-505-8177

* *Barts Carts*
  310-842-8266

* *Big Mama's and Papa's Pizzeria*
  323-851-8111
  310-274-9428

* *Earle's Grill*
  323-299-BUNS

* *Juice C Juice*
  866-824-8758
  www.bartscarts.com

* *Pie 'n' Burger*
  626-795-1123
  www.pienburger.com

Five Best Places to Have a First Birthday Party

1. At your home or a local park
2. Any place with Lou Stratten (310-280-3378)
3. Bright Child (310-393-4844)
4. Creative Space (Eastside 323-462-4600, Westside 310-231-7600)
5. Kidnasium (310-395-6700)

birthday cakes

Everyone's neighborhood market has a bakery that makes perfectly fine birthday cakes (some are even very tasty), but now that you've entered the land of children's birthday parties, all bets are off. Since we started on the birthday party circuit, we have tasted our way through just about every bakery in L.A., and have tried creations from a simple flower-decorated cake to an elaborate sculpted train. We have tasted them all!

Don't feel like you have to spend a ton of money and time on a cake that will be destroyed in less than ten seconds by a pack of two-year-olds; we have many friends who forgo lavish cakes, and instead buy a yummy white cake from their local Ralph's Market. Everyone is just as happy! If you do go for the really intricate cake, give yourself some lead time and note that many bakeries are closed on Sundays and Mondays. Depending on the cake, some bakeries may need as much as four weeks advance notice. Finally, the best tip we heard was to buy cupcakes instead of a cake (especially for first birthdays); cupcakes are great for little hands to hold!

Bluebird Bakery

8572 National Boulevard
Culver City
310-841-0939

This bakery will create and deliver adorable mini-cupcakes ($1.50 each) or large cupcakes ($2.50 each) decorated with sprinkles or flowers in chocolate, vanilla, carrot, or lemon cake. The bakery also makes cakes decorated with simple characters ($70).

Bristol Farms

www.bristolfarms.com

Bristol Farms's bakery section has really good cakes and cupcakes that can be decorated with your child's favorite characters (our favorites are the *Sesame Street* characters).

Cake and Art

8709 Santa Monica Boulevard
Los Angeles
310-657-8694

Cake and Art specializes in intricate, sculptured birthday cakes. They will custom make a cake in any design or character you can imagine. The sculpted character cakes are quite amazing—starting at $85 for fifteen to twenty people—or you can have a character "painted" on a cake instead, starting at $55. They also make cupcakes, starting at $1.50 each.

Cake Collection

2221 South Barry Avenue
Los Angeles
310-479-7783
www.cakecollection.com

The Cake Collection will custom make an elaborate birthday cake that tastes amazing. The bakery does both character "painted" cakes or sculpted cakes in any character or design you like. The standard birthday cake feeds fifteen to twenty people and starts at $52, but the decorative work is anything but standard. Wonderful cupcake towers also are available.

Candy Alley

13020 San Vincente Boulevard
Los Angeles
310-394-0700

This old-fashioned candy store located in the back of Pulp and Hide stationery store in Brentwood reminds us of being kids again. Not only will they do party favors and amazing candy centerpieces, the cakes are really tasty as well. The Barbie cake is our favorite: an actual Barbie doll is decorated with a skirt of cake and icing in your child's favorite colors.

Hansen Cakes*

193 South Beverly Drive
Beverly Hills
310-273-3759

1072 South Fairfax Avenue
Los Angeles
323-936-4332

18432 Ventura Boulevard
Tarzana
818-708-1208
www.hansencakes.com

Many people in L.A. think that Hansen's is the

only place for cakes. The bakeries specialize in intricate and ornate designs, which are displayed throughout their shops. If you or your child wants anything on the cake (and we mean anything), Hansen's can make it. Their cakes are also some of the tastiest we've tried. The buttercream and chocolate chip filling is particularly popular. Cakes with a character design start at $46 and serve fifteen to twenty children.

Heavenly Cake Creations

2916 West Vernon Avenue
Los Angeles
323-290-4700

Heavenly Cakes has some of the most reasonably priced cakes in L.A. The standard character cake starts at $25 and serves fifteen to twenty children. Cupcakes start at 50 cents each.

How Sweet It Is*

2554 Lincoln Boulevard, Suite 458
Marina del Rey
310-821-0140

Not only is Linda Doorbar a great baker, she is an artist too. She can create anything you want for your child's party. You can choose from ten different flavors and more than five cake fillings. The sweetest part is the free delivery—it will save you from worrying about one more thing the day of the party! Prices start at $120 for a cake that serves forty people.

Rosebud Cakes

311 South Robertson
Beverly Hills
310-657-6207

www.rosebudcakes.com

Rosebud Cakes is known for its wedding cakes, but they do magnificent birthday cakes as well. If you don't mind spending some extra money on a cake, the sculpted designs are fabulous. It has a large selection of flavors, including "The Most," which is a chocolate Bavarian cream with fudge and chocolate chips. Prices start at $80 for a cake serving fifteen to twenty people.

Sprinkles Cupcakes*

9636 Santa Monica Boulevard
Beverly Hills
310-871-3844

Sprinkles Cupcakes is the only bakery in town that makes cupcakes exclusively. The cupcakes come in twenty flavors, which owner Candace Nelson decorates with handcrafted sugar fondant designs. They also provide disposable cupcake towers and goody bags.

Susina (formerly Sugar Plum Bakery)

7122 Beverly Boulevard
Los Angeles
323-934-7900

Susina will cater your entire party with the most delectable food you can imagine, pleasing to both parents and children. The cakes are amazing, starting at $35 for a nine-inch cake. All types of party favors are available as well, including custom, hand-decorated sugar cookies and candies tied up in a little bag.

❋ Sweet Lady Jane

8360 Melrose Avenue
Los Angeles
323-653-7145
www.sweetladyjane.com

Sweet Lady Jane has some of the most heavenly desserts at some of the most unbelievable prices. The standard birthday cake (which comes in twenty-two different flavors) starts at $47 and serves twelve to sixteen people. The sculpted creations will cost you $200 and up.

❋ Viktor Benes Bakery

8718 West Third Street (next to Cedars-Sinai)
Los Angeles
310-276-0488

Viktor Benes Bakery is conveniently located inside Gelson's markets and is a great option for those who don't want to go overboard for a child's birthday, but still want a really great bakery cake. Also, cakes can be decorated while you wait. A standard birthday cake starts at $42 and feeds fifteen to twenty people. There is an additional $15 charge for a character design.

Another great alternative to expensive sculpted birthday cakes is an ice cream cake from Haagen-Dazs, Ben & Jerry's, or Baskin-Robbins. Our favorite is Baskin-Robbins, which has many locations around L.A. Cakes start at around $34.99 and serve twelve to sixteen people, and you can choose two flavors of ice cream. Decorations are extra at most locations. Baskin-Robbins also offers mini ice cream cones that are a great addition to any toddler's birthday party. These cost $36 for thirty-six cones and come in a box that can be easily transported to your party.

We've listed a few of the many Baskin-Robbins locations below:

❋ Baskin-Robbins*

271 North Canon Drive
Beverly Hills
310-273-3422

17332 Ventura Boulevard
Encino
818-789-6431

10916 Kinross Avenue
Los Angeles
310-208-8048

578 Washington Boulevard
Marina del Rey
310-821-0031

1026 Swarthmore Avenue
Pacific Palisades
310-459-2800

1227 Wilshire Boulevard
Santa Monica
310-394-0773

15030 Ventura Boulevard
Sherman Oaks
818-990-5209
www.baskinrobbins.com

haircuts

Every baby book has a page for that first lock of hair, for good reason: Your child's first haircut is a momentous occasion. Many moms we know bring their babies along to their own hairdressers, or they try to give them their first haircut themselves. But there are places that specialize in children's cuts that get the job done faster and in a more entertaining fashion. They usually offer fun features, including videos, special chairs, and balloons; some may even present your child with a first haircut diploma. All of the salons listed below recommend making an appointment so your child doesn't have to wait long. If you don't have an appointment, mornings are best for walk-ins; you'll avoid the afternoon chaos when the big kids get out of school.

Before we get to the salons, there's one other hair-related issue we must address. As icky as it may sound, once your child starts school, you are sure to hear about lice. Hair Fairies provides lice removal in its salon or in the privacy of your home, and will end your lice problem once and for all. Many mothers swear by Hair Fairies to remove lice and stop them from coming back. Hair Fairies is located in Los Angeles, at 8250 West Third Street (323-655-6555, www.hairfairies.com).

❋ *Kaleidoscope*
1203 Wilshire Boulevard
Santa Monica
310-656-2725
This salon provides the standard features: videos, toys, and balloons. A first haircut comes with a certificate. Haircuts cost $16. Walk-ins are welcome.

❋ *Kiddie Kuts*
239 South Robertson Boulevard
Beverly Hills
310-659-4790
This popular salon in Beverly Hills cuts both children's and adults' hair. They have a great selection of toys and videos. The salon will provide you with a picture of your child's first haircut, which costs $20. By appointment only.

❋ *Kids Kut**
11701 Wilshire Boulevard, 14B-1
Los Angeles
310-914-9095
This salon was created with kids in mind. Your child can choose which kind of chair he wants to sit in, from a big truck to a motorcycle and a pink jeep. If you have more than one child, there is a play area in the back. Children receive lollipops and balloons after their haircut. A first haircut costs $25, and includes a certificate and before and after digital photos of your child. A regular haircut is $18. Appointments are recommended, but walk-ins are welcome.

❋ *A Little Off the Top Kids Hair**
18957 Ventura Boulevard
Tarzana
818-344-4243
This salon is more upscale than your average children's salon, but they still have toys, videos, balloons, and cookies. A first haircut is $22 and comes complete with a certificate and a lock of hair for the baby book. Appointments are recommended.

Lollicut

18663 Ventura Boulevard
Tarzana
818-342-6171

Lollicut is a terrific place for your child's first haircut. The salon provides a certificate, balloons, cookies, and lollipops! The chairs are shaped like cars, horses, and other fun animals. Haircuts are $18. Appointments are recommended, but walk-ins are welcome.

Over the Rainbow

8300 Tampa Avenue, Suite C
Northridge
818-886-9325

This kids' salon in the Valley has videos and toys to keep your child busy while his hair is being cut. First haircuts come with a keepsake certificate, picture, and lock of hair ($18). The salon also has a play area to keep your other children busy in between. Appointments are recommended, but walk-ins are welcome.

Pacific Coast Hair for Kids

Hugh Slavitt
970 Monument Street, #216
Pacific Palisades
310-573-7777

Hugh is a lifesaver for parents whose kids are petrified of getting their first haircut. Friends rave about his patience and understanding. In fact, one mom we know took her toddler there three times just to talk to Hugh before the big cut—each time without being charged! A child's cut costs $22. By appointment only.

Tipperary

9422 Dayton Way
Beverly Hills
310-274-0294

Tipperary has been around so long that Linda's husband remembers getting his haircut here as a child! Although it's a fairly standard kids' salon, the stylists really know how to give a great first cut, which comes with a Polaroid and lock of hair. Haircuts cost $27; appointments are recommended.

Yellow Balloon

2009 Westwood Boulevard
Los Angeles
310-475-1241

1328 Wilshire Boulevard
Santa Monica
310-458-7947

12130 Ventura Boulevard
Studio City
818-760-7141

Yellow Balloon is a chain of hair salons that caters to children. They do a great job for first haircuts, complete with a picture and a lock of hair for your baby book. Prices vary by location, but start at $16. Appointments are recommended, but walk-ins are welcome.

capturing those moments

A new baby can bring out the shutterbug in anyone. Before you know it, photo albums and picture frames will take over your house. Even the most patient parents may become frustrated trying to get the perfect picture of their child for that beautiful silver frame your in-laws sent. Relax! There are professionals who know exactly how to get even the crankiest, nap-deprived child to smile for the camera.

From our experience, we really recommend choosing a photographer who specializes in children and families. Our list of photographers includes those who specialize in photos of children and pregnant women as well. Most charge a basic sitting fee, which may or may not include the proofs. It is nice to hire someone whose fee includes the proofs; this way you take something away from the shoot before having to order reprints. Many photographers have packages that include a certain number of reprints. Remember, the more reprints you order, the cheaper the prices. Also, don't be afraid to negotiate on price; most photographers don't really make money until you start ordering reprints.

Any photographer who works with children often will have a list of suggestions to help make your shoot go as painlessly as possible. Here are some of ours: keep your child's nap time in mind when scheduling your shoot; don't feed your child too much sugar prior to the shoot (if you do, you may be subjected to the unfortunate sugar crash during your shoot, which is not pretty); and dress your child in something at least semi-comfortable, so the clothes don't become a distraction for her or him during the shoot.

photographers

✳ A La Mode Photo

Heather Hart
Santa Monica
310-770-2676
www.ALaModePhoto.com

Heather Hart specializes in black and white photos of infants, children, and pregnant women. She usually shoots on the beach in Santa Monica, and her pictures evoke a sandy, seaside feeling. Her large package is $425, which includes the sitting, two rolls of film, two enlarged proof sheets, two 8x10 archival prints, and wallet sizes. She also offers gift certificates, which make wonderful presents for a mother-to-be!

✳ Belly Shots

Los Angeles
310-392-2359
www.bellyshots.com

More than just photos of growing tummies, Belly Shots is a pregnancy portraiture photo studio and beauty salon designed exclusively for pregnant women. They indulge you with prenatal massages, manicures, pedicures, hairstyling, and makeovers. In addition to the private studio, the photographers also work on location. Promotional packages start at $340, including a free wardrobe consultation, contact sheet of the thirty-six-image session, and a custom 5x7 print. A gift certificate from Belly Shots makes a great shower gift.

Lee Brubaker Photography

11400 Chenault Street
Los Angeles
310-476-1992
www.brubakerphotography.com

Lee Brubaker shoots traditional pictures of babies, children, and families in a romanticized light with lace, ribbons, and the like. Lee will provide wonderful outfits, such as lace dresses for your little girl to wear for that special picture. Lee charges a $150 sitting fee for one roll of either black-and-white or color film, and if you order a minimum of $200 in reprints, you get to keep all of your proofs in 4x6 format.

Classic Kids

1627 Montana Avenue
Santa Monica
310-395-1468
www.classickids.net

Classic Kids specializes in black-and-white and hand-tinted portraits of families and children taken in its studio. It costs $295 for two to four rolls of film per child.

CMS Design Portraiture

Palos Verdes
310-373-5450

Chris Stillans specializes in location portraiture of families and children. He will take multiple background shots, so you have a good selection to choose from. Although he will take photos in color or black and white, his photographic watercolor images are popular. A session costs $100 for one or two people and $150 for more than two people.

Andy Comins Photography*

10769 Tabor Street
Los Angeles
310-559-5537
www.andycomins.com

Andy Comins will capture your child on film or in digital format, and he really connects with kids of all ages. He has two session fees: $450, which includes three rolls of black-and-white or color film (or equivalent coverage digitally) and three proof sheets; or $350, which includes two rolls of film and two proof sheets. You can purchase the negatives or digital files for $45 per frame.

Leanna Creel*

323-972-3543
creelphoto.com

Leanna Creel's filmmaking background is evident in her documentary-style photography that captures the "story" and "character" of your child. For a fixed rate of $250 per roll, she will come to your home (or another convenient location), and you get to keep the negatives and the 4x6 proofs of everything she shoots. She also has a guaranteed one-week turnaround. We love her one-of-a-kind package that allows your child to star in her or his own vintage-style Super-8 film transferred onto DVD. She'll shoot any event, from your child's birthday party to ballet class.

Victoria Davis Photography

310-456-6311
www.victoriaphotography.com

Children's photographer Victoria Davis's signature is her use of natural lighting in order to capture moments of spontaneity in her subjects; she often photographs her subjects at the beach. She charges $350 for a sitting at her studio in Santa Monica or $400 on location, which includes two rolls of film. You can buy the 4x6 proofs at $25 per roll.

❊ Day One Photography
310-450-8501

www.dayonephoto.com

Day One specializes in pregnancy, birth, and children's photography. If you want photos of your baby's birth but can't get a family member to take them for you, Day One is the answer. A photographer will attend your birth (with a 24-hour on-call service) and stay for five to six hours taking photos.

❊ Dene Feldman
323-662-1146

www.denefeldman.com

Dene Feldman, a transplanted New Yorker living in Silver Lake, is a mother herself, so she knows how hard it is to get just the right shot of your child for that holiday card. She charges $350 for a family sitting, which includes 4x6 proofs, and she also does holiday cards, framing, and matting.

❊ Chuck Gardner Photography
11362 Burnham Street

Los Angeles

310-472-0170

www.chuckgardner.com

People who use Chuck Gardner rave about his rapport with children and the wonderful moments he is able to capture. He shoots in his studio and on location, but his real art is in outdoor environmental portraiture. He charges $175 for a studio session and $275 for location sessions, both with unlimited amount of film (not including proofs). About ten days after your photos have been taken, Chuck will meet with you to help you choose your pictures. He will even project them on a screen, which really helps to determine which are best.

❊ Anita Maya Photography
323-525-0819

www.mayafoto.com

Anita Maya takes great, natural photos of babies and kids. She is based in the Hancock Park area, but works all over L.A. She specializes in using natural light for at-home and location shoots, and she'll spend as much time with you as necessary to help you prepare for your session. Anita's sessions start at $325 for two rolls of either black and white or color (or a combination), and she will include one free 8x10 photo with any of her packages (proofs are not included).

❊ Kat Monk Photography
Manhattan Beach

310-379-0715

www.katmonkphoto.com

Kat Monk does wonderful photography of babies and children. She works in both black and white and color, and her pictures really capture the innocence of childhood. Kat does great holiday cards, too. She charges $195 for a "mini" individual sitting, $275 for a "mini" family sitting, and $375 for a family sitting, all of which take place either at her studio (inside or in the garden) or at the beach, and include three rolls of film and proof sheets.

Nathanson's Photography

902 Broadway
Santa Monica
310-453-0434
www.nathansons.com

Nathanson's Photography has been taking traditional children's and family photos for over twenty-five years. They provide in-studio and on-location shoots. All of the photographers are extremely patient; in fact, they take many of the school photos around L.A. Their hours are flexible and they can usually be booked with little advance notice. They charge a $100 sitting fee, which does not include proofs.

Allyson Nevil Photography

310-458-8089
www.allysonnevil.com

Allyson specializes in fun, candid photos taken either at your home, a park, the beach, or any location you choose. She will gladly time her sessions around a child's schedule, nap times, or feeding times. Her sitting fee is $300, which includes three rolls of film, and all the 4x6 proofs. You can also purchase the negatives for an additional $50 and have reprints made yourself.

Photowow

11950 Wilshire Boulevard
Los Angeles

310-820-3197
www.photowow.com

Although this is not a traditional photography studio, Photowow is a great place to take your photos and have them turned into objets d'art. Photowow does everything from turning your pictures into Warhol-like pop art to digitizing millions of tiny pictures into one large photo of your family (you have to see it to believe it)! Using your photos, they can make just about anything you can imagine, including invitations and puzzles—all of which are great for gifts.

Christopher Rainone

323-243-7450
www.rainonephotography.com

Christopher's background in photojournalism has given him an appreciation for the perfect candid moments. He shoots on location using a digital camera for instant results. He charges $475, which includes 4x6 proofs, and he will provide you with a CD of high-resolution images so you can order reprints.

Trish Reda

626-203-8494
www.trishreda.com

Trish works on location, taking pictures in settings that are unique to your family. She charges $350 for a sitting fee and proofs, and will schedule a follow-up appointment to view the proofs. Trish has a Baby's First Year package that includes four photo sessions during your child's first year and all the 4x6 proofs from each session for $1,650.

Susan Sheridan Photography*

323-969-8559

www.susandsheridanphotography.com

Susan is great at capturing the spontaneous wonder of children, newborns, and pregnancy in her photos. She will print your photos in color, black and white, or sepia. She will also do touch-ups, matting, framing, birth announcements, and holiday cards. Portrait sittings cost $400 for up to five people and two to three rolls of film (either black-and-white or color); you get to keep 4x6 copies of all proofs.

Tiny Toes Photography

Heidi Porat

Los Angeles

310-770-2447

www.tinytoesphoto.com

Heidi Porat's photography captures the pure expressions and playful moments of children and families either at her studio or on location. Private sessions start at $99 for film or digital photography with proof sheets. She also often offers specials, including reduced rates for mini photo days, playgroups, schools, and Mommy and Me groups. Birth announcements, holiday cards, note cards, and photo products can be custom-made with your favorite images.

Torpedo Productions*

818-783-6426

Torpedo Productions will turn your video footage and photographs into a DVD, complete with music, titles, and effects. It's a great way to preserve for posterity your memories of special events, such as your child's birth, par-

ties, and recitals, or just precious everyday toddler moments.

Stacie Isabella Turk

310-459-3777

www.ribbonhead.com

Stacie's prices start at $795 for two rolls of film. Included in the price are hair and makeup for mother, and $100 worth of custom prints. She also has hand-bound custom heirloom books and antique window and door frames that hold between six and ten custom images.

Urban Baby Photography

323-436-0426

www.urban-baby.com

Photographer Carrie Nicol uses high-speed film in order to catch each and every changing expression and movement of your child. She charges $350 for two rolls of film, including proofs.

Village Photo Studio

15200 Sunset Boulevard, Suite 117

Pacific Palisades

310-459-9903

www.village1hourphoto.com

This photo studio is a great place to get pictures taken of your newborn. There is an $89 sitting fee, but new mothers receive a complimentary photo session good for six weeks. Photographs are converted to CDs for safekeeping.

Ken Wolf Children's Photography*

310-264-9464

Ken Wolf takes pictures at just about every kid-related activity in town. He posts fliers of his scheduled visits, giving you the opportunity to have him photograph your child doing what he or she likes best—playing, dancing, karate, whatever! You can view the pictures the following week when Ken and his staff arrive with their computers. There is no sitting fee, and Ken offers a variety of great packages; meanwhile, you are under no obligation to take part in the shoot or purchase anything. If Ken does not visit your local music or karate class, call him and request that he contact the management to schedule a visit.

Other Photography Services

✳ *JCPenney*
Various locations throughout L.A.
www.jcpenny.com

✳ *Portrait Perfect*
2306 Westwood Boulevard
Los Angeles
310-446-7700

18737 Ventura Boulevard
Tarzana
818-654-2500
www.portraitperfect.com

✳ *Picture People*
248 Fox Hills Mall, Suite F10
Culver City
310-398-3597

Northridge Fashion Center
9301 Tampa Avenue

Northridge
818-772-4597
www.picturepeople.com

✳ *Sears*
Various locations throughout L.A.
www.sears.com

scrapbooks and mementos

The toddler years go by fast and you will want to preserve these memories as well as possible. Every mother we know dreams about having her scrapbooks and photo albums in order, documenting each milestone in her baby's life with the perfect keepsake—but who has the time? In order to assist you in this mission, we have scouted out the places that will help you organize and preserve your mementos. If time is as precious to you as your little one is, these tips are sure to help you out!

Scrapbook Essentials

✳ paper: different cardstocks, borders, themes, etc.
✳ stickers
✳ pens
✳ die cuts; precut die cuts in various shapes and sizes
✳ albums
✳ stencils
✳ cutting tools
✳ adhesives

Scrapbooking Resources

Color Me Mine

Various locations throughout L.A.

www.colormemine.com

This paint-your-own ceramics store is a great place to get a lasting impression of those tiny fingers and toes, if you can get your little one to sit still long enough to paint his hand or foot! Older children will love painting their own plates or cups. This is also a great place for personal gifts for family and friends.

Creative Memories

www.creativememories.com

Creative Memories is the premier scrapbooking company. Supplies are only sold through sales consultants, who offer home shows to demonstrate and pitch their products. Check out the website to find a consultant in your area.

Flavor and Flair

3808 Main Street

Culver City

310-202-6567

www.flavorandflair.com

Flavor and Flair is a scrapbook supply store and creative workshop. There are classes for the beginner scrapper as well as a program for the more advanced called Foxxy Scrappers, which offers discounts, monthly incentives, and a monthly contest. The store also hosts birthday parties and baby showers.

Michaels—The Arts and Crafts Store

Various locations throughout L.A.

www.michaels.com

Michaels offers all sorts of scrapbooking supplies from paper cutters and stencils to a large selection of rubber stamps. All products are reasonably priced. We love Michaels for its inexpensive gift wrap, party goods, and craft supplies for kids. There are several Michaels stores in the L.A. area.

Once Upon a Page

2800 Burbank Boulevard

Burbank

818-846-8910

www.onceuponapage.com

This huge scrapbook store offers a wide variety of classes and demonstrations. They will also put together a scrapbook for you if you don't have time to create one yourself. The store is available for parties and showers.

The Photo Fairy/Amy Phillips

310-659-1157

Do you have boxes of photos and mementos stored in boxes? Do you get stressed about not knowing what to do with them, or when you'll have time to do it? The Photo Fairy designs custom scrapbooks for those who do not have the time or inclination to do it themselves. Amy is also available for private groups or private scrapbook lessons.

❉ Scrampers

3754 Sepulveda Boulevard
Torrance
310-375-3454

This store is good resource for South Bay scrappers. Classes and demonstrations are offered.

❉ Scrapbook Safari

6100 Topanga Canyon Boulevard (Westfield Promenade)
Woodland Hills
818-227-9704
www.scrapbooksafari.com

Scrapbook Safari is the Valley's largest resource for scrapbook supplies. Aside from its large selection, classes for beginners as well as the serious archivist are offered.

❉ Scrappers Corner

Northridge Fashion Center
9301 Tampa Avenue
Northridge
818-349-4969
www.scrappers-corner.com

This scrapbooking store offers many classes, crop sessions, and demonstrations. There is a VIP program, and weekly and monthly specials such as coupon day, early-bird discounts, and midnight crop sessions. The store is available for meetings and parties.

❉ Scrapping Blues

1570 Rosecrans Avenue
Manhattan Beach
310-643-2388

This store has all the supplies you need to make a great scrapbook. There are tables in the back where you can work on your scrapbook.

❉ Strictly Scrapbooking

2740 Pacific Coast Highway, #G
Torrance
310-517-0161
www.strictlyscrapbooking.com

Strictly Scrapbooking houses a huge amount of scrapbooking supplies and offers creative classes from the ABCs of Scrapbooking for beginners to Dry Embossing for more advanced scrappers. For those really serious about the craft, check out Late Niter; this Friday night class allows you to work on your scrapbook from 6 P.M.–12 A.M.!

❉ Sweetpeas & Snapshots*

11726 West Pico Boulevard
Los Angeles
310-479-2444

Owner Mary Smilove recently expanded this adorable scrapbook shop, where you can find everything you need to make a great scrapbook. If you don't have the time or inclination to do it yourself, you can drop off your materials, and the store's employees will put it together for you. This is also a great place to throw a baby shower; the new mom leaves with a book made with tender loving care by her guests.

a word on preschools

When your child is almost two years old, you will probably start to hear all the nasty rumors associated with one of the most innocent places in the world: preschool. There is always one school that is impossible to get into and another school that has become so hot they aren't accepting non-siblings anymore. If you are like us, you too will be baffled by the complexity of the preschool admissions process, and wonder if it will be harder to get your kid into preschool than it was for you to get into college! You may suffer a brief panic attack as well: Are you looking too early? Too late? Somewhere in between? Some people begin their search when their child is as young as one.

But try to relax. There are so many preschools that you are guaranteed to find one where your child will be happy. Remember the reality of what you are pursuing: a place for your child to spend three hours a day socializing with other children.

Here are some basic facts to keep in mind as you look for a preschool for your child:

❋ Most schools start children at three years, although some do start as early as two years, nine months. The cutoff dates sometimes vary by gender and may differ from school to school.

❋ Some schools have transition programs that require a parent to be in attendance as often as three times a week. If you are unable to make this commitment, this is not the program and/or school for your family.

❋ Try to limit your search to schools that are no more than a twenty-minute drive from your house. If you spend all your time in the car, you'll have no time between drop-off and pick-up. Remember, most preschools are only two- or three-hours long, although some offer an extended-day option.

❋ Find out about the costs up front. All of the preschools listed below are private and some will cost more than others; also, once your child is a student, you will probably run into additional fees. There are also other options, such as Head Start, day care, and others that are subsidized through different types of governmental funding. To learn more about these kinds of programs, check with your city to find out if any are offered in your neighborhood.

❋ Do the legwork. Talk to as many parents of preschoolers as you can. Make arrangements early to take tours of the facility. Most schools won't accept applications until you have taken the informational tour (usually between October and April). Also, find out what other application policies there are, especially timing. Some schools allow you to fill out an application the day your baby is born, while others won't accept applications until your child's first birthday.

❋ Once you have found a school you are interested in, let the school know it's your first choice.

Additionally, we recommend the book *Coping with Preschool Panic: The Los Angeles Guide to Private Preschools* by Michelle Nitka, PsyD. Michelle also provides private preschool consultation (mnitka@preschoolguide.com, 310-285-9441). Other experts in the field include parenting expert and ex-preschool teacher and administrator Betsy Brown Braun (www.parentingpathways.com, 310-459-9209), and preschool specialist Christy Bergin (www.bestfitschools.com, 310-434-9706).

Once your child is in preschool, you will almost surely look back at this time and wonder what all the fuss was about. The hardest thing for us was finding out exactly what schools were located in our area. Below is a list of most, not all, of the preschools in L.A.; they are sorted by geographical areas. We hope this helps you in your search for that perfect place to get your child's education started.

Beverly Hills/Bel Air/Westwood

❖ **Adat Shalom Karno Nursery School**
3030 Westwood Boulevard
Los Angeles, CA 90034
310-475-4985

❖ **Bel-Air Presbyterian Preschool**
16100 Mulholland Drive
Los Angeles, CA 90049
818-990-6071

❖ **Berkeley Hall School**
16000 Mulholland Drive
Los Angeles, CA 90049
310-476-6421

❖ **Beverly Glen Playgroup**
10409 Scenario Lane
Los Angeles, CA 90077
310-470-0992

❖ **Beverly Hills Presbyterian Preschool**
505 North Rodeo Drive
Beverly Hills, CA 90210
310-271-5197

❖ **Leo Baeck Temple Early Childhood Center**
1300 North Sepulveda Boulevard
Los Angeles, CA 90049
310-476-2274

❖ **Little Village Nursery School**
11827 West Pico Boulevard
Los Angeles, CA 90064
310-479-8468

❖ **St. John's Presbyterian Nursery School**
11000 National Boulevard
Los Angeles, CA 90064
310-477-0507

❖ **Stephen S. Wise Temple Nursery**
15500 Stephen Wise Drive
Los Angeles, CA 90077
310-476-8561

❖ **Temple Emanuel Early Childhood Center**
300 North Clark Drive
Beverly Hills, CA 90211
310-276-9776

West Hollywood/Hollywood/ Los Feliz/Silver Lake

❋ **All Children Great and Small**
4612 Welch Place
Los Angeles, CA 90027
323-666-6154

❋ **Beverly Hills Montessori**
1105 North Laurel
Los Angeles, CA 90046
323-650-2922

❋ **Canyon Co-op Nursery School**
1820 North Las Palmas Avenue
Los Angeles, CA 90028
323-464-7507

❋ **The Center for Early Education**
563 North Alfred Street
West Hollywood, CA 90048
323-651-0707

❋ **Christopher Robin School**
815 North Alta Vista Boulevard
Los Angeles, CA 90046
323-934-6512

❋ **Doheny School**
968 North Doheny Drive
Los Angeles, CA 90069
310-275-3004

❋ **Fountain Day Nursery School**
1128 North Orange Grove Avenue
Los Angeles, CA 90046
323-654-8958

❋ **Hilltop Cooperative Nursery**
3625 Marathon Street
Los Angeles, CA 90027
323-663-3025

❋ **Holloway Preschool**
8510 Holloway Drive
Los Angeles, CA 90069
310-659-4336

❋ **Hollywood Los Feliz Corners**
1839 North Kenmore
Los Angeles, CA 90027
323-661-3448

❋ **Hollywood Schoolhouse**
1248 North Highland Avenue
Hollywood, CA 90038
323-465-1320

❋ **Hollywood Temple Beth El Nursery**
1317 North Crescent Heights Boulevard
Los Angeles, CA 90046
323-656-6964

❋ **Los Angeles Family School**
2646 Griffith Park Boulevard
Los Angeles, CA 90039
323-663-8049

❋ **Los Feliz Cooperative Nursery**
3401 Riverside Drive
Los Angeles, CA 90027
323-662-8300

Pilgrim School
540 South Commonwealth Avenue
Los Angeles, CA 90020
213-385-7351

Play Mountain Place
6063 Hargis Street
Los Angeles, CA 90034
323-870-4381

Rose Scharlin Co-Operative
2414 Lake View Avenue
Los Angeles, CA 90039
323-661-1319

Sunset Montessori Preschool
1432 North Sycamore Street
Los Angeles, CA 90028
323-465-8133

Temple Israel
7300 Hollywood Boulevard
Los Angeles, CA 90046
323-876-8330

Wagon Wheel School
653 North Cahuenga Boulevard
Los Angeles, CA 90004
323-469-8994

The Walther School
1246 North Gardner Street
Los Angeles, CA 90046
323-876-4715

Brentwood/West Los Angeles

Brentwood Presbyterian Nursery School
12000 San Vicente Boulevard
Los Angeles, CA 90049
310-826-2020

Creative Center for Children
10547 Santa Monica Boulevard
Los Angeles, CA 90025
310-475-9004

Crestwood Hills Co-op
986 Hanley Avenue
Los Angeles, CA 90049
310-472-1566

It's a Children's World
1653 South Robertson Boulevard
Los Angeles, CA 90035
310-552-1155

Samuel Goldwyn Foundation Children's Center
2114 Pontius Avenue
Los Angeles, CA 90025
310-445-8993

Sunshine Preschool
11942 Sunset Boulevard
Los Angeles, CA 90049
310-472-2212

Temple Isaiah Preschool
10345 West Pico Boulevard
Los Angeles, CA 90064
310-553-3552

❄ *UCLA Childcare Services*
101 South Bellagio Road
Los Angeles, CA 90095
310-825-5086

❄ *University Synagogue Preschool*
11960 Sunset Boulevard
Los Angeles, CA 90049
310-472-0603

❄ *West L.A. Methodist Preschool*
1637 Butler Avenue
Los Angeles, CA 90025
310-479-1682

❄ *Westwood Presbyterian Church Preschool*
10822 Wilshire Boulevard
Los Angeles, CA 90024
310-474-2889

❄ *Westwood United Methodist Church Preschool*
10497 Wilshire Boulevard
Los Angeles, CA 90024
310-474-8986

❄ *Wilshire Boulevard Temple Early Childhood Center*
11661 West Olympic Boulevard
Los Angeles, CA 90064
310-445-1280

Culver City/Westchester

❄ *B'nai Tikvah Nursery School*
5820 West Manchester Avenue
Los Angeles, CA 90045
310-649-4051

❄ *Happyland Preschool*
4045 Lafayette Place
Culver City, CA 90230
310-839-3739

❄ *The New School West*
12731 Venice Boulevard
Los Angeles, CA 90066
310-313-4444

❄ *New World Montessori School*
10520 Regent Street
Los Angeles, CA 90034
310-838-4044

❄ *Pacifica Montessori*
6405 Green Valley Circle
Culver City, CA 90230
310-417-3087

❄ *Temple Akiba Nursery School*
5249 South Sepulveda Boulevard
Culver City, CA 90230
310-398-5783

❄ *Turningpoint*
8780 National Boulevard
Culver City, CA 90232
310-841-2505

✳ **Westchester Lutheran Preschool**
7831 South Sepulveda Boulevard
Los Angeles, CA 90045
310-670-6093

North Hollywood/Valley

✳ **Adat Ari El Nursery School**
12020 Burbank Boulevard
Valley Village, CA 91607
818-766-6379

✳ **Briarwood Preschool**
12150 Riverside Drive
North Hollywood, CA 91607
818-766-0700

✳ **The Country School**
5243 Laurel Canyon Boulevard
North Hollywood, CA 91607
818-769-2473

✳ **Maggy Haves School**
6100 Coldwater Canyon Avenue
North Hollywood, CA 91606
818-763-8359

✳ **The Neighborhood School**
11742 Riverside Drive
North Hollywood, CA 91607
818-762-1212

4433 Mammoth Avenue
Sherman Oaks, CA 91423
818-783-7289

✳ **Oakdale School**
12140 Riverside Drive
North Hollywood, CA 91607
818-506-4304

✳ **Sherman Oaks Nursery School**
5520 Van Nuys Boulevard
Sherman Oaks, CA 91401
818 787 6481

✳ **Sherman Oaks Presbyterian Nursery School**
4445 Noble Avenue
Sherman Oaks, CA 91403
818-788-3537

✳ **Valley Beth Shalom**
15739 Ventura Boulevard
Encino, CA 91436
818-788-0567

Pacific Palisades/Topanga/ Malibu

✳ **Calmont School**
1717 Old Topanga Canyon Road
Topanga, CA 90290
310-455-3725

✳ **Calvary Christian School**
701 Palisades Drive
Pacific Palisades, CA 90272
310-573-0082

✱ Children's Creative Workshop
6955 Fernhill Drive
Malibu, CA 90265
310-457-2937

✱ Early Childhood Center of Kehillat Israel
16019 Sunset Boulevard
Pacific Palisades, CA 90272
310-459-4413

✱ The Garden of Childhood
6453 Guernsey Avenue
Malibu, CA 90265
310-457-2327

✱ Little Dolphins by the Sea
15601 Sunset Boulevard
Pacific Palisades, CA 90272
310-454-7277

✱ Malibu Jewish Center & Synagogue Preschool
24855 Pacific Coast Highway
Malibu, CA 90265
310-456-2296

✱ Malibu Methodist Nursery School
30128 Morning View Drive
Malibu, CA 90265
310-457-5144

✱ Methodist Preschool of Pacific Palisades
801 Via de la Paz
Pacific Palisades, CA 90272
310-454-5529

✱ Pacific Palisades Presbyterian Nursery School
15821 Sunset Boulevard
Pacific Palisades, CA 90272
310-454-0737

✱ Palisades Lutheran Preschool
15905 Sunset Boulevard
Pacific Palisades, CA 90272
310-459-3425

✱ Palisades Montessori Center
16706 Marquez Avenue
Pacific Palisades, CA 90272
310-454-6497

✱ St. Matthew's Parish School
1031 Bienveneda Avenue
Pacific Palisades, CA 90272
310-454-7767

✱ Topanga Co-op Preschool
1440 North Topanga Canyon Boulevard
Topanga, CA 90290
310-455-3155

✱ Topanga Montessori Preschool
1459 Old Topanga Canyon Road
Topanga, CA 90290
310-455-3373

✱ St. Aidans
28211 Pacific Coast Highway
Malibu, CA 90265
310-457-8899

Santa Monica

❋ *Beth Shir Shalom Temple Nursery School*
1827 California Avenue
Santa Monica, CA 90403
310-829-2517

❋ *Bright Start Learning Center*
1501 Seventeenth Street
Santa Monica, CA 90404
310-315-9353

❋ *Circle of Children Preschool*
1227 Montana Avenue
Santa Monica, CA 90403
310-393-7731

❋ *The Early Years School*
302 Montana Avenue
Santa Monica, CA 90403
310-394-0463

❋ *Evergreen Community School*
2800 Colorado Avenue
Santa Monica, CA 90404
310-453-6255

❋ *First Presbyterian Church of Santa Monica Nursery School*
1220 Second Street
Santa Monica, CA 90401
310-451-9259

❋ *The First School*
1733 Ocean Park Boulevard
Santa Monica, CA 90405
310-452-0095

1810 Broadway
Santa Monica, CA 90405
310-828-0018

❋ *First Step Nursery School*
2650 Second Street
Santa Monica, CA 90405
310-399-8118

❋ *First United Methodist Church Nursery School*
1008 Eleventh Street
Santa Monica, CA 90403
310-395-7292

❋ *The Growing Place*
401 Ashland Avenue
Santa Monica, CA 90405
310-399-7769

1406 Marine Street
Santa Monica, CA 90405
310-392-9737

❋ *Hill 'n' Dale Family Learning Center and Preschool*
1540 Twenty-sixth Street
Santa Monica, CA 90404
310-828-6766

✳ *New Path Montessori*
1962 Twentieth Street
Santa Monica, CA 90404
310-450-2477

✳ *Palisades Preschool*
958 Lincoln Boulevard
Santa Monica, CA 90403
310-434-9917

✳ *Rustic Canyon Co-op Nursery School*
601 Latimer Road
Santa Monica, CA 90402
310-459-1049

✳ *Santa Monica Montessori School*
1909 Colorado Avenue
Santa Monica, CA 90404
310-829-3551

✳ *Tenth Street Preschool*
1444 Tenth Street
Santa Monica, CA 90401
310-458-4088

✳ *Trinity Baptist Children's Center*
1019 California Avenue
Santa Monica, CA 90403
310-395-3282

✳ *Westside Waldorf School*
1229 Fourth Street
Santa Monica, CA 90401
310-576-0788

Venice, South Bay

✳ *American Martyr's Preschool*
1705 Laurel Avenue
Manhattan Beach, CA 90266
310-802-8149

✳ *Carden Dominion School*
320 Knob Hill Avenue
Redondo Beach, CA 90277
310-316-4471

✳ *First Years Preschool*
1010 Amoroso Place
Venice, CA 90291
310-399-3120

✳ *Montessori School of Manhattan Beach*
315 South Peck Avenue
Manhattan Beach, CA 90266
310-379-9462

2617 Bell Avenue
Manhattan Beach, CA 90266
310-545-8104

✳ *Redwood Village Children's Center*
13150 Maxella Avenue
Marina del Rey, CA 90292
310-306-7815

✳ *Sand Tots Parent Participation Nursery School*
2108 Vail Avenue
Redondo Beach, CA 90278
310-370-4300

✽ *Seasprites Children's Center*
417 Twenty-fifth Street
Hermosa Beach, CA 90254
310-318-2429

South Pasadena/Pasadena

✽ *Aria Montesorri School*
693 South Euclid
Pasadena, CA 91106
626-793-3741

✽ *Colonial House*
412 Mission Street
South Pasadena, CA 91030
626-403-7099

✽ *Pacific Oaks*
714 West California Boulevard
Pasadena, CA 91105
626-397-1363

✽ *San Marino Recreation*
1560 Pasqualito Road
San Marino, CA 91108
626-403-2200

✽ *St. James United Methodist Church*
2033 East Washington Boulevard
Pasadena, CA 91104
626-791-1934

index

About the Authors

LINDA FRIEDMAN MEADOW is a Chicago native. After attending Northwestern University and receiving both a B.S. and a J.D., Linda headed out to L.A. to become an entertainment attorney. Most recently, Linda worked at Columbia TriStar Motion Pictures in acquisitions and business affairs. Linda and her husband Cary have two daughters—Sarah, five, and Eve, three-and-a-half—and another one on the way.

LISA ROCCHIO grew up in New Orleans. She holds a B.S. in finance from the University of Alabama and an M.B.A. from the University of Southern California. Most recently she worked as an executive at an investor relations firm. Lisa and her husband John have two sons—Jack, five, and Will, three—and a new daughter, Sarah, who is six months old.